NEW STUDIES IN

Thanksgiving

Titles in this series:

NEW STUDIES IN BIBLICAL THEOLOGY 13

Series editor: D. A. Carson

Thanksgiving

AN INVESTIGATION OF A PAULINE THEME

David W. Pao

APOLLOS

INTERVARSITY PRESS
DOWNERS GROVE, ILLINOIS 60515

APOLLOS (an imprint of Inter-Varsity Press),
38 De Montfort Street, Leicester LE1 7GP, England
World Wide Web: www.ivpbooks.com
Email: ivp@uccf.org.uk

INTERVARSITY PRESS
PO Box 1400, Downers Grove, Illinois 60515, USA
World Wide Web: www.ivpress.com
Email: mail@ivpress.com

First published 2002

British Library Cataloguing in Publication Data
A catalogue record for this book is available from the British Library.

UK ISBN 0–85111–272–2

Library of Congress Cataloging-in-Publication Data
These data have been requested.

US ISBN 0–8308–2613–0

Set in Monotype Times New Roman
Typeset in Great Britain by Servis Filmsetting Ltd
Printed in Great Britain by Creative Print and Design (Wales), Ebbw Vale

Contents

Series preface

New Studies in Biblical Theology is a series of monographs that address key issues in the discipline of biblical theology. Contributions to the series focus on one or more of three areas: 1. the nature and status of biblical theology, including its relations with other disciplines (e.g. historical theology, exegesis, systematic theology, historical criticism, narrative theology); 2. the articulation and exposition of the structure of thought of a particular biblical writer or corpus; and 3. the delineation of a biblical theme across all or part of the biblical corpora.

Above all, these monographs are creative attempts to help thinking Christians understand their Bibles better. The series aims simultaneously to instruct and to edify, to interact with the current literature, and to point the way ahead. In God's universe, mind and heart should not be divorced: in this series we will try not to separate what God has joined together. While the notes interact with the best of the scholarly literature, the text is uncluttered with untransliterated Greek and Hebrew, and tries to avoid too much technical jargon. The volumes are written within the framework of confessional evangelicalism, but there is always an attempt at thoughtful engagement with the sweep of the relevant literature.

In a day with more than its share of whining, self-pity, lawsuits and dissatisfaction, this volume by my colleague Dr David Pao has a prophetic element to it. Numerous studies have treated Paul's 'thanksgiving' sections – exploring parallels in first-century literature, noting their ties to broader themes in the corpus of Paul's writings, and teasing out their rhetorical devices. But very few treatments of this theme in Paul comprehensively reflect on the theology of thanksgiving, and how such theology is deeply embedded in Paul's thought and in the gospel itself. Dr Pao supplies the lack, and does so in a way that is both informed and edifying. His study is not only the stuff of biblical theology and grist for many sermons, but will prove to be the occasion for self-examination, repentance and a new resolve to be thankful.

D. A. Carson
Trinity Evangelical Divinity School

Author's preface

This book grows out of an interest in an aspect of Pauline thought that does not fit comfortably within traditional conceptions of Pauline theology or Pauline ethics. This re-evaluation of an important Pauline theme aims at providing insights into the passion of an apostle who never fails to insist on the significance of both the gospel message and the response this message demands. In highlighting the significance of the wider biblical-theological paradigm as the proper framework of interpretation, it is also my hope that the power and depth of Pauline exhortation can be heard in a fresh way.

Before embarking on this journey, a word of explanation concerning the structure of this work may be helpful. While the bulk of the study is theological and exegetical in nature, the first chapter includes sections that contain detailed arguments of a rather different nature. To establish the foundation of this study, chapter one provides a lexical-semantic examination of ways thanksgiving is expressed. This discussion provides the basis for our understanding of thanksgiving as God-centredness. The following chapters that deal with individual Pauline passages will in turn support this affirmation. For those who are primarily interested in the theological significance of this Pauline theme, chapter two could be a convenient starting point.

I am grateful to Prof. D. A. Carson for his invitation to include this study into the *New Studies in Biblical Theology* series. His insightful advice and continuing encouragement have been critical in the nurturing of this study. I am also indebted to Dr Peter O'Brien for his helpful comments in the early stages of this study. My other colleagues in the New Testament Department of Trinity Evangelical Divinity School also deserve to be mentioned for their support and friendship in the partnership of ministry.

I would also like to acknowledge my teaching assistants, Timothy Swinson and Michael Rice, for their help during the various stages of the writing process.

Finally, this book would not be possible without the love and patience of my wife Chrystal. Her sacrifice has provided me with a model of faithful ministry. To Chrystal, and to our daughters, Charis and Serena, this book is dedicated.

May our Lord be glorified as we attempt to be faithful to his Word.

David Pao

Abbreviations

AB	Anchor Bible
AnBib	Analecta biblica
ANF	*Ante-Nicene Fathers*
ANRW	*Aufstieg und Niedergang der römischen Welt*
ATR	*Anglican Theological Review*
Bib	*Biblica*
BJS	Brown Judaic Studies
BTB	*Biblical Theology Bulletin*
BZ	*Biblische Zeitschrift*
CBQ	*Catholic Biblical Quarterly*
CQ	*Classical Quarterly*
CTJ	*Calvin Theological Journal*
CurTM	*Currents in Theology and Mission*
DRev	*Downside Review*
ECC	Eerdmans Critical Commentary
ETL	*Ephemerides theologicae lovanienses*
ExAud	*Ex auditu*
ExpTim	*Expository Times*
FRLANT	Forschungen zur Religion und Literatur des Alten und Neuen Testaments
HDR	Harvard Dissertations in Religion
HNT	Handbuch zum Neuen Testament
HNTC	Harper's New Testament Commentaries
HTKNT	Herders theologischer Kommentar zum Neuen Testament
HTR	*Harvard Theological Review*
ICC	International Critical Commentary
Int	*Interpretation*
JBL	*Journal of Biblical Literature*
JETS	*Journal of the Evangelical Theological Society*
JHS	*Journal of Hellenic Studies*
JNSL	*Journal of Northwest Semitic Languages*

JPT	*Journal of Pentecostal Theology*
JQR	*Jewish Quarterly Review*
JSNT	*Journal for the Study of the New Testament*
JSNTSup	Journal for the Study of the New Testament: Supplement Series
JSOTSup	Journal for the Study of the Old Testament: Supplement Series
JSPSup	Journal for the Study of the Pseudepigrapha: Supplement Series
JTS	*Journal of Theological Studies*
JTSA	*Journal of Theology for Southern Africa*
LCL	Loeb Classical Library
LXX	Septuagint (Greek version of the Old Testament)
MT	Masoretic Text
MTZ	*Münchener theologische Zeitschrift*
Neot	*Neotestamentica*
NICNT	New International Commentary on the New Testament
NIGTC	New International Greek Testament Commentary
NIV	New International Version
NovT	*Novum Testamentum*
NovTSup	Supplements to *Novum Testamentum*
NRSV	New Revised Standard Version
NSBT	New Studies in Biblical Theology
NTF	Neutestamentliche Forschungen
NTS	*New Testament Series*
OBT	Overtures to Biblical Theology
OTL	Old Testament Library
PNTC	Pillar New Testament Commentaries
RB	*Revue Biblique*
ResQ	*Restoration Quarterly*
RevExp	*Review and Expositor*
RSR	*Recherches de science religieuse*
RTR	*Reform Theological Review*
SBG	Studies in Biblical Greek
SBLDS	Society of Biblical Literature Dissertation Series
SBLMS	*Society of Biblical Literature Monograph Series*
SBLSP	*Society of Biblical Literature Seminar Papers*
SecCent	*Second Century*
SJT	*Scottish Journal of Theology*
SNT	Studien zum Neuen Testament

SNTSMS	Society for New Testament Studies Monograph Series
STDJ	Studies on the Texts of the Desert of Judah
TDNT	*Theological Dictionary of the New Testament*
Them	*Themelios*
TNTC	Tyndale New Testament Commentaries
TynBul	*Tyndale Bulletin*
VE	*Vox evangelica*
VT	*Vetus Testamentum*
WBC	Word Biblical Commentary
WMANT	Wissenschaftliche Monographien zum Alten und Neuen Testament
WUNT	Wissenschaftliche Untersuchungen zum Neuen Testament
ZNW	*Zeitschrift für die neutestamentliche Wissenschaft und die Kunde der älteren Kirche*

Chapter One

Thanksgiving as God-centredness

'Be thankful' (Col. 3:15) is a recurring plea of the apostle Paul. This Pauline emphasis on thanksgiving can be felt through a brief glance at the use of related vocabularies in the New Testament. The verb *eucharisteō* and its cognate noun and adjective, together with *charis*, when it acquires the meaning of thanksgiving, appear sixty-two times in the New Testament. More than three-quarters of such occurrences appear in the Pauline corpus.[1] The rest appear mostly in the gospel feeding stories and in the non-Pauline Lord's Supper account.[2] More significant is the fact that only in Paul does one find a call to be thankful.[3] In none of the other New Testament authors can one find such a sustained emphasis on thanksgiving. The same can be said concerning extra-biblical authors; thus Paul Schubert's claim, made more than fifty years ago, remains uncontested that Paul 'mentions the subject of thanksgiving more frequently per page than any other Hellenistic author, pagan or Christian'.[4]

Despite the recognition of the prominence of the Pauline theme of thanksgiving, most of the major works on Pauline theology[5] and

---

[1] In this study, all the epistles traditionally ascribed to 'Paul' will be considered as 'Pauline'. While some may wish to question the authenticity of certain epistles in the corpus, most will, however, agree that even those disputed letters should be considered as belonging to the Pauline tradition.

[2] In the gospels, outside of the feeding stories and the non-Pauline Lord's Supper account, the *eucharisteō* word-group appears only in Luke 17:16; 18:11 and John 11:41. Two of such appearances are in the context of prayer. Besides the gospels' usage, this word-group appears only in Acts and Revelation. In Acts, the occurrences (24:3; 27:35; 28:15) can all be found in accounts related to Paul. In Revelation, the three occurrences (4:9; 7:12; 11:17) appear in contexts where honour is given to God. The use of *charis* as a reference to thanksgiving can be found only in Heb. 12:28 outside the Pauline epistles.

[3] One possible exception is Heb. 12:28, although this is not strictly a call to thanksgiving in the Pauline sense.

[4] Schubert 1939: 41. As noted below, his statement can be qualified by noting the importance of the thanksgiving theme in the writings of Philo, a rough contemporary of Paul.

[5] See, for example, Bultmann 1955; Whiteley 1974; Witherington 1994; and Dunn 1998.

Pauline ethics[6] fail to wrestle with it. Such a striking absence reflects the perceived ambiguity of the location of the thanksgiving theme within the structural landscape of both the theology and ethics of Paul. Instead of examining this theme in isolation, this study aims at the rehabilitation of the thanksgiving theme within the modern constructions of the theology and ethics of Paul. In this process, a renewed understanding of the 'thought' of Paul may be achieved.

Source and traditions

Previous works on thanksgiving in Paul focus primarily on two issues: (1) the search for the source of and the traditions behind the development of the Pauline theme of thanksgiving; and (2) the formal analysis of the epistolary significance of thanksgiving within Pauline epistles.

The first group is best represented by George Boobyer,[7] who was among the first to attempt to search for the context of certain thanksgiving passages within the Pauline corpus. Highlighting the peculiar connection between thanksgiving and the offering of glory to God in a number of Pauline passages (e.g., 2 Cor. 4:15; 9:12–14; Phil. 2:11), Boobyer argues that such connection shows that Paul was indebted to certain Hellenistic notions that have their roots in Iranian thought. He concludes:

> Paul's conception of increasing the δόξα θεοῦ [glory of God] with εὐχαριστία [thanksgiving] is the result of a mingling of Iranian-Gnostic light speculation with more primitive ideas of the effect of sacrifice and praise upon a deity. The conception of an effect is primitive; the conception of praise as light which increases the light or glory of God is Iranian-Gnostic.[8]

Focusing on only a few verses, Boobyer's study fails to consider other passages that provide a rather different picture of the religious milieu in which the Pauline thanksgiving theme develops. His history-of-religion approach, while popular among critical scholars in the early part of the last century, has now been rejected by most. Nevertheless, Boobyer's study is useful in highlighting the fact that the Pauline

---

[6] See, for example, Enslin 1957; Furnish 1968; Hays 1996.
[7] Boobyer 1929.
[8] Boobyer 1929: 89.

thanksgiving theme should be examined within the context of the ancient thought-world. He is correct in rejecting psychological factors as the major tools in analysing this theme since 'to assert that this is an adequate explanation is most unsatisfactory'.[9]

Since Boobyer's study, there has not been a sustained effort in the search for the context of this Pauline theme. Several studies that focus primarily on the Hebrew traditions of thanksgiving should, however, be noted, especially in light of the recent renewed interest in the Jewishness of Paul. These include studies that allude to the connection between thanksgiving and benediction,[10] confession[11] and praise.[12] Although these are not developed discussions on Pauline thanksgiving, they do pave the way for our analysis of the role of thanksgiving within the structure of Pauline theology and ethics.

Epistolary thanksgiving

Recent discussions on Pauline thanksgiving have centred on the significance of introductory thanksgiving paragraphs in Pauline epistles. The first of such studies is the significant work by Paul Schubert who argues:

> Direct exegesis of the Pauline thanksgivings with reference to their respective letters reveals beyond a shadow of a doubt their strictly epistolary form and function. The reference to the extra-Pauline Hellenistic epistolary thanksgivings confirms the exegetical judgment convincingly.[13]

This emphasis on form instead of theological development of the theme sets the stage for the discussion that follows.[14] A direct consequence is

---

[9] Boobyer 1929: 83.

[10] Guillet 1969: 163–204; and Beyer 1964: 754–765.

[11] Robinson 1964: 194–235; and Bornkamm 1964: 46–63.

[12] Ledogar 1968: 63–89. See also Guthrie 1981, whose study focuses on the development of the *tôḏāh* tradition in the Old Testament. He extends his discussion to the eucharist in the New Testament. While this study is significant in a number of ways, an examination of the Pauline thanksgiving theme is not presented.

[13] Schubert 1939: 183.

[14] See, for example, McFarlane 1966. Despite the title of this thesis, McFarlane focuses primarily on formal elements and linguistic traditions behind the Pauline use without paying sufficient attention to the actual function of the term within the contours of Pauline theology. He limits himself primarily to the Pauline introductory thanksgivings, and this is probably due to his questionable understanding that one cannot affirm 'the centrality of the virtue of gratitude' (35) in the Pauline material.

the conviction to separate the introductory thanksgiving period from the various thanksgiving statements that appear in the body of the Pauline epistles.

In revising Schubert's thesis, Peter O'Brien presents a detailed exegetical treatment of the introductory thanksgiving periods and concludes that 'Paul's introductory thanksgivings were not meaningless devices' but 'were integral parts of their letters, setting the tone and themes of what was to follow'.[15] This study is valuable in that it provides a detailed examination of the various theological themes developed within the Pauline thanksgiving periods.[16] It also emphasizes the pastoral intent of Paul, the primacy of the gospel message, the logical priority of the divine acts that demand a proper response, and the Jewish context within which the content of the thanksgiving period should be read.

While interest in the formal aspects continues to attract scholarly attention,[17] this focus on Pauline introductory thanksgiving has only presented us with a partial picture of the Pauline theme of thanksgiving. Moreover, the focus on epistolary function may at times prevent one from examining the unique emphasis placed on this particular theme. This concern is particularly acute with the appearance of Peter Arzt's study that challenges the scholarly consensus based primarily on Schubert's work.[18] After a re-examination of papyrus letters, Arzt concludes that formal 'introductory thanksgiving' cannot be identified in the beginning sections of letters 'contemporaneous with the Pauline and other New Testament letters'.[19] While the conclusion of Arzt's study is not accepted by all,[20] his study reminds us that epistolary function does not exhaust the significance of thanksgiving in

---

[15] O'Brien 1977. In another article (1975: 144–155), O'Brien repeats the same concern: 'in drawing our attention to the literary nature of these passages Schubert has given the impression that Paul's thanksgiving reports were merely literary devices. One is left wondering whether Paul actually gave thanks (or offered petition) for the churches concerned at all' (146).

[16] O'Brien (1975: 144–155) provides an illuminating study on the mentioning of the 'gospel' in the introductory paragraphs of several of the Pauline epistles (1 Thess. 1:5; 1 Cor. 1:6; Col. 1:5).

[17] See the summary in White 1987: 1730–1756.

[18] Arzt 1994: 29–46. Appearing in the same year, Dippenaar (1994: 147–188) argues for a similar position. Before Arzt, a number of commentators had already questioned the existence of a fixed thanksgiving period in Hellenistic letters. Cf. Best 1972: 65; K. Berger 1974: 190–231; and Lambrecht 1990: 194.

[19] Arzt 1994: 44.

[20] See, for example, Reed 1996: 87–99, who points to additional evidence of formal parallels and suggests that flexibility of formal conventions should be considered as well.

Paul,[21] and a strict separation between introductory thanksgiving and other appearances of the thanksgiving theme cannot be maintained.

It is clear that both the source-critical approach and the formal one that focuses on the introductory paragraphs fail to provide us with an appropriate appreciation of Paul's emphasis on thanksgiving. Here, O'Brien's article on 'Thanksgiving within the Structure of Pauline Theology' should also be mentioned.[22] In this study that moves beyond the introductory paragraphs, O'Brien provides a catalogue of the various appearances of the thanksgiving word-group. The listing is arranged according to forms (e.g., colloquial uses, thanksgivings said over food, exhortations to thanksgiving, short expressions of thanksgivings, and so on) and is followed by an insightful conclusion that highlights the fact that in Paul 'thanksgiving is always a response to God's saving activity in creation and redemption'.[23] Such a statement could be supported by and be further examined within the Hebrew traditions of thanksgiving, and an attempt to detect the underlying theological sub-structure behind the listing can be further extended. Due to the self-imposed limits of O'Brien's article, several peculiar statements related to the thanksgiving theme remain unexplored. More importantly, the exact categories that one should use in examining themes such as thanksgiving need to be articulated.

A cross-cultural examination

To begin to discuss the Pauline theme of thanksgiving, the historical and cultural distance between the ancient text and modern readers should be recognized. It is in this sense that a 'cross-cultural'[24] analysis is needed. Modern Western conceptions of thanksgiving are dominated by the model that privileges the emotional sense of gratefulness in response to a certain act of kindness and the need to fulfil the 'debt' to achieve the balance of personal relationship.[25] Within this model,

---

[21] See also Wiles 1974: 160, who argues against the dominance of epistolary convention in explaining the introductory thanksgiving in Pauline epistles. According to Wiles, Pauline epistolary practice is derived fundamentally from Jewish liturgical traditions. Cf. Robinson 1969: 149.

[22] O'Brien 1980: 50–66.

[23] O'Brien 1980: 62.

[24] The term is used not in the missiological sense but it aims at highlighting the temporal and cultural distance between the ancient text and the modern readers.

[25] For a helpful analysis of modern Western conceptions of thankfulness, see McConnell 1993. Cf. Amato 1982: 26–33. For a discussion of thanksgiving among non-Christian and non-Western religious systems, see Carman and Streng 1989.

thanksgiving is detached from social ethics and theological discourse and is reduced to the level of etiquette that is functionally limited to the realm of individual interchange. Several observations from the Pauline texts are sufficient to question the adequacy of such a model.

First, in the introductory paragraphs, thanksgiving is not offered because of the reception of a certain gift on the part of the author. The grounds are usually acts of God within the lives of the believers and the faithful response of the audience.[26] Thankfulness as a result of the experience of grace by others became a dominant category. It is the prominence of such an emphasis that should be noted.

Second, thanksgiving in Paul is reserved for God and not human beings.[27] This fact alone requires an explanation, and it forces one to search for a wider theological basis for understanding the various forms of appearance of the theme.

Third, while thanksgiving is usually offered in response to past acts of kindness, in Paul thanksgiving is also offered for the future acts of God. This is most clearly stated in 1 Corinthians 15:56–57 where Paul thanks God for the future resurrection of the saints: 'The sting of death is sin, and the power of sin is the law. But thanks be to God! He gives us the victory through our Lord Jesus Christ.' The distinct eschatological orientation of such acts of thanksgiving goes beyond modern conceptions of reciprocity of grace and thanksgiving.

Fourth, moving from the future to the present concern, the ethical significance of thanksgiving as a continuing commitment is depicted in a surprising way through the contrast found in Ephesians 5. In verse 4 of that chapter, instead of 'obscenity, foolish talk or coarse joking', Paul exhorts the church to offer 'thanksgiving'. Here, thanksgiving is used as a summary term to characterize the proper behaviour of the people of God.[28] The contrast is further developed in verse 5 where the one who performs evil deeds is described as an 'idolater'. The contrast between the one who offers thanksgiving and one who worships idol is most striking;[29] this cannot be understood apart from

[26] Rom. 1:8; 1 Cor. 1:4; 2 Cor. 1:11; Eph. 1:16; Phil. 1:3; Col. 1:3; 1 Thess. 1:2; 2 Thess. 1:3; and Philem. 4.

[27] The only possible exception is Rom. 16:4. Even here, however, while Paul was thanking Prisca and Aquila for risking their lives for him, the qualification that not only is Paul the one who is to give thanks but also 'all the churches of the Gentiles' shows that the wider concern for the ministry of God and thus the work of God is in sight.

[28] See also Eph. 5:18–20 and Col. 3:17.

[29] See also Rom. 1:21 where the connection is made between idolaters and those who refuse to offer thanks to the one true God.

the wider biblical narrative concerning the acts of God and the proper response that is required.

Related to the above point is the understanding of ingratitude as one of the distinguishing marks of non-believers. In Romans 1:21, unbelieving Gentiles were condemned since 'they neither glorified him as God nor gave thanks to him'. Similarly, in the vice list of 2 Timothy 3:1–5, 'ungrateful' is mentioned together with 'unholy'. The understanding of ungratefulness as one of the cardinal acts of disobedience should not be easily dismissed.

Finally, the call to thanksgiving without reference to past gracious acts points to the peculiar characterization of the people of God. In Colossians 3:15, the body of Christ is simply called to be thankful: 'Let the peace of Christ rule in your hearts, since as members of one body you were called to peace. And be thankful.' Such an absolute use of the term again presupposes a wider historical and theological framework. Similarly, the call to 'give thanks in all circumstances' (1 Thess. 5:18) moves beyond the modern conception of reciprocity.[30]

From this cursory survey, it is clear that an alternate interpretive model is needed without which numerous Pauline statements on thanksgiving cannot be properly understood. Such a model should not be an arbitrary one constructed apart from the consideration of the structure that forms the foundation for the other theological motifs articulated in the Pauline corpus. In this study, it will be suggested that Hebrew covenant traditions form the basis for both theology and ethics in Paul, and that thanksgiving can be understood as the bridge between the two. Before getting to the explication of these traditions, we should focus on the heart of Pauline thanksgiving: God-centredness.

To say 'Thanks'

In Hellenistic Greek literature, various terms came to be used to express gratitude and acts of giving thanks. Prominent among them are terms related to the word *charis*, which in itself can acquire the sense of 'gratitude'. This usage survives in the Pauline literature where it is at times used to express thanksgiving (e.g. 1 Cor. 10:30; Rom. 7:25). Related to *charis* is the term *charistērion*. Xenophon was

---

[30] See also Col. 2:6–7: 'So then, just as you received Christ Jesus as Lord, continue to live in him, rooted and built up in him, strengthened in the faith as you were taught, and overflowing with thankfulness.'

the first to use the term. After Xenophon this term was used mainly by Greek writers in their descriptions of Roman affairs, including cultic settings where religious gratitude was discussed.[31]

A more common term for thanksgiving is *eucharistein* and its related forms. The adjectival form can be found in Herodotus to express sense of gratitude. According to Schermann (1910: 376–377), the verb and the noun became common only in the late Hellenistic period.[32] At first, the term was used to refer to the condition of well-being. With the use of the preposition, the verb came to refer to the condition of being the beneficiary of gracious acts and thus the disposition of gratitude.[33] By the first century BC, the term is used to refer to public expressions of gratitude.[34] In the papyri, the term is commonly used in the sense of 'giving thanks',[35] and inscriptions from the first century BC confirm the use of the term in this sense.[36] Further development of the verb in connection with different cases to specify 'thanks given to someone for something' takes place after the New Testament period. In the Pauline material, this word-group dominates expressions of thanksgiving, although other ways of expressing thanksgiving can also be found.[37]

Turning to the canonical portions of the Septuagint, it is striking that the *eucharistein* word-group is virtually absent.[38] There are a number of ways to account for this. First and most importantly, as noted above, the use of the verb *eucharisteō* in secular Greek literature to convey the sense of 'thanksgiving' became common only in the late Hellenistic period. This explains why the earlier Greek trans-

[31]   See the discussion in Bremer 1998: 127–128.

[32]   A search in the *Thesaurus Linguae Graecae* (1992) confirms and qualifies the conclusion of this earlier study. The *eucharistein* word-group is used by a number of authors from the fourth century BC onwards, but it became widely used in Greek literature only after the first century BC.

[33]   Schermann (1910: 377) also notes that the term continues to bear the senses of gratitude and giving thanks well into the Christian era.

[34]   See Ledogar 1968: 92.

[35]   See the examples in Schubert 1939: 145–146. Among the many examples listed here are those with references to thanksgiving to deities.

[36]   Schermann 1910: 378.

[37]   While *eucharisteō* is almost always used by Paul in reference to God, other forms of expressions of thanks can be detected, especially when the reference is to a human being. Peterman (1991: 161–170), for example, has suggested that explicit acknowledgment of debt, as found in Phil. 4, can be understood as a way to express thanks to another human party.

[38]   The only instance where the word-group appears is in Prov. 11:16, but it is not used in the sense of 'gratefulness' or 'thanksgiving'. See the discussion below in the next note.

lation of the Hebrew Bible lacks this verb.[39] Also worth noting is the suggestion that the term *eucharisteō* does not have an exact Hebrew equivalent. Related to this is the fact that Hebrew words of thanksgiving already had their Greek equivalents.[40]

A more radical suggestion is provided by Westermann, who argues that not only do we have no Hebrew equivalent of the Greek word-group, but the 'concept' of thanksgiving is also absent in the Old Testament:

> The fact that there is no word for 'to thank' in Hebrew has never been properly evaluated. The ignoring of this fact can be explained only in that we live so unquestionably in the rhythm between poles of thanks and request, of 'please!' and 'thank you!', and the thought does not occur to anyone that these concepts are *not* common to all mankind, and have *not* been present as a matter of course, do *not* belong to the presuppositions of human intercourse nor to those of the contrast of God and man.[41]

The assumptions behind this statement should be questioned. First, the absence of one particular word-group does not signify the absence of a concept. In the same way, the absence of a Greek equivalent of the Hebrew term *ḥeseḏ* ('covenantal faithfulness' or 'loving-kindness') in the New Testament does not signify the absence of such a concept in the teachings of the early apostles. More importantly, Westermann is assuming that the concept of thanksgiving as found in later Christian writings is utterly distinct from ideas embedded in the Hebrew traditions. Apart from the Pauline development, it is doubtful whether Westermann's thesis can stand the challenge when one examines the Old Testament itself.[42] Despite his questionable conclusion, Westermann does correctly remind us of the cultural gap between our understanding of thanksgiving and the ancient world of thought. Nevertheless, it is not that the idea of thanksgiving is missing in the Old Testament. It is our conception of the very notion of thanksgiving that should be re-evaluated.

---

[39] This is confirmed by the fact that in Prov. 11:16, where the word-group makes its only appearance, it is used in the sense of graciousness, a usage common in early secular Greek literature.

[40] Ledogar 1968: 102. See also the discussion below concerning the relationship between thanksgiving and other praise verbs.

[41] Westermann 1965: 25.

[42] See the detailed critique in Miller 1994: 403–404.

Moving to the apocryphal writings in the Septuagint, one begins to find the *eucharisteō* word-group being used to express thanksgiving:[43] thanksgiving towards other human beings[44] and towards God.[45] Not only are these books written after the canonical books, these are also the books that are more heavily influenced by contemporary Hellenistic culture. One has to admit, however, that the word-group is not yet in wide circulation even in these Jewish writings.

A rather different picture can be found in the Hellenistic Jewish author Philo. In his writings, the *eucharistein* word-group takes on a new significance. Not only is the term used to express gratitude and for expressions of thanksgiving, it also represents the heart of all religious ideals. The word-group appears more than 150 times in Philo's writings.[46] The term *eucharistia* is used in both the singular and the plural to refer to thank-offering in literal form as well as verbal expressions of thanks. Any act of thanksgiving is understood as an act of sacrifice. Therefore, moral conditions were imposed as one offers thanks to God (*De Specialibus Legibus I*, 167). For Philo, outward acts of thanksgiving are considered to be the natural expression of the blessed soul.[47] These are not isolated acts, however. They reflect the commitment of the entire person as one who acknowledges the centrality of God the Creator. The following quotation best reflects Philo's emphasis on thanksgiving:

> Having learned, then, that, in all that has to do with shewing honour to God, one work only is incumbent upon us, namely thanksgiving, let us always and everywhere make this our study, using voice and skilful pen. Let us never tire of composing eulogies in prose and poetry, to the end that, whether with or without musical accompaniment whichever of its appointed functions the voice may exercise, be it eloquent speech or song, high honour may be given both to the world and to the Creator of the world; the former, as one has said, the most perfect of things produced, the latter the best of producers. (*De Plantatione* 131 [Colson and Whitaker, LCL])

[43] At this stage, the word-group is used to express both the disposition of gratitude and acts of giving thanks.

[44] Additions to Esther 8:12; 2 Maccabees 2:27; 12:31. Sirach 37:11 should probably be included here although the exact sense of the term is uncertain.

[45] Judith 8:25; 2 Maccabees 1:11; 3:33; 3 Maccabees 7:16; Wisdom of Solomon 16:28; 18:2.

[46] The exact number cannot be determined since part of his writings did not survive in Greek. See the discussion in LaPorte 1983: 4–6.

[47] Ledogar 1968: 95–97; LaPorte 1983: 38.

The significance of Philo's writings in our discussion of Pauline thanksgiving cannot be dismissed. Without arguing for any literary dependence between the two authors, Philo's writings do provide us with a precedent whereby thanksgiving depicts the essence of one's personal relationship with God. Thanksgiving is therefore related to other theological affirmations and to expressions that reflect such affirmations. More importantly, thanksgiving is not simply a reaction to random acts of kindness, it is a way to affirm the supremacy of God the Creator and the mighty acts he has done on our behalf. Philo has therefore prepared us to widen our perspective as we encounter the significance of thanksgiving in Paul. In Philo, as in Paul, thanksgiving approximates acts of praising God, and it is precisely these acts of praising that touch upon the central claims of the Old Testament.

Thanksgiving and worship

In reading the Old Testament, instead of questioning whether the idea of thanksgiving exists or not, one should focus on particular ways in which thanksgiving is expressed and how the idea of thanksgiving itself is construed. In the modern usage of the term, the one who offers 'thanks' is one who is reacting properly in response to a gift. In the Old Testament, one also finds ways to respond to the reception of gifts or gracious acts of God. The response, however, is more profound than simply noting the reception of favours. One of the prominent ways to express thanks to God for what he has done for his people is to offer him praise.

In the Old Testament, the Hebrew noun *tôḏāh* is often used to describe the praise that accompanies a thanksgiving sacrifice. In Aquila's translation of the Old Testament, *eucharistia* is often used to translate this word.[48] While *eucharisteō* floods the Pauline material, *aineō*, the word that is most frequently used to translate Hebrew verbs of praise, is strikingly missing in the Pauline epistles.[49] It would be irresponsible to argue that Paul is not interested in offering praise to God. A more likely and obvious explanation is that another word was used to express such praises to God. In light of the

---

[48] Ledogar 1968: 121.

[49] The only exception appears in Rom. 15:11 within the quotation from Ps. 117:1. The noun *epainos*, in reference to the praise for God, is also limited to two passages (Eph. 1:6–14 and Phil. 1:11).

fact that both praise and thanksgiving are proper responses to God, praise is likely to be at the centre of the Pauline emphasis on thanksgiving.

Despite the connections between thanksgiving and praise in the Old Testament, differences between the two have frequently been noted. Nitzan (1994: 175), for example, has suggested that in songs of praise, all creatures honour God, 'extolling His sovereignty over the Creation as a whole and upon all mankind'. Songs of thanksgiving, on the other hand, 'express the sense of gratitude of an individual or of a specific group of people for kindness which God has performed specifically for them'. Brueggemann (1985: 68) has further noted that thanksgiving is rooted in concrete action while praise is related to the general attributes of God.

Such distinctions are based on Gunkel's formal categories for the different settings of the psalms, and one wonders if such clear-cut classification can indeed be made. Mowinckel's use of terms such as 'laudatory thanksgiving' (1962: 32) reflects this ambiguity. Walter Brueggemann (1985: 68) himself admits that in a number of psalms such distinction cannot be made.[50] Moving beyond formal distinctions, the differences between thanksgiving and praise become even more arbitrary, and analysis often depends on how they are defined. For the study of Old Testament theology, Patrick Miller (1985: 10–11) rightly notes that thanksgiving and praise 'have come together so thoroughly in the Old Testament that one cannot really sift out one from the other as a legitimately separate theological subject'. Marvin Tate (1990: 66) further notes that praise and thanksgiving 'have a symbiotic relationship' in that 'one cannot live without the other'. In both praise and thanksgiving, God is acknowledged as the powerful God who alone can deliver his people from distress and evil. More importantly, he deserves endless thanksgiving because he alone is God. Therefore when one reads the Pauline call to '[s]ing and make music in your heart to the Lord, always giving thanks to God the Father for everything, in the name of our Lord Jesus Christ' (Eph. 5:19–20), one is reminded of the words of the psalmist:

> I will extol the LORD at all times;
> his praise will always be on my lips.
>
> (Ps. 34:1)

---

[50] See, for example Pss. 66 and 100; 2 Chron. 29:10–16.

The juxtaposition of praise and thanksgiving can also be found within the Old Testament. In Psalm 35, thanksgiving and praise can be found in parallel construction:

> I will give you thanks in the great assembly;
> among throngs of people I will praise you.
>
> (v. 18; cf. 109:30)

Praise and thanksgiving also appear together elsewhere: 'With praise and thanksgiving they sang to the LORD' (Ezra 3:11).

Even if distinctions between thanksgiving and praise can be made in the Old Testament,[51] such distinctions dissolve in the theology of Paul. The distinction between universal praise and thanksgiving for a specific group breaks down with Paul's emphasis on the cosmic lordship of Christ and the universal impact of the eschatological dawn of salvation. To separate the acts of God from his attributes is also foreign to Paul's thought and to the ancient Hebrew mentality. God's 'attributes' are revealed through his mighty acts in history, and the climax of such divine acts in the death and resurrection of Jesus Christ is understood as the ultimate revealed act through which God can be known.

Another distinction that has been suggested is the factor of emotional or actual distance. C. Mitchell (1987: 134–135), for example, has suggested that 'When people are thanked, the thanks turn to praise when the person to be thanked is remote or unknown, since a person to whom one is not directly speaking cannot be thanked.' For our purpose, the distinction is less critical, since in terms of content both thanksgiving and praise are identical. Nevertheless, if we accept this distinction, the use of thanksgiving (instead of praise) in Paul then signifies the closeness of God as the effects of his mighty acts in history can be felt continuously.

The connection between praise and thanksgiving is not limited to Old Testament traditions. For the ancient Greeks, the proper way to express gratitude was to offer praise.[52] In the classical period, hymnic

---

[51] Our discussion does not aim at showing that praise and thanksgiving are 'synonymous' terms in the Old Testament on a linguistic level. The point is rather that the two concepts are related and one cannot fully appreciate the force of either term without also taking into consideration the connotation of the other.

[52] This is established by the important study of Quincey (1966: 133–158). Likewise, Versnel (1981: 50) notes that 'the term with which the Greek of the classical period expressed his gratitude is not so much a word of the family of *charis*, as both in religious and secular texts, above all *(ep)ainos, epainein.*'

texts narrating the praise of gods were used to express thanksgiving.[53] In Hellenistic and Roman periods, praise was always offered in the sense of 'thanks'. Such use survives in the Pauline text, as the praise vocabulary in 1 Corinthians 11:2 should probably be understood to express thanksgiving: 'I praise you for remembering me in everything and for holding to the teachings, just as I passed them on to you.'[54] The distinction between praise and thanksgiving is often established through criteria based on modern usage.

Our modern usage of the term 'thanksgiving', in reference to human interaction in everyday life, assumes that a gift or favour can be returned and an appropriate return can thus be understood as the proper expression of thanksgiving. This becomes problematic in hierarchical societies where there is significant difference in the status of the giver and the receiver. In such conditions there is 'no real possibility of exchange because all of the power, the entire source of gifts, is on one side in this relationship' (Carman 1989: 158). In the case of the God of the universe, such possibility of return dissipates as no human beings can offer anything in return that can do justice to the gift received. The only proper response, then, is praise and worship. In describing divine–human encounter, therefore, thanksgiving and praise understandably merge and become the one and only proper response to God who is the source of all power and goodness.

Pauline thanksgiving transcends modern understanding of the distinction between praise and thanksgiving in yet another way. In everyday life, praise may be appropriate from a third-party individual observing the transfer of a gift from A to B, while gratitude is only expected from B.[55] For Paul, however, thanksgivings are often offered in the introductory paragraphs of his epistles for the relationship between God and the church that he was addressing. Again, the distinction between praise and thanksgiving dissolves in the theology of Paul, and the functional identification between the two becomes a significant theological emphasis in Paul.

It is within such a context that one can understand the significance of thanksgiving in Paul. Paul is not concerned with teaching his churches proper etiquette. It is the proper response to the salvific acts of God that is at the centre of both his 'theology' and 'ethics'. Thanksgiving in Paul is an act of worship. It is not focused primarily

[53] See Bremer 1998: 127–137.

[54] For other examples in the Hellenistic and Roman periods, see Quincey 1966: 149–150.

[55] For a philosophical analysis of this distinction, see D. Lyons 1968: 92–97.

on the benefits received or the blessed condition of a person; instead, God is the centre of thanksgiving. This understanding of thanksgiving as worship is shared by other New Testament authors. In Hebrews, for example, one reads: 'since we are receiving a kingdom that cannot be shaken, let us be thankful, and so worship God acceptably with reverence and awe' (12:28). In thanksgiving, God is being honoured.

Closely related to praise in the Old Testament is the term *bārak* ('to bless'). When an individual blesses God, he is often offering him praises. The relationship between the two is illustrated by Psalm 135:21:

> [Blessed be] the LORD from Zion,
>   to him who dwells in Jerusalem.
> Praise the LORD.

In Psalm 145:21, both terms are translated as 'praise' in the NIV:

> My mouth will speak in praise (*hillel*) of the LORD.
>   Let every creature praise (*bārak*) his holy name
>   for ever and ever.

In these instances, God is praiseworthy because of what he has done for his people. Blessing turns into praising when God is the object.[56] Blessings are offered to God when blessings from God are received (e.g. Gen. 24:27; Ps. 18:46–48). In the Old Testament, when human characters become recipients of divine favour, 'grateful response is by benediction'.[57] In these cases, honour and glory replace material benefits when God is blessed. God is acknowledged as the one from whom all goodness comes.[58] In the term 'blessing', one again finds the merging of praise and thanksgiving. The convergence of the three terms can be found in one verse in the Old Testament:

---

[56] C. Mitchell (1987: 147) offers a discussion of the process in which *bārak* came to be used as a praise-verb. In 1 Sam. 25:33 and Jer. 20:14 we find instances where *bārak* is used to refer to impersonal entities that cannot receiving any 'blessing'. In those instances, *bārak* is understood as 'praise'.

[57] Greenberg 1983: 31. Greenberg also argues that 'to bless God' should be understood as 'may YHWH be praised' (35). Cf. Blank (1961: 88) who defines blessing God as 'a return for a favor experienced'.

[58] S. Dawes (1995: 295–296) argues that 'affirmation' is the basic meaning of 'blessing' as God is acknowledged as the Lord of all. Clearer examples include Exod. 18:10; Deut. 8:10; Josh. 22:33.

Enter his gates with thanksgiving
and his courts with praise;
give thanks to him and bless his name.

(Ps. 100:4)[59]

At the root of praise and blessing, therefore, is thanksgiving.

In the Septuagint, *eulogeō*, the verb used to translate *bārak*, is also used to translate verbs of praise, including *hillel*. At the turn of the Christian era, *eulogeō* is used together with *eucharisteō*.[60] While many have considered this as a uniquely Jewish phenomenon, evidence shows that *eulogeō* in secular Greek literature has also been used to express praise and thanksgiving.[61] The word-group has been used in inscriptions from the third century BC onwards in the sense of 'words of praise'. After a preliminary survey, Pleket (1981: 187) suggests that in secular Greek, as in the Septuagint, the term was the 'non-secularized Greek word for "praise"'.[62] Behind such praise is the grateful response to deities for benefits received.

When we come to the New Testament, we have further evidence for the interchangeability of these terms. The various accounts of the Lord's Supper provide the most obvious examples. While *eulogeō* is used for the bread and *eucharisteō* for the cup in the Matthean (26:26–27) and the Markan (14:22–23) accounts, *eucharisteō* is used for both in Luke (22:17–19) and Paul (1 Cor. 11:24). Similarly, while *eulogeō* is used in Synoptic accounts of the feeding of the five thousand (Matt. 14:19; Mark 6:41; Luke 9:16), *eucharisteō* is used in the accounts of the feeding of the four thousand (Matt. 15:36; Mark 8:6). Jeremias (1966: 113) suggests that here we have the 'Graecizing' tendency where the *eucharisteō* word-group is beginning to replace the *eulogeō* word-group. One can also suggest that *eucharisteō* is being Hebraized as thanksgiving is understood primarily as a proper way to respond to God. In any case, Audet (1959: 646) is probably correct is claiming that *bārak* is the 'true parent' of Christian thanksgiving.

The connection between blessing and thanksgiving is not limited

---

[59] NIV has translated the final phrase as 'praise his name'.

[60] See the important articles of Robinson 1964: 194–235 and 1969: 124–158. Robinson notes that 'to bless' and 'to thank' are used as interchangeable terms in the Qumran hymns. When thanksgiving becomes an important term in early Christianity, Judaism increasingly uses blessing terminology. Cf. Bickermann 1962: 524–532.

[61] Contra Beyer 1964: 754–765.

[62] See the references provided by Pleket (1981: 186–187). One has to admit, however, that the use of blessing-terminology in this sense is far less pervasive in secular Greek literature.

to meal accounts. The clearest Pauline example comes from 1 Corinthians 14:16: 'If you are [blessing] God with your spirit, how can one who finds himself among those who do not understand say "Amen" to your thanksgiving, since he does not know what you are saying?'[63] Blessing and thanksgiving are virtually synonymous in this context;[64] both can be understood as acts of praise. On a linguistic level, the two terms are not 'identical'. On a theological level, however, one cannot be understood without the other.[65]

Formal parallels can be found in the introductory paragraphs of some of the Pauline epistles when 'thanksgiving' is substituted by an extended 'benediction'. In 2 Corinthians (1:3–4) and Ephesians (1:3–14),[66] Paul introduces his letters with a benediction in which the gracious acts of God are recounted. These introductory paragraphs have their precedent in the letters embedded in the first chapter of 2 Maccabees[67] where benedictions also open the letters. The benediction form may reflect Paul's indebtedness to the Jewish traditions while thanksgiving can be understood as a Hellenistic adaptation.[68] The exact reasons for Paul's choice remain unclear,[69] but both forms obviously are acceptable in the time of Paul.[70] In light of other parallels,

---

[63] NIV rightly translates 'blessing' as 'praising'.

[64] See Fee 1995: 672 n.35 and Thiselton 2000: 1114.

[65] For the use of 'bless' as 'praise', see Rom. 1:25; 9:5; and 2 Cor. 11:31.

[66] See also 1 Pet. 1:3–5. In the case of Ephesians, the benediction does not entirely replace the thanksgiving since thanksgiving comes right after the benediction in 1:15–16. The relationship between the two in the context of Ephesians continues to be a subject of scholarly debate. See the survey in Lincoln 1990: 47–54.

[67] See 2 Maccabees 1:1–9 and 1:10–17. For other related examples, see 1 Kgs. 5.21f.; 2 Chron. 2.10f.; Eusebius, *Praeparatio evangelica* 9.34; Josephus, *Jewish Antiquities* 8.53; and the discussion in McFarlane 1966: 26; and Best 1987: 79–91; 1998: 105 (cf. O'Brien 1999: 89).

[68] O'Brien 1977: 239; 1979: 504–516; 1999: 124–126. O'Brien also notes the distinction between the two as thanksgiving-formula is used to recount God's work in the lives of others while benediction-formula is used for blessings in which he himself participated. This distinction should be qualified because (1) Paul's participation is frequently implied in the thanksgiving paragraphs where he is the implied instrument through which God has blessed the churches; and (2) the number of samples for both is limited and a firm conclusion cannot be made.

[69] Schubert (1939: 183) has argued that benediction was used when a hostile audience was addressed. This does not apply to Ephesians; and in 2 Corinthians God's gracious acts are noted right after the benediction.

[70] Also worth noting is the possible relationship between these 'introductory benedictions' and the paradigmatic blessings that accompany the establishment of Old Testament covenants. Newman (1998: 89–101), for example, has pointed to the parallels between Eph. 1:3 and Gen. 12:1–3. If this can be accepted, the significance of the use of the benediction form in Ephesians and plausibly in 2 Corinthians has to be re-evaluated. As we shall see, the reference back to the covenantal relationship between God and his people is an essential element in Pauline thanksgiving as well.

the relationship between the two is again affirmed. Thanksgiving recounts the gracious deeds of God in the context of prayer; likewise benediction recounts the mighty acts of God in a liturgical context. In terms of content and function, both are acts of praise and both are acts of worship when God is recognized as the one from whom all blessings flow.

Our understanding of thanksgiving as praise in the context of worship would not be complete without a note concerning the connection between thanksgiving and doxology. To give glory to God is to ascribe honour to him for what he has done. In this sense, it is again related to acts of praise. In Psalm 66, for instance, the psalmist issues a call of praise and doxology for what God has done:

> Shout with joy to God, all the earth!
>   Sing to the glory of his name;
>   make his praise glorious
> Say to God, 'How awesome are your deeds!
>   So great is your power
>   that your enemies cringe before you.
> All the earth bows down to you;
>   they sing praise to you,
>   they sing praise to your name.'
>
> (66:1–4)

Praise and glory are offered as a grateful response to the awesome work of God. Praise, thanksgiving and glory can be distinguished by the fact that glory is often due only to the kingly ruler whose majesty demands the humble response of his people. In the case of the Creator of the universe, however, all three again collapse when the ultimate being is addressed.[71]

In the Pauline epistles, to give glory to God is likewise a proper response to the gracious acts of God. In the final section of Romans, one that points to the climax of the history of salvation, Paul writes that 'Christ has become a servant of the Jews on behalf of God's

---

[71] Frequently, praise and thanksgiving are primarily verbal acts, but one can give glory to God through one's behaviour and pattern of living. This distinction breaks down, however, in Paul when thanksgiving is also a way of life. See, for example, the interchangeability of the two terms when Col. 3:17 ('And whatever you do, whether in word or deed, do it all in the name of the Lord Jesus, giving *thanks* to God the Father through him') is read in the light of 1 Cor. 10:31 ('So whether you eat or drink or whatever you do, do it all for the *glory* of God'). For a discussion of the ethical implications of a life of thanksgiving, see ch. 4 below.

truth, to confirm the promises made to the patriarchs so that the Gentiles may glorify God for his mercy' (Rom. 15:8–9). More explicit connections between thanksgiving and glory can also be found. Again, in reference to what God had done in the life of his Son, Paul writes: 'All this is for your benefit, so that the grace that is reaching more and more people may cause thanksgiving to overflow to the glory of God' (2 Cor. 4:15).[72] Thanksgiving and glory are connected in the context of worship in light of the gracious and mighty deeds of God.[73]

Thanksgiving as God-centredness

When thanksgiving is understood in the sense of praise, it touches upon the centre of worship. D. A. Carson (1993: 13) has rightly noted that 'biblical religion is God-centredness: in short, it is worship'. In the context of worship, one affirms God to be the Lord of all. When giving thanks, God the creator of all is acknowledged to be the source of all goodness. Thanksgiving thus understood belongs properly to theological affirmation as well as ethical concern. It centres on who God is and what he has done and is doing for us; but it is also concerned with ways in which we can align our lives to such creedal affirmations. It is a spontaneous response in the presence of the awesome God, but it can also be 'practised'. In the words of Clement of Alexandria, '"if thou shalt love the Lord thy God," . . . let its first manifestation be towards God in thanksgiving and psalmody' (*Pedagogus* 2.4 [*ANF* 2:249]).

This sense of thanksgiving as acknowledging God as the Creator is made explicit in Revelation. In Revelation 4, the living creatures worship God, ascribing him with three attributes: 'glory, honour and thanks to him who sits on the throne and who lives for ever and ever' (v. 9). The twenty-four elders respond by laying their crowns before the throne saying:

---

[72] This is one of the key passages used by Boobyer (1929) to argue that glory is understood as a light substance and thanksgiving is offered to increase the glory of God. He traces this connection to 'Iranian–Gnostic light speculation' (85). Such a conclusion is unjustifiable and unnecessary in light of the previous discussion concerning the relationship of these concepts in the Old Testament.

[73] Related to glory is the act of confessing the mighty deeds of God. In Phil. 2:11, the two are connected when confessing is understood as grateful remembrance of the work of God: 'and every tongue confess that Jesus Christ is Lord, to the glory of God the Father'. In this sense, one can agree with Ledogar (1968: 70) who claims that the 'confess' word-group 'come[s] closest of all . . . to the basic notion of praise'.

'You are worthy, our Lord and God,
   to receive glory and honour and power,
for you created all things,
   and by your will they were created
   and have their being.'

(v. 11)

In this passage, 'glory, honour and thanks' are paralleled by 'glory
and honour and power'. Thanksgiving is tied with honour and glory.
Moreover, it is reasonable to see the connection between the third
term of each series: 'thanks' and 'power'. To thank God is to
acknowledge that he alone is the powerful one. To support the acclamation of God as the powerful one, God's act of creation is alluded
to. In light of the ancient conceptions of creation as the manifestation of power, it is thus expected that God's act of creation be mentioned.[74] This connection between thanksgiving and power is
confirmed by Revelation 11:17, where one finds the doxology by the
same twenty-four elders in terms of thanksgiving:

'We give thanks to you, Lord God Almighty,
   the One who is and who was,
because you have taken your great power
   and have begun to reign.'

In Paul, thanksgiving is also the way to acknowledge the power
of God over all creation. In 1 Corinthians 10, concerning the par-
taking of meals sacrificed to idols, Paul claims freedom for taking
part in the meal 'with thankfulness' (v. 30) and the foundation for
such freedom is the theology of creation: 'The earth is the Lord's,
and everything in it' (v. 26).[75] Other Pauline references to thanksgiving over food should also be considered in light of this creation
theology.[76] In Romans 14:6, the one who 'gives thanks to God' is

---

[74] For the connection between power and creation, see the studies of Levenson
(1988) and Lee (1993: 199–212).
[75] This is a verbatim quotation from Ps. 24:1, and the verse that follows in this psalm
will make it clear that the author had the creation event in mind: 'for he founded it
upon the seas and established it upon the waters' (v. 2).
[76] The theological significance should not be reduced by formal classification.
Behind this meal-time practice is the affirmation of God as the creator of all. Labelling
these as 'thanksgiving said over food' (e.g., O'Brien 1980: 57) often assumes that they
cannot be integrated into the Pauline understanding of thanksgiving.

one who 'eats to the Lord'. The centrality of the issue of lordship is evident. Creation theology resurfaces in 1 Timothy 4, when food taken with thanksgiving is affirmed (v. 3) since 'everything God created is good, and nothing is to be rejected if it is received with thanksgiving' (v. 4). In all three of these passages, Paul is turning the Jewish meal-time practice on its head, as the food that is blessed is expected to be that which conforms to the acceptable food-laws. Instead, Paul is justifying the eating of all food with the Jewish practice of meal-time thanksgiving that affirms the universal Lordship of God.[77]

When God is acknowledged as the Lord of all, thanksgiving becomes a humbling act admitting the dependency of human existence. Modern psychologists have taught us that ingratitude is a sign of narcissism when a person is not able to acknowledge his or her need of others. In the words of Nancy McWilliams and Stanley Lependorf (1990: 444-445):

> Gratitude seems to us to be an integral expression of our dependency on one another. To thank someone acknowledges our need to have been helped or enriched in the first place . . . Although those of us with predominantly narcissistic concerns may go through the motions of thanking, we frequently resist expressing whole-hearted appreciation, since that would acknowledge a previous insufficiency of some sort, an insult to the grandiose self.

In biblical theology, the failure to acknowledge one's dependency upon the Creator is the root of all sins. In the Old Testament, the connection between human insufficiency and thanksgiving is always assumed though not always made explicit. In David's prayer in 1 Chronicles 29:10–19, we do find this conglomeration of themes. David begins by acknowledging God as the creator of all:

> 'Yours, O Lord, is the greatness and the power
> and the glory and the majesty and the splendour,
> for everything in heaven and earth is yours.'
>
> (v. 11)

---

[77] Cf. Fee 1987: 482; and Dunn 1988: 2.807.

He then continues by giving thanks to God:

> 'Now, our God, we give you thanks,
> and praise your glorious name.'
>
> (v. 12)

This is immediately followed by an admission of human weakness: 'But who am I, and who are my people, that we should be able to give as generously as this? Everything comes from you, and we have given you only what comes from your hand' (v. 13).

Early Church Fathers have already pointed to the acknowledgment of dependency as the centre of thanksgiving. Origen, for example, illustrates the biblical concept of thanksgiving by pointing to another prayer of David in 2 Samuel 7:18–22 (*De Oratione* 33.2):[78]

> 'Who am I, O Sovereign LORD, and what is my family, that you have brought me this far? . . . How great you are, O Sovereign LORD! There is no-one like you, and there is no God but you, as we have heard with our own ears.'

In his writings, Paul's emphasis on justification by grace draws our attention solely to the righteousness of God in Christ. Human beings are without merit since 'all have sinned and fall short of the glory of God' (Rom. 3:23). Any boasting apart from the work of God is to be condemned as trusting on one's ability in the presence of God. In the presence of the cross, one can only rely on the grace of God: 'May I never boast except in the cross of our Lord Jesus Christ, through which the world has been crucified to me, and I to the world' (Gal. 6:14).[79]

On the foundation of the recognition of divine grace and human weakness, the connection between petition and thanksgiving can be properly appreciated.[80] When petition is grounded on thanksgiving, God and not self-interest becomes the focus. On the other hand, thanksgiving without petition proclaims God to be the Creator without trusting that he indeed is one who is able to provide for his

---

[78] This reference is noted in Ledogar 1968: 100.

[79] For a recent treatment on 'boasting', see Seifrid 2000: 67–76.

[80] Schaller (1990: 6) rightly notes: 'Only where our prayer of petition and lament arises on the foundation of such thanksgiving does it become different from a human arrogance, the idea that in a presumptuous and arrogant way we can make God concerned with our petty human life.'

people. In the Pauline epistles, petitions are often found precisely in the thanksgiving paragraphs that introduce the epistles.[81] The two cannot be separated in the Pauline model of prayer: 'Do not be anxious about anything, but in everything, by prayer and petition, with thanksgiving, present your requests to God' (Phil. 4:6; cf. 2 Cor. 9:14; 1 Tim. 2:1).[82]

God, and not his gifts, is the primary focus of Pauline thanksgiving.[83] In the constant act of thanksgiving, the relationship with God is nurtured. Through thanksgiving, the gracious acts are remembered and the life of a person is thereby changed. Thanksgiving then becomes an act of submission when the performance of such an act is not aimed at coercing God to act, but is a way to acknowledge him to be the Lord of all. In this sense, thanksgiving becomes subversive when the Lordship of God is acknowledged even when the one who is in control seems to be invisible. We are changed in thanksgiving then, as we encounter this gracious God. In the words of Karl Barth (1957: 669), thanksgiving signifies 'the change of the being of man before God brought about by the fact that God has altered His attitude to man'.

As the 'image of the invisible God' (Col. 1:15), Christ becomes the Lord of all. In this context, creation language is again invoked: 'For by him all things were created: things in heaven and on earth, visible and invisible, whether thrones or powers or rulers or authorities; all things were created by him and for him' (1:16). It is precisely in this epistle, where the Lordship of Christ is emphasized, that one finds the Pauline emphasis on thanksgiving. To be 'in Christ' and to acknowledge Christ as the Lord of all, then, is expressed by acts of thanksgiving: 'just as you received Christ Jesus as Lord, continue to live in him, rooted and built up in him, strengthened in the faith as you were

---

[81] Petitions can be in the form of prayer-report or actual prayer. Phil. 1:3–4 best illustrates petitions in the form of prayer-report: 'I thank my God every time I remember you. In all my prayers for all of you, I always pray with joy . . .' Rom. 1:8–10 provides an example for an actual petition-prayer (together with a prayer-report) in the thanksgiving itself: 'First, I thank my God . . .; and I pray that now . . .'

[82] Wiles (1974: 161) also points to the fact that in Jewish liturgical traditions, petitions were often enclosed by praises and blessings to God, expressing thankfulness to God along with requests for deliverance.

[83] Of course one cannot separate the gifts from the giver. Furthermore, Pauline thanksgiving is based on the greatest gift of all: salvation through the death and resurrection of Christ (cf. Rom. 5:15, 17; 2 Cor. 9:15). Nevertheless, we should focus on the giver and not the gifts in the examination of Pauline thanksgiving. In focusing on the gift, a 'thank-you' might have been sufficient. In focusing on the Lord of all, however, worship and submission are required.

taught, and overflowing with thankfulness' (2:6–7). The fact that thanksgiving focuses on the Lordship of God in Christ and is not simply a response to certain favours received explains the appearance of the absolute call to thanksgiving in 3:15: 'And be thankful'.

The distinct theocentric and christocentric focus of Pauline thanksgiving may explain why thanksgiving is directed only towards God.[84] God alone deserves worship and praise. When all goodness is recognized to be coming ultimately from God, gifts offered by other human beings also invoke thanksgiving to God. In 2 Corinthians 1:11, Paul mentions that others will give thanks to God on account of what God had done for Paul and his co-workers. Later in the same epistle, Paul calls the Corinthians to give to the Jerusalem church. Paul notes that the reception of the gifts by the Jerusalem apostles will 'result in thanksgiving to God' (9:11). In this context, the wider theological basis can also be detected. The gift that the Jerusalem church is expected to receive is given in response ultimately to the salvific acts of God and 'the surpassing grace' from God (9:14).[85] Both the Corinthians and the Jerusalem church therefore are to give thanks to God himself.[86]

---

[84] See the discussion in note 27 above.

[85] For the word-play on grace and gift in 2 Cor. 8 – 9, see Georgi 1992: 107–109. Georgi also notes that thanksgiving in this context is concerned with the result of the climactic acts of God when Jews and Gentiles can now become one body in Christ. The collection for the saints precisely aims to maintain such unity.

[86] Other short expressions of thanks in the Pauline epistles should also be considered in this light. These expressions are not simply rhetorical devices or emotional outbursts of Paul but they point to a central Pauline theme that salvation comes only from God (e.g., Rom. 6:17; 7:25; 1 Cor. 15:57; 2 Cor. 2:14).

Chapter Two

Thanksgiving within the covenantal traditions

We have established that Pauline thanksgiving requires appropriate analytic categories that may be foreign to modern sensibilities. In this chapter, a biblical-theological category that stretches beyond one particular corpus in the Christian canon will be discussed. This category is not explicitly evoked with every appearance of the Pauline call to thanksgiving, but without a proper appreciation of the importance of the function of this category within the thought-world of Paul, Pauline thanksgiving will not be fully explicable.

God and his people

In the Old Testament, the relationship between God and his people is expressed primarily within the context of the covenant.[1] Covenant does not simply assume the relationship between God and his people in an abstract sense. The relationship is developed within history through actual time and space. Through the development of this relationship, the nature of God is revealed.[2] In covenant traditions, Israel defines her past and finds her future.

Covenant lies at the heart of Old Testament theology. In covenant theology, one finds 'the key to a question that has long occupied the attention of Old Testament scholars: the question of the distinctiveness of Israel's religious faith'.[3] Not only is this the distinctive

---

[1] No attempt will be made here to recover the origin of the term 'covenant'. The failure to achieve any consensus is noted by Barr (1977: 23–28).

[2] The best example appears within the wider context of the Sinai covenant when God revealed his own name to Moses (Exod. 3:14; cf. 6:3).

[3] Nicholson's (1986: 191) statement reflects the consensus of Old Testament scholars, although many would point to other distinctive elements in Israel's faith. What is being debated, however, is the way covenant theology developed. Nicholson, for example, argues that the notion of a covenant between Yahweh and Israel was conceived in the eighth century BC. This is to assume the Documentary Hypothesis, one that is increasingly under attack. In this chapter, these historical concerns will not be our focus.

element, the covenant in turn aims at maintaining the distinctiveness of Israel's faith.

It is not the idea of an agreement between human beings and the deity that is distinct. Rather, it is the concept that God is one, and the implications of such an affirmation, that is foreign to Israel's neighbours. Right after the establishment of the Mosaic covenant,[4] one that is in continuity with the Abrahamic covenant,[5] we find the delivery of the Ten Commandments, the first of which reads: 'I am the LORD your God' (Exod. 20:2; Deut. 5:6) together with the prohibition: 'You shall have no other gods before me' (Exod. 20:3; Deut. 5:7). These affirmations hold prominent place in the 'words of the covenant' (Exod. 34:14–17) and they lie at the core of the covenant renewal ceremony during the time of Joshua (Josh. 24). The significance of these commandments extends beyond the Mosaic Torah. In Psalms 50 and 81, psalms that reflect covenant renewal ceremonies,[6] one finds allusion to these commandments: 'I am God, your God' (Ps. 50:7) and 'I am the LORD your God' (Ps. 81:10). The *Shema* that has been dear to the Jewish life of worship for centuries also begins with the same affirmation (Deut. 6:4). In the Old Testament, to violate the covenant is to do evil in the eyes of God. The worst of such 'evil' is to worship anything or anyone other than the true God of Israel:

> If a man or woman living among you in one of the towns the LORD gives you is found doing evil in the eyes of the LORD your God in violation of his covenant, and contrary to my command has worshipped other gods . . . you must investigate it thoroughly. If it is true . . . take the man or woman who has done this evil deed to your city gate and stone that person to death (Deut. 17:2–5).

---

[4] Exod. 19 represents the first stage of a long process through which the covenant is established. See also the account of the confirmation of the covenant in Exod. 24.

[5] Cf. Lev. 26:42–45 where God's paradigmatic act of deliverance is understood as the fulfilment of the covenant to the patriarchs. New Testament authors seem to share the same understanding (cf. Acts 3:25; 7:8; Gal. 4:21–31). In this chapter, various covenants in the Old Testament will be alluded to without highlighting the relationship and differences among them. Instead, continuity will be assumed. For helpful treatments of the various covenants, see Dumbrell 1997; McComiskey 1985; Beckwith 1987:93–118; and the recent study of McKenzie 2000.

[6] See the discussion in Weinfeld (1990: 21–22).

A number of titles have been ascribed to God who is the Lord of all. Prominent among them is the title 'king'.[7] The mere use of suzerainty treaties as the model for the Sinai covenant reflects the fact that royal ideology forms the framework of this agreement.[8] The affirmation of God as king can be found in the Song of Moses in Exodus 15 where the power and sovereignty of God is affirmed. The Song concludes with the acclamation: 'The LORD will reign for ever and ever' (v. 18). The kingship of God is further developed in the covenant with David (2 Sam. 7). In the reign of King David, the Abrahamic covenant is recognized with the promise of kingly descendants (Gen. 17:6, 16). The Davidic dynasty represents a symbol of the kingly rule of God. Furthermore, an everlasting covenant is established with the house of David:

> I will maintain my love to him for ever,
>   and my covenant with him will never fail.
> I will establish his line for ever,
>   his throne as long as the heavens endure.
>
> (Ps. 89:28–29)

For a fulfilment of these promises, one has to wait for the arrival of the Messianic era in the life and ministry of Jesus Christ.

In addressing Israel, the affirmation does not simply state that God is 'the' only God. Instead, the affirmation makes it clear that God is 'your' God. Monotheism is not stated in an abstract form. It is manifested in the relationship between God and his people. 'I will be your God', therefore, finds its completion with the phrase 'and you shall be my people'.[9] When he established his covenant with Abraham, God already had the creation of his people in mind: 'I will establish my covenant as an everlasting covenant between me and you and your descendants after you for the generations to come, to be your God and the God of your descendants after you' (Gen. 17:7). This promise is reaffirmed and in some sense realized in the Mosaic covenant: 'the LORD has declared this day that you are his

---

[7] Dumbrell (1997: 42) notes that '[t]he presupposition of covenant is the present kingship of God'. He also notes that the full exposition of this aspect of the covenant can be found only in the New Testament with Jesus' proclamation of the kingdom of God.

[8] See Mendenhall 1955. For a survey of the scholarly debate concerning the implications of the parallels between the two, see Nicholson (1986: 56–82).

[9] See Exod. 6:7; Lev. 26:12–13; Deut. 29:13; Jer. 7:23; 30:22; 31:33.

people, his treasured possession as he promised' (Deut. 26:18). The God who calls Israel from among all the nations is not, however, a tribal God. It is precisely because of God's universal sovereignty that he can call a people for himself to be a blessing to others: 'Although the whole earth is mine, you will be for me a kingdom of priests and a holy nation' (Exod. 19:6; cf. Gen. 12:2–3; Is. 61:6). For the people of Israel, the proper response to the establishment of this covenantal relationship is to offer God praise and glory (Exod. 15:11).

God created his people and he became their God. Throughout the entire process of establishing the covenantal relationship with Israel, God is the one taking the initiative. After the flood and the tower of Babel, God has shown his love by calling Abram (Gen. 12:1). In the exodus narrative, it is God who likewise took the initiative in building up his people (Deut. 10:15). With David, it is also God who called him to be the leader of his people (2 Sam. 7:8), thus continuing the promise to the patriarchs (Gen. 22:18). In this covenantal relationship, therefore, Israel's role is to provide a proper response to the divine initiative.[10] Throughout the history of the covenantal relationship, God is at the centre of the drama.

Also unique to the covenant(s) between God and Israel is the sense of history embedded in the definition of this relationship. This covenantal relationship is defined by the history of the mighty acts of God, the present obligations of the people of God, and the promises that point to the future hope. The past, present and future aspects highlight the importance of the temporal framework in the outworking of God's relationship with his people.

The past in covenantal traditions

The mighty acts of God in the past form the basis for the present relationship. This is well illustrated by the historical prefaces found in the covenant formula.[11] In the establishment of the covenant with Abraham, God 'introduces' himself by reciting what he had done for Abraham and his family: 'I am the LORD, who brought you out of Ur of the Chaldeans to give you this land to take possession of it' (Gen.

---

[10] This also highlights a related distinctive element of Old Testament history. Unlike the literature of surrounding nations, the history of Israel is not aimed at honouring her ancestors and founding fathers. Glory belongs solely to God, while human characters are simply recipients of divine grace.

[11] The historical preface is a critical part of the suzerainty treaties as shown in Mendenhall 1955: 30.

15:7). Similarly, in the presentation of the Ten Commandments, this history is proclaimed immediately after the affirmation of the one God of Israel: 'who brought you out of Egypt, out of the land of slavery' (Exod. 20:2; Deut. 5:6). Even in the case of David, past inter-action forms the basis for present relationship: 'I took you from the pasture and from following the flock to be ruler over my people Israel. I have been with you wherever you have gone, and I have cut off all your enemies from before you' (2 Sam. 7:8–9). In the Old Testament, the recitation of the mighty acts of God frequently appears in covenantal context. It is precisely these mighty acts that constitute the 'history' of Israel. Mendenhall (1955: 44) is therefore correct in noting that 'the covenant form itself furnished at least the nucleus about which the historical traditions crystallized in early Israel'.

The connections between covenant and history provide insight into aspects of Israel's faith. First, unlike other nations that trace their history back to the mythic past, history is the plane where Israel's identity is formed. The fact that God is the subject of this history also means that God is the primary character in the forma-tion of the identity of the community. Related to this is the fact that God is revealed in history. 'Theology' in the biblical sense, then, is the account of what God did for his people.[12] When 'theology' is con-structed in this way, the proper action of the covenantal partners is also defined accordingly. God is the faithful God who will not abandon his people as witnessed through the establishment of the various covenants.[13] Human beings are called to 'remember' what God has done for them. This remembering takes centre stage in the cultic life of Israel.[14] Furthermore, because this history is an account of the power of God and Israel's reception of divine grace, obedience is demanded in the response to the remembering of the past.[15]

---

[12] This is established already in the classic work of von Rad (1966: 1–78).

[13] *Hesed*, a term that is used to express God's concern for his people, can, therefore, be understood as 'covenantal faithfulness'. Sakenfeld (1985), in particular, has traced the theme of the faithfulness of God through the various Old Testament covenants.

[14] This again reflects the uniqueness of the way Israel worships her God (see de Vaux 1961: 217–213). In this sense, the term 'cultic' is to be understood in the widest sense when the everyday life of Israel is also considered as an act of worship. For a further discussion of the theme of remembering, see chapter three below.

[15] See the classic statement in Auberbach (1953: 15) who suggests that unlike the Homeric epic, biblical accounts of Israel's history 'do not flatter us that they may please us and enchant us – they seek to subject us, and if we refuse to be subjected we are rebels'.

Finally, when the history of Israel is understood as the account of promises fulfilled by God, the future is built on the same basis. Israel has a future precisely because she has a past. In the covenants, the past is celebrated in anticipation of the future when Israel remains loyal in her life of praise in the present.

The present in covenantal traditions

Covenant stipulations follow the affirmation of the one God of Israel and the history of God's dealings with Israel. As God recognizes Israel to be his 'treasured possession', Israel acknowledges God as her Lord by committing to 'walk in his ways' (Deut. 26:17–18). The Ten Commandments, then, becomes the classic symbol of covenantal obligations,[16] and the entire Pentateuch comes to be recognized as primarily serving as a code for the covenant people. When the covenant was confirmed, Israel provided the expected response: 'Everything the LORD has said we will do' (Exod. 24:3). These commandments are not abstract rules to be fulfilled, however. They represent the will of God. To observe the commandments is to acknowledge God to be Lord. To keep the commandments is therefore frequently understood as a way to 'love' God (cf. Exod. 20:6; Deut. 5:10; 7:9; 10:12; 19:9).[17]

It is clear that keeping the commandments is not to be understood as a way to earn favour in the presence of God. Rather, it is a response to the divine acts of grace. Furthermore, with respect to God himself, to keep the commandments of God is to acknowledge his sovereignty, 'for the LORD, whose name is Jealous, is a jealous God' (Exod. 34:14). In the same way, for the people of God, to keep God's commandments is to keep themselves holy and distinct from other nations (cf. Exod. 19:5–6; Lev. 18:24). Circumcision (Gen. 17:2, 9–10) in the Abrahamic covenant functions in a similar way. Understood in this way, a strict separation between 'ritual' and 'ethical' laws in their covenantal context cannot be made.[18]

---

[16] For the function of the Decalogue as the symbol of covenantal stipulations in the rest of the Old Testament and in Second Temple Judaism, see Weinfeld 1990: 1–44; and Freund 1998: 124–141.

[17] Baltzer (1971) has argued, on the basis of a comparison between Old Testament covenants and Ancient Near Eastern treaties, that 'to love God' is the main requirement of biblical covenants. See also Nicholson (1986: 215) who points out that these covenantal stipulations reflect a different understanding of the nature of Israel's God as he is not simply the Lord and master but also a partner in this covenantal relationship.

[18] The distinction was made in the prophetic writings only when Israel failed to perform portions of the commandments according to their intended function. See, for example, Is. 1:11–17 and Hos. 6:6.

In any discussion of covenantal stipulations, Israel's failure to remain a faithful partner should be noted. Even when Moses was still on the mountain where the covenant was being confirmed, Israel turned against Moses and their God who brought them out of Egypt. By building the golden calf, they broke the basis of the covenant that affirms Yahweh to be their only God. They were called 'a stiff-necked people' (Exod. 32:9). Moreover, their disobedience is not limited to this earlier rebellion. The accusation through the mouth of the prophets applies to the entire history of Israel: 'They followed worthless idols and became worthless themselves' (Jer. 2:5). This reverses the condition of Israel when the covenant was first established. They were called God's 'treasured possession' (Exod. 19:5) and they were supposed to follow the true God who brought them out from Egypt. In breaking the covenant, one can only expect to see the departure of the presence of God and the blessings that were promised. In spite of the acts of faithless Israel, however, God has shown himself to be a forgiving God. After the golden calf incident, God further revealed himself to be 'the compassionate and gracious God, slow to anger, abounding in love and faithfulness, maintaining love to thousands, and forgiving wickedness, rebellion and sin' (Exod. 34:6–7). The future of the covenants rests on such promises.[19]

The future in covenantal traditions

Building on the creedal recognition of the sovereignty of Yahweh and the history of his gracious dealings with Israel, the covenant points to the future when the people of God will be delivered from their distress and suffering.

In the Abrahamic and Mosaic covenants, the blessings to Israel are symbolized by the promise of the land. When Israel was found to be an unfaithful partner, she was forced out of the land. In the midst of such catastrophes, the prophets offer interpretation within the context of the covenant. Jeremiah, for example, accuses the people for not obeying the terms of the covenant (Jer. 11:3–4). Although the people turned from their God, God did not forget his people. The future is articulated in terms of what God had done in the past. The people will no longer say: 'As surely as the LORD lives, who brought the Israelites up out of Egypt.' Instead, they will say: 'As surely as the LORD lives, who brought

---

[19] After the exile, an event that was understood to be a punishment of Israel's wickedness, the same affirmation was repeated (Neh. 9:16–18).

the Israelites up out of the land of the north and out of all the countries where he had banished them' (Jer. 16:14–15; cf. Is. 49:8).[20]

The true hope for Israel, however, lies in the distant future when the people will finally be able to remain faithful to their God. In this context, the new covenant is introduced:

> 'The time is coming,' declares the LORD,
>   'when I will make a new covenant
> with the house of Israel
>   and with the house of Judah.'
>
> (Jer. 31:31)

Unlike the previous covenant, the law will be inscribed 'in their minds' and 'on their hearts' (Jer. 31:33; cf. Ezek. 36:26). The novel element in this covenant is not what God will do or what he will become. The new covenant promises that God's people will be able to remain faithful in the covenantal relationship.[21] God's faithfulness remains unchanged as he again takes the initiative to re-establish the covenantal relationship with his people.[22] The people 'will come and bind themselves to the LORD' and this will be 'an everlasting covenant that will not be forgotten' (Jer. 50:5).

This new covenant signifies the climactic moment in the relationship between God and his people. Therefore, not only is it the fulfilment of the Mosaic covenant, this 'everlasting covenant' is also the realization of God's 'faithful love promised to David' (Is. 55:3). With the establishment of this covenant, the people will 'remember' all that God had done for them (Ezek. 16:63), and the presence of God will be with them for ever (Ezek. 37:26). The promised reconciliation between God and his people is also depicted in terms of marital bliss (Hos. 2:16; Jer. 31:32; Ezek. 16:59–63), unity among Jews and Gentiles (Is. 42:6), and cosmic harmony (Ezek. 34:25; Hos. 2:18). Such metaphors point to the finality of this new covenant.

The vision for the future is not an accidental development of Old Testament covenantal traditions. It is a natural extension of God's

---

[20] The use of the exodus typology in the description of the coming salvation of God can be found elsewhere in both the Old and the New Testaments. For a further discussion, see Pao (2000: 37–69).

[21] It is not the power of the people that is being emphasized. God is the one who will keep them in his love. See also Is. 59:21 where the descent of the Spirit is mentioned in the context of the provision of the new covenant.

[22] This is made explicit in Ezek. 20:37 when God promises: 'I will bring you into the bond of the covenant.'

past promises and of what he had done for his people.[23] It reflects God's character as a faithful covenant partner. Moreover, it touches directly on the centre of Israel's faith: God will not cease to be the Lord of all because his name is 'I am'.[24]

Paul and the covenantal traditions

The promise of the new covenant points to the person of Jesus.[25] He stood at the climax of all promises (2 Cor. 1:20); in him all promises find their fulfilment (Luke 24:44). At the beginning of Luke's gospel, Zechariah praises God for remembering 'his holy covenant' (Luke 1:72). The rest of the Lukan narrative is therefore understood as a continuation of God's covenantal relationship with his people. In the second volume of the Lukan writings, the Jews are referred to as heirs of the covenant God made with their fathers (Acts 3:25). In this covenantal context, Jesus is understood as the initiator of the 'new' covenant. His death was understood as critical to the establishment of the covenant as his blood is the 'blood of the covenant, which is poured out for many for the forgiveness of sins' (Matt. 26:28; cf. Mark 14:24).[26] In the Lukan and Pauline accounts of the Lord's

[23] Not only is the idea of the 'new covenant' not an accidental development, it is also not a 'late' development in Old Testament covenantal traditions. The realization of Israel's failure to be the faithful covenant partner from the very beginning is accompanied by the recognition of God's continued gracious and creative acts in his dealings with his own people. Rendtorff (1998: 72) is correct when he states that the idea of the 'new covenant' is 'implicit in the whole of the Bible's covenant theology from early on: Israel is no longer living in the covenant originally concluded before God and with him, but now lives in the covenant which God has renewed, in spite of Israel's breach of the covenant'.

[24] The connection between the name of Yahweh and his sovereignty over both the past and the future is made explicit in Revelation where God is the one 'who is, and who was, and who is to come' (1:8; cf. 11:17).

[25] Covenantal traditions also play an important role in Second Temple Jewish literature. E. P. Sanders (1976: 11–44; and 1977), for example, has argued that covenant was the controlling paradigm within which the relationship between God and his people is understood. While Sanders is correct in noting the importance of covenant in Jewish traditions, he has defined covenant too narrowly in terms of election especially in a sociological sense. His understanding of covenantal nomism as the primary soteriological category is also open to question. Furthermore, to say that this kind of covenantal nomism is '*the* religion of Judaism' (1976: 41; italics his) is also an overstatement, to say the least. For a detailed critique of Sanders' understanding of covenant, see Elliott 2000: 245–307.

[26] This is an allusion to the Sinai covenant ceremony where one finds reference to 'the blood of the covenant' (Exod. 24:8). The Lord's Supper itself also reminds one of the mentioning of eating and drinking in Exod. 24:11. For a discussion of the sacrificial aspects of the Last Supper in 1 Corinthians, see, among others, Kilpatrick 1983: 53–54.

Supper, the terms 'new covenant' are used in reference to the cup (Luke 22:20; 1 Cor. 11:25). Outside of the Pauline corpus, the epistle to the Hebrews provides the strongest argument that Jesus fulfilled the promises of the new covenant. In Hebrews 8:8–12, the new covenant promise of Jeremiah 31:31–34 is quoted (cf. Heb. 10:16–17). Jesus is called 'the mediator of a new covenant' and those who believe in him will receive 'the promised eternal inheritance' (Heb. 9:15). The finality of this covenant is also signified by the use of the phrase 'eternal covenant' (Heb. 13:20). In early Christianity, therefore, the life and death of Jesus is interpreted within the context of Old Testament covenantal situations.

When we turn to Paul, a similar picture can be found. Covenant language is found in passages where the continuity and discontinuity with Israel's past is discussed. The reference to the 'new covenant' in the Pauline account of the Lord's Supper (1 Cor. 11:25) reappears in 2 Corinthians 3 where Paul describes his ministry as that of the 'new covenant' (v. 6). Together with the use of the phrase 'written on our hearts' (v. 2) in this context, one seems justified to see Jeremiah 31:31 behind this passage.[27] The context provided by Jeremiah 31 is important for our understanding of the Pauline understanding of the 'new covenant'. With the words,

> 'It will not be like the covenant
> I made with their forefathers
> when I took them by the hand
> to lead them out of Egypt.'
>
> (Jer. 31:32)

the new covenant is depicted precisely through the contrast with the old (i.e., Sinai) covenant.[28] The same contrast can also be found in Paul. In 2 Corinthians 3:8, Paul notes that the ministry of the Spirit will be more glorious. With this statement, Paul is acknowledging both the continuity with the past (cf. v. 7) and the radical discontinuity that came with the dawn of the eschatological era.[29]

[27] E.g., Furnish 1984: 19–96; Barnett 1997: 163–165, 175. For a discussion of the importance of Ezek. 11:19 and 36:26–27 in this context, see also Hafemann 1986: 206–218.

[28] Weippert (1979: 336–351) has rightly noted that the exodus generation is primarily in view in the context of Jer. 31. For a further discussion of the use of Jeremiah in the interpretation of the exodus narrative, see the recent study of Shead (2000: 33–61).

[29] This discontinuity is expressed by the use of the term 'old covenant' in 2 Cor. 3:14.

This contrast between the new and the old covenants is not limited to 2 Corinthians. In Galatians 3, the same emphasis on continuity and discontinuity can be found. First, more recent covenants that God made with his people do not invalidate previous ones (vv. 15–17). On the other hand, one finds the affirmation that the new covenant accomplished by Christ is a fulfilment of the Abrahamic covenant, thus qualifying the role of the Mosaic covenant.[30] Similarly, in Galatians 4:21–31, the superiority of the covenant established by Christ is asserted through the allegory of the covenants of Hagar and Sarah. Without invalidating the law, Paul highlights the fundamental notion of God's grace and human depravity by pointing to God's promises in the Abrahamic covenant.

In Romans 11, the discussion of the relationship between Israel and the church is presented. In the quotation from Isaiah 59:21, one finds a reference to the covenant God made with Israel: 'And this is my covenant with them' (v. 27). The reference to the covenant points to the continuity of God's promises (cf. Rom. 9:4). In the context of the wider arguments of Romans, these promises are fulfilled in the work of Christ and the covenant to Israel is then 'fulfilled' in the establishment of the new covenant.[31] The phrase that immediately follows ('when I take away their sins', cf. Is. 27:9) should also be understood through the christocentric lens provided by Romans 1 – 8. Therefore, even if distinction between ethnic Israel and the church can be made, soteriologically they both look to the new covenant established by Jesus Christ himself.

This christocentric emphasis of the new covenant and the continuity of the covenants can be found in Ephesians 2:12–13:

> [R]emember that at that time you were separate from Christ, excluded from citizenship in Israel and foreigners to the covenants of the promise, without hope and without God in the world. But now in Christ Jesus you who once were far away have been brought near through the blood of Christ.

---

[30] Paul also makes it clear, however, that the law is not 'opposed to the promises of God' (Gal. 3:21). For a further discussion of the role of the law in Pauline thought, see Seifrid 2000: 95–127. Seifrid highlights one contrast between the Abrahamic and Sinai covenants: 'God takes an obligation upon himself in his promise to Abraham in Genesis 15 and in contrast places an obligation upon his people in the giving of the law at Sinai' (111). This is a helpful distinction although covenantal stipulation is not entirely missing in the Abrahamic covenant, and God's promise for his people continues in the Sinai covenant.

[31] This is supported by the possible allusion to Jer. 31:33 here.

The inclusion of the Gentiles points to one of the distinctive elements in the new covenant. In emphasizing the discontinuity of this new covenant, continuity is also noted. While reference to the covenant in Romans 11 points to the continuity of promises to Israel, in Ephesians the emphasis is placed on the conversion of the Gentiles. In both cases, references are made to the covenants of Israel.[32] Gentile inclusion is therefore placed firmly within the covenantal promises of the Old Testament.

We have seen that covenantal terminology usually appears in contexts when continuity and discontinuity with the Old Testament promises is at issue. The limited appearances of these terms in these contexts do not, however, sufficiently reflect the importance of covenantal traditions in Pauline writings. It would be better to understand covenantal traditions as the foundation or presupposition of his theology.

As in the Old Testament covenantal traditions, the affirmation of one God who has a special relationship with his people lies at the heart of the Pauline gospel. The affirmations 'God is one' (Gal. 3:20) and 'there is no God but one' (1 Cor. 8:4) reflect Paul's fundamental conviction. In the era of the new covenant, the affirmation of the one God is now understood in a christological sense when the Lordship of Jesus is affirmed without betraying the monotheistic emphasis. In 1 Corinthians 8:6, for example, one reads: 'yet for us there is but one God, the Father, from whom all things came and for whom we live; and there is but one Lord, Jesus Christ, through whom all things came and through whom we live' (cf. Col. 1:15–20; 1 Tim. 2:5). Even in Trinitarian formulae, the affirmation of 'oneness' is not compromised (Eph. 4:4–6).

The affirmation of the one God is accompanied by the emphasis on the elected status of his people. Believers are the 'elect' (e.g., 2 Tim. 2:10; Titus 1:1) and the 'beloved' people of God (e.g., Rom. 1:7; 11:28; Eph. 5:1; Col. 3:12; cf. 1 Thess. 1:4), a term understood in the sense of election.[33] Paul's claim to be the true circumcision (Phil. 3:3;

---

[32] The plural 'covenants' in Eph. 2:12–13 is comparable to Rom. 9:4 where the plural is also used (although the singular form does appear in Rom. 9:4 in some manuscripts). In these two passages, Paul is likely to be referring to both the Abrahamic and Mosaic covenants. The distinction between covenants is not always emphasized, however, when the salvation of Jews and Gentiles cannot be entirely separated in the Old Testament covenantal traditions. See Getty 1987: 92–99. Cf. Talbert 1987: 299–313.

[33] See, for example, Mal. 1:2–3 where metaphors of human emotions are used to describe God's sovereign choice within his covenantal relationship with Israel. See also Deut. 7:9, where the Mosaic covenant is explicitly called the 'covenant of love'.

cf. Rom. 2:27; Col. 2:11) also alludes to the symbol of the covenant people of God.[34] With cultic terms of separation such as 'holy' and 'blameless', the church is depicted as the chosen people: 'For he chose us in him before the creation of the world to be holy and blameless in his sight' (Eph. 1:4; cf. Col. 1:22). The corresponding noun 'saints' further points to the elected status of the people (e.g., Rom. 8:27; 1 Cor. 6:2; Eph. 1:15–18; 6:18; Col. 1:2, 4). Moreover, since the temple represents God's presence among his own people, Paul's understanding of believers as the temple should not be ignored: 'For we are the temple of the living God. As God has said: "I will live with them and walk among them, and I will be their God, and they will be my people"' (2 Cor. 6:16; cf. 1 Cor. 3:16–17; 6:19). In the context of Ezekiel, this is precisely the promise made when God establishes the 'eternal covenant' with his people (Ezek. 37:27; cf. Jer. 32:38).[35]

As in the Old Testament, the covenant theology of Paul is also portrayed in terms of the past, the present and the future relationship between God and his people. In the Mosaic covenant, the historical preface depicts God's mighty acts of deliverance when Israel was delivered from the hands of the Egyptians. In the new covenant, the covenantal relationship between God and his people reached its climax when God delivered his people from sin through the death and resurrection of his own Son.[36] The Pauline version of the Lord's Supper points to the establishment of the 'new covenant' (1 Cor. 11:25). For Paul, his 'gospel' is nothing but what Christ did, and this is what we are called to remember: 'Remember Jesus Christ, raised from the dead, descended from David. This is my gospel, for which I am suffering even to the point of being chained like a criminal' (2 Tim. 2:8–9).[37]

As in the case of the covenant people in the Old Testament, the church is also called to reflect the holiness of God. In covenantal terms, believers are called to 'live a life worthy of the calling you have received' (Eph. 4:1; cf. Phil. 3:14). This call is related back to the

---

[34] See, in particular, Gen. 17:10: 'This is my covenant with you and your descendants after you, the covenant you are to keep: Every male among you shall be circumcised.' The spiritualization of circumcision already appears in Deut. 10:16: 'Circumcise your hearts . . .'

[35] Divine presence is understood as the essence of the covenantal relationship between God and Israel (cf. Lev. 26:12–13).

[36] The contrast between the faithful Son of God, Jesus Christ, and the unfaithful Israel who failed to fulfil the covenantal relationship is critical to Paul's argument. See the recent treatment of Gal. 2:15–21 in light of the covenantal relationship between God and Israel in B. Longenecker 1996: 75–97.

[37] The mentioning of David and election in the context (2:10) reflects the use of the covenantal framework in this call of remembrance.

mighty acts of God in Christ when the Christian's triumph over sin is understood in terms of the death and resurrection of Christ (Col. 3:1–4; cf. Rom. 6:4, 11–14; 1 Cor. 5:6–8; Gal. 5:24–25; Eph. 5:1–2; 2 Tim. 2:11).[38] As a covenant people, holy living is the only appropriate way to respond to the gracious acts of God in Christ (2 Cor. 6:1). It is divine grace, however, that enables believers to accomplish this goal: 'The one who calls you is faithful and he will do it' (1 Thess. 5:24; cf. 1 Cor. 1:8; Phil. 1:6; 1 Thess. 3:13).

Naturally, the new covenant also looks forward to the future when the promises of God will be fully realized.[39] In reference to the establishment of the new covenant, we are called to remember what Christ did for us 'until he comes' (1 Cor. 11:26). Christ's return will mean that God will be present with his people for ever and that the people of God will receive final deliverance. Therefore, the Day of the Lord is understood as 'the day of redemption' (Eph. 4:30). Corresponding to this deliverance is the recognition of God as the one Lord and the ultimate king of all (1 Cor. 15:24; cf. 2 Tim. 4:1).[40]

Among the metaphors used in describing the future promises is one that plays a prominent role in Old Testament covenantal tradition. Believers were promised that they 'will receive an inheritance from the Lord' (Col. 3:24; cf. Eph. 1:14, 18; 5:5),[41] one that is promised to the people of Israel, and that they will become 'heirs according to the promise' (Gal. 3:29; cf. 4:1–7; Rom. 8:17; Titus 3:7) of such inheritance. In the Old Testament, the Greek word for 'inheritance' (*klēronomia*)[42] and its related forms are used in the context of the Abrahamic and Mosaic covenants in reference to the promised land (e.g., Gen. 15:7; Exod. 15:17; Josh. 11:23). In Isaiah 49:8, the same promises are given in reference to the future of Israel as a covenant people:

---

[38] Christian living is also described in cultic terms as believers are called to offer themselves 'as living sacrifices, holy and pleasing to God' (Rom. 12:1; cf. Eph. 5:2). For a further discussion, see chapter four below.

[39] It should be noted that for Paul, 'the old has gone, the new has come' (2 Cor. 5:17). The coming of the promised Messiah ushered in the eschatological era. Nevertheless, future consummation is yet to come (cf. 1 Cor. 15; 1 Thess. 4:13 – 5:3).

[40] The use of the term *parousia* in reference to the return of Christ may also support our understanding of the eschatological Day of the Lord as essentially the royal presence and reign of God. Oepke (1967: 866) is probably correct in suggesting that while the term is Hellenistic, in 'essential content, however, it derives from the OT, Judaism, and primitive Christian thinking'.

[41] In the speech of Paul to the Ephesian elders as recorded in Acts 20, the same use of the metaphor of 'inheritance' appears (v. 32).

[42] The term most frequently used for 'inheritance' is *klēronomia*. See also the use of *klēros* in Col. 1:12.

'In the time of my favour I will answer you,
    and in the day of salvation I will help you;
I will keep you and will make you
    to be a covenant for the people,
to restore the land
    and to reassign its desolate inheritances.'

The fact that Paul's use of the term alludes to the Old Testament covenantal promises is confirmed by Galatians 3:18 when Paul writes that the 'inheritance' was given 'to Abraham through a promise'. Therefore, even when referring to the future consummation, Paul articulates our hope within the framework provided by Old Testament promises.

In the affirmation of the one God and the status of his people, Paul builds upon Old Testament covenantal traditions. As in the Old Testament, the new covenant is also historically grounded with references to the past, the present and the future. It is within this framework that Pauline thanksgiving should be examined.

Thanksgiving and the covenantal traditions

In biblical-theological terms, thanksgiving is a covenantal act. In the Old Testament, when the covenant was remembered and renewed, the people of God recommitted themselves to their God. The faithfulness of God was acknowledged and his mighty acts were remembered. It is not outward ritual that God demands. Rather, a heart of thanksgiving is called for. This is illustrated in Psalm 50 where God called his people to gather around him:

'Gather to me my consecrated ones,
    who made a covenant with me by sacrifice.'

(v. 5)

It is not animal sacrifice that God requires (v. 9). Rather, the people are called to '[s]acrifice thank offerings to God' (v. 14). To those who were unfaithful, God questions:

'What right have you to recite my laws
    or take my covenant on your lips.'

(v. 16)

The contrast between the wicked people and those who are faithful in the covenantal relationship is expressed in verses 22–23 in these terms:

> 'Consider this, you who forget God,
>   or I will tear you to pieces, with none to rescue;
> He who sacrifices thank-offerings honours me,
>   and he prepares the way
>   so that I may show him the salvation of God.'

When covenant is understood as the relationship between God and his people, one can affirm with Peter Craigie (1983: 367) that '[j]ust as the covenant was the very heart of the religion of Israel, so too Ps. 50 lies at the heart of the meaning of the covenant'. Within the covenantal context, thanksgiving is not simply an emotional outburst but a response that has theological, ethical and social implications.[43]

The premise of the covenantal relationship is the recognition of God as the one Lord of all. In the previous chapter, we have shown how thanksgiving should be understood as a theological affirmation of the sovereignty of God. In acts of thanksgiving, we acknowledge that God is the source of all goodness. The distinction between creator and creature becomes clear when thanksgiving is offered. When monotheism became an element that set Israel apart from her neighbours, the corresponding call to thanksgiving within the covenantal relationship also reflects the uniqueness of the cultic and ethical practices of Israel.[44] In the context of the new covenant, the

---

[43] In a study of thanksgiving from a comparative perspective, Streng (1989: 5) highlights four dimensions of thanksgiving that can be further explored: 'They are: (1) the attitudes and feelings in a state of mind, (2) a conceptual formulation of a value system, (3) formal ritual expressions at specific occasions, and (4) a communal everyday style of life, or set of social obligations.' All these are relevant for our exploration of thanksgiving within the covenantal relationship in the Old Testament and in Paul. Moreover, in the words of K. Barth (1957: 669), thanksgiving in the Bible does not simply characterize a way to act or a mental state, it is 'the very being and essence' of God's creature. This 'essence' is to be reflected in one's submission to Christ's sovereignty: 'It is the Creator and Lord of this new creature, the new man who lives in it, Jesus Christ Himself, who rules and sustains and motivates this creaturely work, giving it its start and course and goal.'

[44] It is in this way that thanksgiving can be compared to a drastically different command in the Old Testament. The people of Israel are called to 'fear' their Lord. As in thanksgiving, fear may evoke an emotional response, but it should not be understood solely or even primarily in psychological terms. The implicit theological affirmation behind both 'fear' and 'thanksgiving' is the affirmation of the one God who

Pauline call to thanksgiving is then to be understood as making a distinct theological claim.

As Israel is elected by God as his chosen people, thanksgiving also acquires a communal aspect. While the mighty acts of God provide the definition of who the people of God are, thanksgiving provides further affirmation of the identity of God's people when God's gracious acts are remembered. Therefore, while thanksgiving is directed towards God, his people learn from the performance of such acts when they are built up through worship.[45] In the Old Testament, thanksgiving and praise are frequently offered by the covenantal community as a whole. This communal aspect of thanksgiving in the Pauline writings demands further study.[46]

The covenantal relationship between God and Israel is expressed within a temporal framework. The past, the present and the future are defined in light of this relationship. In the Old Testament, this historical consciousness also characterizes thanksgiving and praise. In reference to the manifestation of God in the past as well as in the future, Patrick Miller (1985: 9) claims that 'no aspect of the Old Testament serves as a vehicle for getting at the biblical notion of God in so full and extended a fashion as do the songs of praise and thanks'. The understanding of thanksgiving as embracing the past, the present and the future is already noted by an early Christian author:

> Therefore we ought to give great thanks to the Lord that he has given us knowledge of the past, and wisdom for the present, and that we are not without understanding for the future. (*Barnabas* 5.3 [Lake, LCL])

Thanksgiving is naturally related to the past. In David's psalm of thanksgiving in 1 Chronicles 16, for example, the call to 'Give thanks to the LORD' (v. 8) is followed by a reference to the past:

---

cannot be manipulated but demands to be worshipped as one Lord of all. It is this aspect that sets Israel apart from her neighbours. For a helpful study of the 'fear of the Lord', see Waltke (1992: 17–33), who affirms that this call to fear the Lord 'combines both the rational and non-rational, the ethical and the numinous, in an inseparable unity' (24).

[45] Koenig's (1992: 76) understanding of praise as 'paradoxical' applies here when the people of God also benefited from acts of thanksgiving.

[46] For a discussion of the covenantal relationship between God and Israel as a people, see also the treatment in chapter four below.

> Remember the wonders he has done,
>> his miracles, and the judgments he pronounced.
>>
>>> (v. 12)

This call to remember is precisely the call to remember 'the covenant he made with Abraham' (v. 16) and the 'everlasting covenant' made to Israel (v. 17). The hymn is concluded with another call to thanksgiving:

> Give thanks to the LORD, for he is good;
>> his love endures for ever.
>>
>>> (v. 34)[47]

For Paul, thanksgiving is as much a reference to what God did as it is a reflection of the state of mind of the readers.[48] The understanding of Pauline thanksgiving as a remembrance of what God has done will be discussed in the next chapter.

Thanksgiving is a way of life and it characterizes the covenant people. When God is acknowledged to be one who created his people, he is also claimed to be their Lord and master. Thanksgiving, therefore, is not a static act but it draws out the implication of the past in the everyday living of the covenant people.[49] Images of God that appear in songs of praise and thanksgiving point to the present as the realm of God's sovereignty. In Psalm 93, for example, God is acknowledged as the king of all: 'The LORD reigns, he is robed in majesty' (v. 1). The psalm concludes by mentioning his commandments:

> Your statutes stand firm;
>> holiness adorns your house
>> for endless days, O LORD.
>>
>>> (v. 5)

His kingship and sovereignty also point to his perfect ordinances that must be observed. When God is recognized as the king who is also

---

[47] Guthrie (1981), who argues that theology in the Old Testament is expressed through thanksgiving, further highlights the importance of the act of remembrance in a political context: 'A divine sovereignty which was essentially political required a recitative, historical mode of praise' (40).

[48] Cf. O'Brien 1977: 107–140.

[49] See Brueggemann (1988) who argues that praise and thanksgiving should be rooted firmly in the present experience of God's people.

the judge, it is recognized that he will 'judge the world in righteousness and the peoples in his truth' (Ps. 96:13). Similarly, as Psalm 97:1 begins with a call to praise and thanksgiving: 'The LORD reigns, let the earth be glad', the psalmist continues to remind us of the implications of this declaration: 'Let those who love the LORD hate evil' (v. 10). In thanksgiving, not only do the people count God's gracious acts on their behalf, they also allow him to rule over them. The present implications of thanksgiving in Paul can only be understood in this context. Chapter four will be devoted to the study of this aspect of Pauline thanksgiving.

Finally, thanksgiving also points to the future when the covenantal promises of God are fulfilled. When thanksgiving is understood as establishing the fact that God is a powerful and faithful God who can and will fulfil his promises, thanksgiving becomes the basis for trusting God in the face of an uncertain future. In the Old Testament, the constant mentioning of creation and exodus as the basis of God's future acts reflects this connection between the past and the future. In Isaiah 48:20–21, thanksgiving is offered to God for an act in the future when God would deliver his people from the hands of the Babylonians. The confidence that underlies this thanksgiving for an act that is yet to be accomplished is founded on God's mighty acts during the exodus event:

> Leave Babylon,
>   flee from the Babylonians!
> Announce this with shouts of joy
>   and proclaim it.
> Send it out to the ends of the earth;
>   say, 'The LORD has redeemed his servant Jacob.'
> They did not thirst when he led them through the deserts;
>   he made water flow for them from the rock;
> he split the rock
>   and water gushed out.

In this passage, the future merges with the past, and the past makes the future possible. When the past is remembered in thanksgiving, trust for God to act again is developed and nurtured. If thanksgiving looks back to God's faithfulness, 'it almost spontaneously becomes at the end asking for the future'.[50] In Paul, therefore, thanksgiving

---

[50] Lambrecht 1990: 192.

also points to the future. In chapter five, this aspect will be examined within this covenantal framework.

Thanksgiving in Paul points us back to the past, exhorts us to live our present lives in light of the past, and provides hope as we anticipate the consummation of God's promises in the future. Old Testament covenantal traditions supply the interpretive key to unlock the richness in the Pauline call to be a thankful people.

Chapter Three

Thanksgiving and covenantal history

Pauline thanksgiving focuses on God and what he has done for his people. The past is evoked when the people of God seek to identify the one whom they are worshipping. In this chapter, aspects of Pauline thanksgiving will be examined in light of the historical consciousness embedded in the covenantal traditions.

Thanksgiving as remembrance

The relationship between thanksgiving and remembrance can be found, as expected, in literature of various cultures. In secular Greek, thanksgiving is related to acts of remembrance. It has been suggested that the genuine Greek word for the call to thanksgiving can be found in *mnēmē* and *mimnēskesthai*. Furthermore, the word *mnēsidōrein* is always used in the sense of 'to offer public thanksgiving'.[1] Beyond these linguistic connections, the connections between gratitude and remembrance appear in context where the memory of gifts prompts the offer of thanksgiving.[2]

This connection resurfaces in the Hellenistic Jewish writer Philo. In *De Specialibus Legibus II* 146, Philo discusses the establishment of the Passover feast: 'the festival is a reminder and thank-offering for that great migration from Egypt' (Colson and Whitaker, LCL).[3] In the description of the sacrifice of the first fruit, it is recognized that the sacrifice is 'given in thanks' for God's provision, and first among

---

[1] See Versnel 1981: 59.

[2] Ledogar (1968: 92–93) points to Polybius 6.14.7 and 39.7.2. The role of memory is fundamental to Plato who considers knowledge and truth to be based fundamentally on memory (*Phaedrus* 249–250). Later writers influenced by Plato represent a tradition quite distinct from Polybius and others who see memory as something that transcends the psychological state and epistemological status of an individual and therefore provides a basis for action in the present moment. See also Childs (1962: 26) who points to the parallels between usages of memory-related terms in ancient Greek writers such as Homer and those in Semitic traditions.

[3] See also Ledogar 1968: 93.

the benefits that come with the first fruits is the memory of God (*De Specialibus Legibus II* 171 [Colson and Whitaker, LCL]). Jean LaPorte (1983: 43) has further pointed to *De Plantatione* 126–131 where Philo uses the figure of the virgin Memory in discussing the virtue of gratitude as the only response human beings can give to God since all things belong to God the creator of all.

The Old Testament certainly plays a critical role in the writings of Philo.[4] To give thanks to God is to remember what he has done for us. The call to thanksgiving is therefore a call to transcend the present moment as one searches for an anchor in which reality can be comprehended. In the Old Testament, thanksgiving points backwards to the faithfulness of God, and remembrance forms the basis of any act of thanksgiving. In Psalm 45:17, for example, one reads:

> I will perpetuate your memory through all generations;
>   therefore the nations will thank you for ever and ever.[5]

What is significant is the role 'remembering' plays throughout the Old Testament. Acts of remembering lead one back to the point when God establishes his relationship with his people. It is in this context that remembering becomes one of the most significant covenantal terms expressing how generations of the people of God understand themselves in relationship to the God who has revealed himself in their history.

Remembrance as a covenantal act

The history of the people of God is characterized not by their political might nor by their moral power. Their distinctiveness is determined by their origin in the calling of God and their continued covenantal relationship with their God.[6] To understand who they are, therefore, they have to look back at their own 'history'. For Israel, then, to remember is to situate oneself in the midst of the ongoing relationship with their covenantal partner.

---

[4] In this connection, LaPorte (1983: 14, 43) in particular has drawn attention to the importance of Deut. 8:17–18 in Philo's discussion of thanksgiving.

[5] Instead of 'thank', NIV has 'praise' in this verse (MT: 45:18). See also the discussion of 1 Chron. 16 in chapter two above.

[6] See, for example, Deut. 32:18 where the origin of Israel is located in God although she may not remember him: 'you forgot the God who gave you birth'.

In Exodus, to remember[7] God is to remember the relationship God has established with his people. In Exodus 3:15, immediately after revealing his own name, God said to Moses: 'Say to the Israelites, "The LORD, the God of your fathers – the God of Abraham, the God of Isaac and the God of Jacob – has sent me to you." This is my name for ever, the name by which I am to be remembered from generation to generation.' In this fundamental text, the name of God is the object of remembrance. God is identified both as 'I am who I am' and also in relation to his relationship with the patriarchs. To remember God, then, is to remember his faithfulness within the covenantal relationship. More importantly, this call to remember originated from God himself.

As we have noted, central to the covenant is the affirmation of God as the only God. This becomes the one element that Israel needs to remember as the covenant is being honoured: 'Be careful not to forget the covenant of the LORD your God that he made with you; do not make for yourselves an idol in the form of anything the LORD your God has forbidden. For the LORD your God is a consuming fire, a jealous God' (Deut. 4:23–24; cf. 2 Kgs. 17:38–39; Is. 46:9; Ezek. 6:9). If the people of Israel fail to remember their Lord, they 'will surely be destroyed' (Deut. 8:19). To forget God, then, is to break the covenantal relationship.[8] To remember him, on the other hand, is to move away from a focus on oneself and to put God at the centre of one's life.[9]

Throughout the Old Testament, the 'memory' of God and his covenant is sustained in the living memory of the generations. This call to pass on the traditions is issued in the Song of Moses at the end of the life of Moses:

---

[7] In the Old Testament, 'to remember' is usually expressed through the use of two Hebrew stems: *zkr* and *škḥ*. We will not make distinctions between the two in our analysis of the theological significance of acts of remembering in the Old Testament. For a helpful discussion of the development of the covenantal use of the memory motif in the Old Testament, see Price 1962. His study relies too heavily, however, on the outdated model of the reconstruction of Old Testament traditions.

[8] See Ps. 44:17:

> All this happened to us,
> though we had not forgotten you
> or been false to your covenant.

Here, the act of forgetting parallels that of being 'false' to the covenant. For a further discussion of forgetting as worshipping other gods, see chapter six below.

[9] Wilkes' (1981: 90) observation should be noted: 'A central ingredient in remembering is the belief that the self has its centre of being in something other than itself. The religious person may see his centre in God, or may feel somehow dependent on God for his existence; he feels that he himself is not the centre of the universe.'

Remember the days of old;
consider the generations long past.
Ask your father and he will tell you,
your elders, and they will explain to you.

(Deut. 32:7; cf. Deut. 4:9)

When the covenant with God was being renewed, Israel was called to 'remember the LORD' as the covenantal relationship was confirmed (Deut. 8:18).

In the context of the covenant, to remember God is not simply to bring God back to one's mind. Instead, acts of remembering lead one to be obedient to the covenant stipulations and the will of the sovereign Lord. In this way, remembering is not concerned simply with the past but it forces one to deal squarely with one's present life within the covenantal relationship.[10] In Deuteronomy 8:11, to remember God is to obey him: 'Be careful that you do not forget the LORD your God, failing to observe his commands, his laws and his decrees that I am giving you this day.' In the same book, the call to remember a certain historical event is frequently connected with the call to follow the commandments of God (Deut. 5:15; 8:2; 15:15; 16:12; 24:18, 22). Elsewhere, the object of remembering is explicitly identified as 'all the commands of the LORD' (Num. 15:39). The connection between remembering and observing the commandments of God is further developed by the parallel accounts of the Decalogue. The Exodus version has: 'Remember the Sabbath day' (Exod. 20:8) while the Deuteronomy version has: 'Observe the Sabbath day' (Deut. 5:12). This apparent discrepancy prompted the rabbinic sages to suggest that both 'remember' and 'observe' were pronounced 'in a single utterance', an act that is only possible with God.[11]

This connection between remembering and obedience is not limited to the Mosaic Torah. Already in Joshua, the object of remembering is the words of the Lord through his servant Moses (1:13). Remembering God is to remember the ordinances that he gave to his people. Again, in Psalm 119:55, one reads:

[10] See, in particular, Schottroff 1964. Childs (1962: 51) rightly notes that '[m]emory serves to link the present commandments as events with the covenant history of the past'.

[11] Rabbinic references are provided by Melammed 1990: 191–217. Melammed notes that the discrepancy is only noted in the Babylonian sources, while the Palestinian sources consider the two terms as synonymous in their contexts. Modern scholars, represented by Weinfeld (1990: 7), have pointed to the distinction between sacral and historical aspects in explaining the use of the different verbs.

> In the night I remember your name, O LORD,
> and I will keep your law.

The connection between remembering God and observing his commandments can best be understood within the context of the covenantal relationship between God and his people.

The covenantal focus of the remembering motif is even more explicit when God becomes the subject of acts of remembering. Throughout the Old Testament, God is said to have remembered the covenant that he made with his people. The exodus event began when God 'remembered his covenant with Abraham, with Isaac and with Jacob' (Exod. 2:24; cf. Exod. 6:5; Lev. 26:42–45; Ps. 105:42). Immediately after the Sinai covenant was established, Israel sinned against God. In response, Moses pleaded with God to overlook 'the stubbornness of this people' and 'remember' the covenant with Abraham (Deut. 9:27; cf. Exod. 32:13). Again, when the people sinned against their God, the Lord was asked to remember his covenant: 'Remember your covenant with us and do not break it' (Jer. 14:21).[12]

Despite the frequent failings of the people, the psalmist reaffirms God's commitment to his people:

> [F]or their sake he remembered his covenant
> and out of his great love he relented.
>
> (Ps. 106:45)

This commitment of God already appeared when the Sinai covenant was established: 'For the LORD your God is a merciful God; he will not abandon or destroy you or forget the covenant with your forefathers, which he confirmed to them by oath' (Deut. 4:31). Throughout the Old Testament, one finds the affirmation of the continued goodness of God and his love and faithfulness that will last for ever (e.g., 1 Chron. 16:34, 41; 2 Chron. 5:13; 7:3, 6; 20:21; Ezra 3:11; Ps. 100:5; 106:1; 107:1; 118:1–4, 29; 136:1–26; 138:8; Jer. 33:11).[13]

It is this faithfulness of God to his covenant that leads to his promise of a new covenant when he again remembers his people: 'I

---

[12] See Childs (1962: 34) who points out that action is always implied when God remembers his people. Child's further distinction between God's remembering as action-oriented and human remembering as a psychological process needs to be qualified, however. See Carasik 1996: 88–89.

[13] See Shipp (1993: 29–39), who also notes the frequent juxtaposition of *ḥeseḏ* with remembering in Ps. 25:6–7; 98:3; 106:6; and 109:16.

will remember the covenant I made with you in the days of your youth, and I will establish an everlasting covenant with you' (Ezek. 16:60). Unlike the previous covenants, this is one 'that will not be forgotten' (Jer. 50:5). With the establishment of this covenant, God 'will remember their sins no more' (Jer. 31:34); but Israel will repent by remembering her sins (Ezek. 16:61; Jer. 31:33). Israel will also remember the past when God is faithful to his covenant.[14]

The call to remembrance, therefore, becomes a way to ask God to continue to act in history on behalf of his people. For God's people, the same call is an exhortation to be faithful covenantal partners. Remembering therefore brings the past into the present, and on the basis of the memory of the past, the future is also opened up when God is expected to fulfil his promises.

Confessing the mighty acts of God

'Confession is thanksgiving', according to Clement of Alexandria (*Stromata* 7.3 [*ANF* 2:528]). To thank God is to remember and recount his mighty deeds. Thanksgiving therefore moves beyond the sphere of private sentiments to the public acknowledgment of the mighty and faithful God. In the Septuagint, *exomologeomai* ('to confess') is frequently used to translate terms for thanksgiving.[15] For example, in Psalm 35:18:

> I will give you thanks (*exomologēsomai*) in the great assembly;
> among throngs of people I will praise you.[16]

This Greek word, used for the Hebrew term for giving thanks, points to the fact that thanksgiving entails the remembering and recounting of the mighty deeds of God.

---

[14] The mutual remembering appears in Is. 44:21 where Israel is called to remember, while God in turn promises that he will never forget his people. In Isaiah, the people are called both to remember the former things (46:9) and not to remember the past (43:18). The call to remember points to the recognition of the same God who is faithful to his covenant. The call to forget points to the radical novelty of the new covenant that will last for ever.

[15] While the term *exomologeomai* has been used in the context of the confession of sins (e.g., Dan. 9:4, 20), in the LXX the verb is almost always used for 'praise' or 'thanks'. The same use can also be found in the New Testament (e.g., Matt. 11:25; Luke 10:21; Rom. 15:9). The interchangeability of thanksgiving and confession is further confirmed by the writings of Philo where *eucharisteō* frequently replaced *exomologeomai* of the Septuagint. See Schubert 1939: 41, 198; and Audet 1959: 654.

[16] Cf. Pss. 9:1; 18:49–50; 28:6–7; 30:2–13; 118:21.

The connection between thanksgiving and confession is illustrated by the dialogue between Jethro and Moses in Exodus 18:8–11, a passage that 'contains the most fundamental dimensions of thanksgiving':[17]

> Moses told his father-in-law about everything the LORD had done to Pharaoh and the Egyptians for Israel's sake and about all the hardships they had met along the way and how the LORD had saved them.
> Jethro . . . said, 'Praise be to the LORD, who rescued you from the hand of the Egyptians and of Pharaoh, and who rescued the people from the hand of the Egyptians. Now I know that the LORD is greater than all other gods, for he did this to those who had treated Israel arrogantly.'

The confessional report of Moses prompted Jethro to respond in praise and thanksgiving as the marvellous work of God is remembered. More importantly, this recounting also leads to the recognition by an outsider of the unrivalled status of God.

When Israel offers thanksgiving, the mighty acts of God are being published. The call to thanksgiving is therefore a call to remember how God has been a faithful God. In Psalm 77, for example, the psalmist 'remembered God' (v. 3) by remembering all that he had done:

> I will remember the deeds of the LORD;
> yes, I will remember your miracles of long ago.
> (v. 11)[18]

As in Exodus 18, one of the most significant events that Israel is to remember is the paradigmatic moment when God delivered his people from the hands of the Egyptians. When the Sinai covenant was established, the exodus event was naturally recalled (Exod. 19:3–6; 20:2). The recitation of this defining moment in the history of Israel naturally plays an essential role in the covenant renewal ceremonies found throughout the Old Testament. The first of these is in Deuteronomy 29 where Moses reminds Israel of God's deliverance

[17] Miller 1994: 183.
[18] Similarly, in Ps. 105, to remember God's 'covenant' (v. 8) is to '[r]emember the wonders he has done' (v. 5).

(vv. 2–6); Israel will in turn 'enter into a covenant' (v. 12) with their Lord. When the covenant is renewed at Shechem, the history of God's people is recounted and the exodus event is emphasized (Josh. 24:5–7). In the covenant renewal in the time of Nehemiah, the history of Israel is again recited with the exodus event recounted in detail (Neh. 9:9–21).[19]

The significance of the exodus event is also reflected in the fact that this event forms the basis for the way Israel is to act within the covenantal relationship. In Deuteronomy, in particular, to remember this event characterizes the life of the faithful people of God. The Sabbath commandment is accompanied by the call to 'remember' Israel's days in Egypt (Deut. 5:15). The freeing of servants during the Sabbatical year is grounded on the remembrance of their status in Egypt and the deliverance by their God (Deut. 15:15). The observance of the Feast of Weeks is likewise grounded on this memory (16:12). The same refrain reappears when the proper treatment of foreigners and those who are oppressed is discussed (24:17–18, 21–22). Indeed, all the commandments are to be followed when Israel remembers the exodus event that defines the relationship between God and herself (8:2). Moreover, when Israel faces the future expecting to encounter nations upon entering the promised land, she was comforted by a call to remember: 'do not be afraid of them; remember well what the LORD your God did to Pharaoh and to all Egypt' (Deut. 7:18).

In discussing the exodus event, the significance of the Passover celebration deserves special mention. The call to remember is emphasized once again in the narrative of Exodus 12 – 13. The institution of the Passover marks the dramatic beginning of a new era in the history of salvation. The month of the Passover is to be 'the first month' of their year (12:2), and this event is marked by a temporal marker noting the 430 years Israel spent in Egypt (12:40–41). The festival is to be a 'lasting ordinance' (12:14, 17, 24) and the call to remember this night 'for the generations to come' is repeatedly emphasized (12:14, 17, 42). Equally important is the reason for such emphasis: 'because the LORD brought you out of it [Egypt] with a mighty hand' (13:3; cf. 12:17, 27, 51; 13:8, 14, 16). In Deuteronomy, the reason for the Passover celebration is explicitly linked to the memory that must not fade away: 'so that all the days of your life

---

[19] Several psalms that recount the exodus event probably also have covenant renewal as their setting (e.g., Pss. 78, 105, 136).

you may remember the time of your departure from Egypt' (Deut. 16:3).

The Passover is celebrated specifically by the covenant people. Phrases like 'the whole community of Israel' (Exod. 12:3, 47), and 'all the people of the community of Israel' (12:6), point to the importance of the entire people of God being the recipient of divine deliverance, and those who fail to remember this feast properly 'must be cut off from the community of Israel' (12:19).[20] The significance of Israel as the covenant people is further stressed in Exodus 12:48 when it is emphasized that '[n]o uncircumcised male' may participate fully in the celebration.[21] Remembering the exodus event, therefore, also touches on the very identity of the covenant people. To understand who they are, they have to remember. In remembering, they are also able to understand who their God is.[22]

Outside of the Pentateuch, the exodus event is frequently connected with the creation story. In the thanksgiving psalm of Psalm 136, for example, the psalmist gives thanks to God both for creation (vv. 1–9) and for his deliverance during the exodus event (vv. 10–22). The conclusion of the psalm points to the present (vv. 23–16). The God who manifested himself in creation and in the exodus event is the one who 'remembered us' (Ps. 136:23).[23] More striking are Psalms 74, 77, 89 and 114 where one finds the merging of the creation and exodus stories.[24] The two are considered together when the power of God is in focus. Exodus can be understood as the historical manifestation of the divine creative power. Israel is called to remember both as she grows in the knowledge of her covenantal partner.

---

[20] The Hebrew stem *zkr* appears in these two chapters to refer to acts of observing, remembering and commemoration. Modern distinction between these acts should not be imposed in these contexts.

[21] This aspect becomes especially important when Israel finds herself in foreign lands. After the return of the exiles and the rededication of the temple, the Passover was celebrated. In this context, the line between Israel and her neighbours becomes clearer. Concerning the eating of the Passover lamb, it is said: 'So the Israelites who had returned from the exile ate it, together with all who had separated themselves from the unclean practices of their Gentile neighbours in order to seek the LORD, the God of Israel' (Ezra 6:21).

[22] Léon-Dufour (1987: 105) is correct in noting that 'the element that is characteristic of Israelite cult is not sacrifices or feasts' but 'the role which memory plays in it'. See also the earlier study of Groß (1960: 227–237) who sees 'remembering' as a cultic term.

[23] Allen (1983: 234) rightly notes: 'As contemporary members of the covenant nation, "we" were there in principle, participating in the divine salvation and certainly now living in the good of it.'

[24] Cf. Exod. 25; Is. 50:2; 51:3, 12–16. See also footnote 74 in ch. 1 above.

To remember the past, therefore, is to recognize who God is. When the covenant is renewed in Deuteronomy 29, the point of remembering the past is that Israel might know that God is her Lord and God (v. 6). In Psalm 71, the psalmist declares the 'marvellous deeds' (v. 17) of God that provoke the expected response: 'Who, O God, is like you?' (v. 29). Similarly, in Psalm 77, the psalmist exclaims: 'What god is so great as our God?' (v. 13) and the psalm concludes with a reference back to the exodus:

> You led your people like a flock
> by the hand of Moses and Aaron.
>
> (v. 20)

In remembering and proclaiming his mighty acts, the people thank God for who he is and what he has done for his people:

> 'Give thanks to the LORD, call on his name;
>   make known among the nations what he has done,
>   and proclaim that his name is exalted.
> Sing to the LORD, for he has done glorious things;
>   let this be known to all the world.'
>
> (Is. 12:4–5)

Thanksgiving here becomes the vehicle for the development of the 'theology' of ancient Israel.[25] This theology cannot be separated from the public proclamation of the wonderful name of God.[26] The remembering that leads to such proclamation becomes a call to the nations to remember and therefore submit to God's sovereignty:

---

[25] For the doxological nature of Old Testament theology, where songs of praise and thanksgiving function as creedal confession, see Anderson (1963: 277–285) who recognizes the canonical psalms to be 'the first of all Old Testament theologies' (285). Similarly, Miller (1994: 203) notes: 'Thanksgiving in the Old Testament is where prayer and creed are joined.'

[26] Praise is often explicitly identified as the result if not purpose of remembering. E.g., Ps. 45:17:

> I will perpetuate your memory through all generations;
>   therefore the nations will praise you for ever and ever.

The connection between praise and remembering is further established by the parallel uses of the two terms. See, for example, Ps. 6:5:

> No-one remembers you when he is dead.
> Who praises you from the grave?

> All the ends of the earth
>   will remember and turn to the LORD,
> and all the families of the nations
>   will bow down before him,
> for dominion belongs to the LORD
>   and he rules over the nations.
>
> (Ps. 22:27–28)

Climax of history

When we come to Second Temple Jewish literature, remembering remains a prominent motif. This is reflected in Psalms of Solomon 3:3: 'The righteous remember the Lord all the time.'[27] Significant differences in emphasis can be detected, however. While Israel is called to remember the mighty hands of God in the Old Testament, God is now frequently called to remember his people.[28] More importantly, the call to remember the Torah begins to overshadow the call to remember the divine acts of old.[29] Both can be explained by the awareness of the absence of God's acts among his people[30] and the presence of suffering as the people found themselves being ruled over by foreigners. To have further grounds for thanksgiving and remembering, they are waiting for God to reveal himself again in history.

When the dawn of the eschatological age appeared with the coming of the promised Messiah, God's people again find reasons for thanksgiving. As the object of remembering changes, one also finds a restructuring of time when the reckoning of time is redefined by the arrival of the climax of history. Thanksgiving and acts of remembering therefore carry significant theological weight as they point to the fulfilment of covenantal promises.

---

[27] Translation taken from Charlesworth 1985: 2.354.

[28] Nitzan (1994: 89) points to examples from the Qumran where the appeal to God to remember has often replaced words of praise or blessing in prayer literature.

[29] This is the conclusion of Price (1962: 256) who further points to the move from community interests to individual concerns to be obedient to the Torah. Guthrie (1981: 146) likewise argues that 'torah had replaced todah as the norm of theological understanding in Judaism'. It should be noted, however, that remembering Torah also has an important role to play in the Old Testament (Exod. 20 – 24; 2 Kgs. 23:1–3), and that both the Torah and the mighty acts of God should be understood as complementary components within the context of the covenant.

[30] If the responsibility of a prophet is to provide proper interpretation of the mighty acts of God, the awareness of the absence of prophets (e.g., 1 Maccabees 4:46) may reflect the realization that God is no longer actively working in history as he had in the past.

In the gospels, notes of thanksgiving often point to the remembering of what God has done for us and thus also to the need to place our trust in him. Thanksgiving is not simply related to individual gifts but it recalls the mighty acts of God. In the thanksgiving prayer of Jesus in Matthew 11:25–30, for example, Jesus thanks God because of the hidden things now revealed 'to little children' (v. 25; cf. Luke 10:21).[31] Thanksgiving here points to a new chapter in salvation history. The address to the Father as 'Lord of heaven and earth' (v. 25) points to the power of God and his control of history. Moreover, the content of the prayer points to Jesus himself, the Son who becomes the ultimate revelation of God: 'All things have been committed to me by my Father . . . and no-one knows the Father except the Son and those to whom the Son chooses to reveal him' (v. 27). Christ is at the centre of the thanksgiving as he has now become the focus to which all thanksgiving, remembering and proclamation should be directed.[32] In the days of old, the Song of Moses (Exod. 15) was written to commemorate the deliverance of God from Egypt; at the end of times 'the song of Moses the servant of God and the song of the Lamb' (Rev. 15:3–4) will be sung when the power of Christ is established on earth.[33]

On the other hand, this focus on God's work in Christ also points to God's remembrance of his people as he renewed his covenant with them. In this 'renewal' God brought salvation history to its climax. In Mary's song of thanksgiving in Luke 1:54–55, the coming of the Messiah signifies God's remembering of his covenantal promises:

> 'He has helped his servant Israel,
>   remembering to be merciful
> to Abraham and his descendants for ever,
>   even as he said to our fathers.'

---

[31] The term used for thanksgiving here is *exomologoumai*. Normally used for confessing, here it refers to thanksgiving directed to God. See Hagner 1993: 318; and Davies and Allison 1991: 273–274.

[32] With regard to the public nature of thanksgiving, Ledogar (1968: 132) has pointed to John 11:41–42 where, after the raising of Lazarus, Jesus gave thanks to God 'for the benefit of the people . . . that they may believe that you sent me'.

[33] In Rev. 15, allusions to Is. 12 can also be identified when Isaiah points to the end of times with a song of thanksgiving:

> 'Give thanks to the LORD, call on his name;
>   make known among the nations what he has done,
>   and proclaim that his name is exalted.' (v. 4)

Is. 12:1–6 is, however, also indebted to the Song of Moses in Exod. 15. For a further discussion of Is. 12 and Exod. 15, see Aune 1998: 863–864.

In the words of Zechariah, this remembering is a remembering of 'his holy covenant, the oath he swore to our father Abraham' (Luke 1:72–73).

While the great act of God in Christ is understood to be God's remembering of his covenant, the reception of the work of God is also understood in terms of thanksgiving. This is best illustrated in the story of the ten lepers (Luke 17:11–19). When Jesus healed the ten lepers, only one returned to thank him (v. 18). In response to the thanksgiving offered, Jesus said to him: 'Rise and go; your faith has made you well' (v. 19). To offer thanks is to acknowledge Christ's act of healing. With this acknowledgment, faith is expressed. Thanksgiving, therefore, is understood as an act of faith. Thanksgiving becomes 'an expression of faith'[34] as it remembers what God has done for us in Christ.

'Do this in remembrance of me'

The celebration of the Lord's Supper provides a clear overlap between the gospels and the Pauline writings in terms of thanksgiving and remembrance. To understand Pauline thanksgiving we need to begin with the tradition that Paul had 'received' (1 Cor. 11:23). While the Lord's Supper has been examined within the context of various Jewish meal settings,[35] the Passover provides the best framework for the appreciation of the significance of this institution. First, the Synoptic gospels specifically date the meal on the Day of Passover, the day 'when it was customary to sacrifice the Passover lamb' (Mark 14:12).[36] Second, the location is also important since it is customary to have the Passover meal in Jerusalem. Third, the Last Supper was held in the

[34] See Soares-Prabhu (1990: 41) who points to the connection between thanksgiving and saving faith.

[35] Some (e.g. H. Anderson 1964: 194–197) have considered the Last Supper as an ordinary Jewish meal, but the majority of scholars attempt to understand the Last Supper against the background of a certain type of Jewish festive meal. It has been compared to the Kiddush meal (e.g., Brilioth 1939) but the temporal references in the gospel accounts make this unlikely. Others (e.g., Kilmartin 1965) have compared it with the *Haburoth*, the meals of the Pharisees in their 'guilds'. This suggestion fails to gain support due to the lack of evidence and the date of relevant source material. Finally, some (e.g., Kuhn 1957) have pointed to the Qumran meals but as Groh (1970: 291–292) has reminded us, the Qumran meal itself is connected with, if not based on, the Passover meal.

[36] See also the Johannine account that makes reference to the 'Passover Feast' (John 13:1). For a discussion of the temporal reference in John 13:1 and the issue of Johannine temporal placement of the Last Meal, see Carson 1991: 455–458, 475.

evening (Mark 14:17; 1 Cor. 11:23), a fact consistent with the Passover meal that was eaten in the evening and not earlier.[37] Fourth, Mark tells us that the meal ended with singing (14:26), and Jeremias has suggested that this refers to the second part of the Passover *hallel*.[38] In light of these considerations, the connection between Passover and the Lord's Supper should be further examined.[39]

The mention of the (new) covenant in all four accounts (Matt. 26:28; Mark 14:24; Luke 22:20; 1 Cor. 11:25) points to the establishment of the new covenant through the coming death of Jesus. As in the establishment of the Sinai covenant (Exod. 24:3–8), this new covenant is established through the perfect sacrifice of Jesus.[40] The Lord's Supper should, therefore, be understood as fulfilling the Passover because the death of Christ fulfils the promises of the previous covenants.[41]

When disciples of Christ are called to observe the Lord's Supper, they are also called to remember the new act of God. The call to remember appears in Luke 22:19[42] but is emphasized by Paul with the two appearances in 1 Corinthians 11:24–26. As discussed above, the command to remember plays an important role in the Passover ordi-

---

[37] Jeremias 1966: 44.

[38] Jeremias 1966: 54–55.

[39] This is not to deny other influences behind the accounts of the Lord's Supper. The expression 'for many' (Mark 14:24; Matt. 26:28), for example, points to Is. 53:12 where the servant will bear the sins 'of many'. It should be noted, however, that Isaiah also draws heavily on the exodus traditions. Hugenberger (1995: 105–140), for example, has further argued that the Isaianic servant is modelled upon the figure of Moses.

[40] Beyond the connection with the Passover sacrifice, the mention of blood and the use of *hyper*-phrases point to a sacrificial context. Furthermore, the allusions to the stories of Korah and his company (Num.16) and that of King Uzziah (2 Chron. 26) in 1 Cor. 11:27–30 point to a sacrificial context in which improper conduct in a cultic setting results in divine punishment. See Kilpatrick 1983: 53–54.

[41] The precise relationship between the Lord's Supper and the subsequent death of Jesus on the cross needs further clarification when both are understood in a sacrificial context. It seems best to understand the Last Supper in light of Old Testament symbolic acts (e.g., Ezek. 5:1–12; Jer. 19:1–15) where such symbolic acts not only foreshadow but also actualize the process of the corresponding ultimate acts. As explicitly stated in Heb. 7:26–27, the institution of the Lord's Supper by Jesus himself points to the fact that he himself is both the high priest who offers the sacrifice and the sacrificial victim who is being sacrificed. For a further discussion, see von Rad 1968: 75; Beck 1970: 194; Grayston 1990: 207; and Wright 1996: 554–563. Cf. Wenham (1995: 11–16) who calls this a 'parable in action'; and Tinker (2001: 18–28) who examines the Lord's Supper through modern speech–act theory.

[42] This call to remember is found in the longer version of the Lukan Last-Supper account. This longer text is supported by most Greek manuscripts, and its parallel with the Pauline texts may point to Luke's familiarity with the practices of Pauline churches and quite possibly Paul's own teachings as well. For a further discussion, see Metzger 1994: 148–150.

nances in the Old Testament. With the death of Christ, the disciples are called to remember this new act.[43] Instead of the lamb of the Old Testament Passover, believers now focus on 'Christ, our Passover lamb' (1 Cor. 5:7). Indeed, in the wider context in 1 Corinthians 10 – 15, the exodus event is constantly alluded to, but it is what Christ did that provides the proper interpretation of the past.[44]

While thanksgiving in the context of the Old Testament is frequently a public act when the mighty deeds of God are published, in the Pauline Last Supper account, the call to remember is also accompanied by a call to 'proclaim the Lord's death' (1 Cor. 11:26). This proclamation of the climactic moment in salvation history is an important element in Paul's call to remember the death of Christ. When thanksgiving points one back to a climactic point in history, one is called to remember and to proclaim. This understanding of thanksgiving is made explicit in the account of the Lord's Supper in the *Didache*, where the celebration of the Lord's Supper is essentially an act of 'thanksgiving'[45] for what Christ has done for us. The instruction in *Didache* begins with these words: 'concerning the giving of thanks, give thanks thus . . .' (*Didache* 9:1 [Lake, LCL]). Prayers of thanksgiving are then offered for both the cup and the bread. In both prayers thanksgiving is offered to God for the revelation he has provided through his son Jesus. After the meal, a third prayer of thanksgiving is offered, and included in the prayer are the following words:

> Thou, Lord Almighty, didst give food and drink to men for their enjoyment, that they might give thanks to thee, but us hast thou blessed with spiritual food and drink and eternal light through thy Child. (*Didache* 10:3 [Lake, LCL])[46]

[43] See Davies (1948: 250) who argues that the death of Christ 'has been substituted for the "the day thou camest forth out of Egypt"' of the Passover traditions. See also Jones 1955: 183–191.

[44] Cf. Farrow (2000: 199–215) who argues that the Pauline account of the Last Supper cannot be understood apart from both the context in 1 Corinthians and the references to the exodus event.

[45] The Lord's Supper is now called the 'Eucharist', and thanksgiving has been elevated to the centre of the celebration.

[46] As in the psalms, the connection between creation and salvation here is noteworthy. This emphasis on creation can also be found in the New Testament. In Col. 1:15–20, for example, the discussion of creation serves to highlight the superiority of Christ. In the context of thanksgiving, creation and deliverance again come together in a statement of Justin Martyr where he urges believers to 'thank God for having created the world, with all things therein, for the sake of man, and for delivering us from the evil in which we were, and for utterly overthrowing principalities and powers by Him who suffered according to His will' (*Dialogue with Trypho* 41 [*ANF* 1:215]).

In these words, the provision of Israel's past is now culminated in the giving of eternal life through Jesus. What is implied in New Testament accounts of the Lord's Supper is now emphasized in the *Didache*: through the death of Jesus we are delivered from the bondage of sins,[47] and this is now the centre for acts of remembering.[48] In acts of thanksgiving, therefore, time is being 'restructured' when the climax of salvation provides the perspective through which all past and future events find their anchor point.

The Pauline gospel

When the Lord's Supper points to the establishment of the new covenant, it signifies God's continued interest and engagement with his covenant people. Consistent with other New Testament witnesses, the primary focus of Pauline thanksgiving is the redemptive work of God through his son.

In Pauline theology, the cross symbolizes the radical nature of God's saving act. Those who oppose this fundamental gospel are the 'enemies of the cross of Christ' (Phil. 3:18). For Paul, reality can be understood only through the lens of the cross, and the gospel of grace can be appreciated only by a thorough understanding of the nature of the cross (cf. 1 Cor. 1:18–25). The cross points to a new chapter in salvation history in which, through God's redemptive act, sinners can have hope.

In the first chapter of Colossians, Christ's redemptive act provides grounds for thanksgiving. Thanks is given to the Father because 'he has rescued us from the dominion of darkness and brought us into the kingdom of the Son he loves, in whom we have redemption, the forgiveness of sins' (Col. 1:13–14).[49] In the thanksgiving in 2 Corinthians 1, the redemptive act of God through Christ is presented in terms of God's 'comfort' for his people, a term used in the Old

---

[47] Although the 'blood' saying is missing in the *Didache* account, the death of Jesus as the setting of the Lord's Supper is assumed, and the focus on 'revelation' points to the totality of Jesus' life and death as a saving act. See also the reference to the eucharist as a sacrifice in *Didache* 14. Cf. Tsirpanlis 1983: 45–47; Jefford 1989: 140.

[48] The importance of acts of remembering in *Didache* should be highlighted. Not only are we called to remember the perfect revelation in Jesus the Son of God, God is also called to remember the church and 'to deliver it from all evil and to make it perfect' (10:5 [Lake, LCL]).

[49] In the previous verse (v. 12), the grounds for thanksgiving is also expressed through a relative pronoun. In reference back to the mighty acts of God in Old Testament exodus-conquest, Paul thanks God for the audience's 'share in the inheritance of the saints'.

Testament to refer to the expected salvation of God.[50] The significance of this reference to God's comfort is confirmed by the phrase 'comfort and salvation' in verse 6. God is thanked when God accomplishes his redemptive acts for his people.

When the cross event is followed by the resurrection, Christ's power overcame the power of death. For Paul, both death and sin reflect the power of the evil one, and when Christ overcame death, the bondage of sin was also broken (e.g., Rom. 6:1–14). In 1 Corinthians 15:56–57, thanks is offered for the overcoming of sin and death: 'The sting of death is sin, and the power of sin is the law. But thanks be to God! He gives us the victory through our Lord Jesus Christ.'[51]

The Pauline gospel centres on the climactic redemptive acts of God, and Christ is naturally the focus of Pauline thanksgiving. Because of the accomplished act of redemption, we can approach God and become acceptable in his sight. When Paul issues a call to thanksgiving, one is to give thanks 'in the name of our Lord Jesus Christ' (Eph. 5:20). 'In the name' refers to the power and authority of Christ that makes such thanksgiving possible.[52] In Colossians 3:17, the same point is made when the Colossians were called to give thanks to God 'through him'.[53] The phrase 'through him' is paralleled by the phrase 'in the name of the Lord Jesus'. The two seem to be synonymous in this context, as both refer back to the work of Christ through whom God 'reconcile[s] to himself all things' (Col. 1:20).[54] Finally, in Romans 7, where Paul discusses his struggle with

---

[50] See Is. 40:1–11, for example, where 'comfort' signifies the dawn of a new era in salvation history (cf. Is. 49:13; 51:3; 52:9). The fact that comfort is understood by ancient interpreters to signify the salvation of Israel as promised is further established in the LXX by the insertion of the phrase 'the salvation of God' in 40:5. Outside of Paul, the term also appears in Luke 2:25. See Pao 2000: 46–47.

[51] For a further discussion of this passage as a reference to the future realization of God's redemptive acts, see chapter five below.

[52] Cf. 2 Thess. 3:6 where the command of Paul is given in Jesus' name. This authority is established through the saving acts of God in Christ. In 1 Cor. 1:2, believers are those 'who call on the name of our Lord Jesus Christ – their Lord and ours'. The Lordship of Christ is emphasized as he is the one through whom we have received our new lives.

[53] Similarly in Rom. 1:8 thanksgiving is given 'through Jesus Christ'. In its context, redemptive acts of God through Christ are alluded to by the use of this prepositional phrase: 'Through him and for his name's sake, we received grace and apostleship to call people from among all the Gentiles to the obedience that comes from faith' (Rom. 1:5). For a further discussion of the 'through him' formula in the context of Pauline prayer, see Gebauer 1989: 139–141.

[54] In the introductory blessing in Eph. 1, the same point is being made where Christ is recognized as the head of all (v. 10).

sin,[55] the thanksgiving note at the end provides a firmer ground for the understanding of the various 'through him' references: 'Thanks be to God – through Jesus Christ our Lord!' (Rom. 7:25). In this context, the prepositional phrase does not simply refer to the act of thanksgiving but also to the fundamental basis upon which thanksgiving could be offered (cf. 1 Cor. 15:57). Here, as elsewhere, thanksgiving can be offered to God only because of what Christ had done for us.

In covenantal language God's redemptive acts are expressed through the language of 'calling' and 'election'. In the introductory paragraph in 1 Thessalonians 1, the language of covenantal love and election is used to provide the ultimate grounds for thanksgiving: 'For we know, brothers loved by God, that he has chosen you . . .' (v. 4).[56] Similarly, in 2 Thessalonians 2:13–14, a constellation of election language appears: 'we ought always to thank God for you, brothers loved by the Lord, because from the beginning God chose you to be saved . . . He called you to this through our gospel, that you might share in the glory of our Lord Jesus Christ.' Again, in Ephesians 1:4–6, a similar constellation appears: 'For he chose us in him before the creation of the world . . . In love he predestined us to be adopted as his [God's] sons' (cf. Eph. 1:18). In these passages, God's covenantal acts are remembered and published. As in the days of old, God is creating a people for himself and this people are called to remember his mighty acts.[57]

In emphasizing the initiative of God as the subject of the mighty acts among his people, the focus on 'gospel' as the powerful agent is often found in connection with Pauline thanksgiving. The reference to the gospel appears in almost all of the Pauline introductory paragraphs,[58] and the gospel message lies behind many of the other

[55] Whether Paul is referring to his pre- or post-conversion experiences will not affect our interpretation of Rom. 7:25. For a further discussion of this verse in its context, see chapter five below.

[56] O'Brien (1977: 150) has rightly noted the Pauline use of the causal participle *eidotes* here to point to the ultimate grounds for thanksgiving.

[57] The continuity between believers and Israel is emphasized throughout the Pauline corpus. The emphasis on God as a faithful God highlights this continuity that is based on covenantal promises in the Old Testament. In the introductory thanksgiving of 1 Corinthians, for example, one finds the emphasis on the faithfulness of God in the context of the calling of his people: 'God, who has called you into fellowship with his Son Jesus Christ our Lord, is faithful' (1:9).

[58] In 1 Cor. 1, although the term 'gospel' is absent, the phrase 'testimony about Christ' (v. 6) serves the same purpose. In Eph. 1:15–23, despite the absence of the term, the content of the gospel is recounted in detail.

Pauline calls to thanksgiving. This gospel is 'the gospel of his [God's] Son' (Rom. 1:9). Gospel as the agent of God's redemptive act is noted in another thanksgiving paragraph in 2 Thessalonians, where thanksgiving is offered for God's calling (2 Thess. 2:13–15): 'He called you to this through our gospel' (v. 14). The power of this gospel is emphasized in the introductory thanksgiving in Colossians. This gospel is the subject of divine acts and is responsible for carrying out the mission of God: 'All over the world this gospel is bearing fruit and growing' (Col. 1:6).[59] Similarly in 1 Thessalonians 1:5, the power of the gospel is noted: 'our gospel came to you not simply with words, but also with power'.[60] This gospel is identified as the 'word of God' (1 Thess. 2:13). Punishment is promised to those who are disobedient to this gospel (2 Thess. 1:8). In these references, the gospel becomes almost an independent agent of God who is able to accomplish the goal within the context of salvation history.

According to O'Brien (1975: 149), this emphasis on the gospel and the word of God is 'one of the most striking features of the [thanksgiving] paragraphs'. In light of our analysis above, the focus on the gospel points to the fulfilment of covenantal promises captured in the gospel of the cross. The Old Testament background for this term should be noted. The term 'gospel' in Paul recalls the use of the word in Isaiah in reference to the coming salvation of God.[61] In Isaiah 40 – 55, this good news that is proclaimed to Jerusalem announces the arrival of the time when the presence of God returns to his people and when their sins are forgiven (cf. 40:1–11). Likewise, the active and powerful word of God also plays a role in this Isaianic vision. In Isaiah 40:8, one reads:

[59] Elsewhere Paul talks about 'partnership in the gospel' (Phil. 1:5) but always in the context of the primacy of the work of Christ and the power of the gospel message.

[60] In the Pauline message, the gospel serves as the link between the divine acts of God and their impact among his people. This understanding of the power of the gospel in salvation-historical categories is best expressed in Rom. 1:16: 'I am not ashamed of the gospel, because it is the power of God for the salvation of everyone who believes: first for the Jew, then for the Gentile.'

[61] Stuhlmacher (1968: 109–179, 218–225) points to Is. 40:9; 41:27; and 52:7 as the proper context for understanding the Pauline use of the term *euangelion*. Another passage that needs to be highlighted is the verse within the frequently quoted Servant Song in Is. 53:1. The connection is explicitly made in Rom. 10:16 with the quotation from Is. 53:1: 'But not all the Israelites accepted the good news (*euangelion*). For Isaiah says, "Lord, who has believed our message?"' Moreover, in Rom. 1:2, 'the gospel of God' is identified as 'the gospel he promised beforehand through his prophets in the Holy Scriptures'.

> The grass withers and the flowers fall,
> but the word of our God stands for ever.

Again, in Isaiah 55:

> As the rain and the snow
> come down from heaven
> and do not return to it . . .
> so is my word that goes out from my mouth:
> It will not return to me empty,
> but will accomplish what I desire
> and achieve the purpose for which I sent it.
>
> (vv. 10–11)[62]

The active word, coming from the mouth of the faithful God, is the divine agent through which God can accomplish his will at the age of salvation. In the Pauline epistles, therefore, when thanksgiving is offered in response to the work of the gospel and word of God, one is called to 'remember' the fulfilled promises.

Divine acts through human agency

Since thanksgiving is essentially an act of remembering, the focus is always on God and his acts. In Pauline thanksgiving, various kinds of 'human works' are mentioned but they are always in the context of the prior and ultimate work of God. The most obvious of these is the acceptance of the gospel in response to the redemptive acts of God. In 1 Thessalonians 1, Paul thanks God because the Thessalonians 'welcomed the message' (v. 6). Immediately preceding this, Paul focuses on God's act of election and the 'power' of the Holy Spirit (v. 5). In the same passage, immediately after the reference to the reception of the gospel, the joy 'given by the Holy Spirit' (v. 6) is mentioned. This is not to deny the importance of sinners converting in the theology of Paul. Conversion of sinners is part of redemptive history as God himself is responsible for sinners turning to himself. Within the same thanksgiving paragraph the conversion of believers is presented as the turning 'to God from idols' (v. 9). Again the verse that follows emphasizes that it is Jesus 'who rescues us from the coming wrath' (v. 10).

---

[62] Isaianic influence can also be identified elsewhere where the active word of God is emphasized: e.g., Acts 6:7; 12:24; 19:20; Rev. 19:13–15.

The same emphasis is found in 1 Thessalonians 2 where thanksgiving is offered because the Thessalonians accepted the gospel as the word of God. Paul goes on to define this word of God further as one 'which is at work in you who believe' (2:13). The active nature of the word of God as discussed above is again apparent. Human response prompts one to give thanks to God, but through the mere act of thanksgiving, God is recognized as the author of all goodness.

This Pauline theology that focuses solely on God finds its fullest expression in the epistle to the Romans. In Romans 6:17, Paul offers thanks for deliverance from sin: 'thanks be to God that, though you used to be slaves to sin, you wholeheartedly obeyed the form of teaching to which you were entrusted'. The ultimate agent of this deliverance is again God, as he is the implied subject of the passive verb: 'You have been set free from sin' (v. 18). In Pauline thanksgivings the same emphasis appears in various forms. For example, in Philippians 1:6, God is the one who 'began a good work' in believers, and in Colossians 1:6, the reception of the gospel is described as the working of the gospel itself. God is always the subject of salvific acts and therefore the ultimate object of thanksgiving.

This discussion allows us to examine other references to the 'good works' of believers. These good works are also subjects of 'remembering' (1 Thess. 1:2) as they are the outworking of the power of the gospel (cf. 1 Thess. 1:5; 2 Thess. 2:13). The proclamation of the gospel and the manifestation of this good news through the lives of the believers are therefore emphasized in Pauline prayers.[63] Paul gives thanks for the 'work' and 'labour' of the believers (1 Thess. 1:3) and their faithful 'partnership in the gospel' (Phil. 1:5).[64] In 2 Corinthians 4:15 Paul explicitly states that the gospel that is 'reaching more and more people' will cause 'thanksgiving to overflow to the glory of God'.

For the believers themselves, thanksgivings are offered because of the evidence of the power of the Spirit in their lives. In Pauline

---

[63] This is where one finds the focus on mission in Pauline prayers. Carson (2000: 182) rightly points out that mission is part of the gospel message and should not be understood as a separate entity: 'the glory of God, the reign of Christ, the declaration of the mystery of the gospel, the conversion of men and women, the growth and edification of the church . . . these are all woven into a seamless garment'.

[64] Needless to say, Paul's own labour in the gospel ministry is also understood as grounded on the power of God. In the introductory thanksgiving/blessing paragraph in 2 Cor. 1, for example, Paul further emphasizes that the point of his own suffering is that he and those around him might rely solely on God (v. 9). Watson (1983: 391) is correct in stating that 'this verse expresses in a nutshell, though in different terminology, the meaning of faith for Paul'.

thanksgiving, this is frequently expressed through elements taken from the triad of faith, love and hope (Rom. 1:8; Eph. 1:15; Col. 1:4; 1 Thess. 1:3; 2 Thess. 1:3; Philem. 5).[65] In Paul, these are considered as the work of the Holy Spirit (cf. Rom. 5:1–5). Other gifts that the believers have received provide no grounds for boasting because it is 'in him' that believers 'have been enriched in every way' (1 Cor. 1:5). The primacy of the gospel that focuses on God's work in Christ is never compromised as all the good works are understood as acts that reflect one's obedience to the gospel (Rom. 6:17; cf. 2 Cor. 9:13).

In a more general way, the unique focus on God in Pauline acts of remembering becomes clear when Pauline epistles are compared with Hellenistic letters. In discussing 1 Thessalonians as an example of early Pauline writings, Helmut Koester (1979: 36) has highlighted distinctive elements in Pauline introductory thanksgiving. First, he notes the disproportionate length of the thanksgiving section in Paul. More importantly, he points to the fact that while the opening of the Hellenistic letters reminds the recipients of the author's personal relationship with them in the past, in Paul's letters his relationship with the church is no longer a private matter but 'an event before God in which the Holy Spirit is the primary agent'. Pauline thanksgiving sections, therefore, are flooded with references to God. This change moves to introduce God as the primary concern with whom relationship is to be nurtured. Koester concludes: 'Rather than binding writer and addressee more closely together in their personal relationship, it establishes a situation for the addressee that is independent of the writer and seen within the context of a universal eschatological event.'

Koester's analysis has not been accepted by all,[66] but he is correct

---

[65] See O'Brien 1980: 56–57 who rightly notes that these are the immediate and not final cause of thanksgiving. The use of these terms seem to predate Paul and is common to early Christian preaching (cf. Heb. 6:9–12; 10:22–24; 1 Pet. 1:3–9). In Pauline introductory thanksgivings, the relationship between the three (or two) is not consistently presented. For example, in 1 Thess. 1:3, love, faith and hope are parallel terms understood as sources of the corresponding virtues: work, labour and endurance. In Col. 1:4, however, hope is the source of both faith and love. These variations reflect Paul's use of traditional material to express his own concerns. For a further discussion on this triad and its power in shaping the self-understanding of the early Christian communities, see Bossman 1995: 71–78.

[66] Malherbe's recent work (2000: 125), for example, provides significant qualification to Koester's thesis by emphasizing the importance of personal relationships in Pauline writings. Malherbe provides a more nuanced conclusion concerning the uniqueness of Pauline thanksgiving as 'it stresses how the relationship between Paul and his readers came about, namely through God's initiative in their election and the exercise of his power in Paul's preaching'.

in emphasizing the unique role of God in the construction of the web of relationships. The relationship between God and his people is the primary concern in Pauline writings, and the relationship between individual believers is not ignored but is transformed and determined by their relationship with God.

In addition to the interjection of the vertical relationship into the thanksgiving paragraphs, one may also add that the temporal framework in Pauline thanksgiving is also expanded as the 'past' relationship between the author and his audience is now extended to the ancient past when God established his relationship with his covenant partner. Ephesians, for example, begins with the emphasis on election 'before the creation of the world' (1:4). This relationship forms the basis for thanksgiving (cf. 2 Thess. 2:13). In Pauline thanksgiving, this relationship is also extended to the future when Christ is to appear to fulfil all promises.[67] The relationship that is in view here is the covenantal relationship between God and his people. Thanksgiving, therefore, is an act of remembering what God has done for his covenantal partner.

Grace and thanksgiving

Thanksgiving is an act of covenantal remembering. In our previous discussion, we have noted that all good works are to be understood as gifts from God, and one of the most important tasks for the recipients of such gifts is to proclaim what God has done for us. Thanksgiving becomes a critical element in this message that focuses solely on God and his son Jesus. In Pauline terms, this is divine 'grace'. In this sense, thanksgiving touches on the core of Pauline theology, and it is not by accident that it is precisely in Paul that one finds this emphasis on thanksgiving.

The fact that *charis* ('grace') and *eucharistia* ('thanksgiving') share the same stem has been noted by many.[68] In the context of Pauline theology, the two words also point to the same fundamental premise. Divine grace and the constant call to thanksgiving in Paul points to an undeserving act that alters one's fundamental

---

[67] The future aspect of Pauline thanksgiving will be discussed in ch. 5 below.

[68] Ledogar (1968: 91–92), for example, points to the fact that both terms were used in classical Greek literature to refer to gratitude until the first century when *eucharistia* and its related forms express outward expressions of gratitude. For the connection between *eucharistia* and yet another related term, *chairō* ('to rejoice'), see Silva 1988: 235.

orientation and relationship with God.[69] The term *charis*, while not a particularly religious term in Hellenistic literature, came to be used by Paul in reference to the culmination of covenantal acts as God himself fulfils his promise to his people.[70] Similarly, thanksgiving, as we have seen, is also used to point to the proper remembering of God's act within the context of the covenant. Moving beyond etymological concerns, therefore, one can maintain the connection between the two.

Given the actual usage of these terms in Pauline writings, the connection between the two is even more apparent. First of all, in a number of passages, the term *charis* is actually used in the sense of thanksgiving (Rom. 6:17; 7:25; 1 Cor. 10:30; 15:57; 2 Cor. 2:14; 8:16; 9:15; Col. 3:16; 2 Tim. 1:3).[71] More relevant for our purposes, however, are those Pauline passages in which one finds the word-play between grace and thanksgiving.

Among the introductory thanksgivings in Paul, the one in 1 Corinthians 1 points directly to God's grace given in Christ Jesus as grounds for thanksgiving (v. 4). Although it is true that the term in this context focuses on the 'effect produced',[72] the use of the term also points to God who is the ultimate source of goodness as expressed in the covenantal relationship. Beyond the numerous references to salvation by the grace of God, the use of the term in connection with Paul's identification of himself as an apostle (e.g., Rom. 1:5; cf. Rom. 12:3; 15:15; Gal. 2:9; Eph. 3:2, 7–8) points to the outworking of salvation history when salvation is to reach the Gentiles. Behind these Pauline references is the affirmation that the power of God is manifested through grace (Rom. 5:20–21; 2 Cor.

[69] In concluding a study of thanksgiving from a comparative perspective, Carman (1989: 166) rightly notes that the justification of sinners in Paul's gospel calls for continuous thanksgiving: 'Only a gracious act that permanently changes the order of human relationship can evoke a continuing gratitude. Grace is by definition something from outside the existing human situation, but it does evoke a response and create a relationship between unequal partners.'

[70] Mounce (2000: 10) is correct in noting that grace in Paul does not refer simply to divine favour but should be understood within the same semantic domain as the Hebrew term *ḥesed*, a term that signifies 'covenantal faithfulness'.

[71] In most of these instances, the use of *charis* in the sense of thanksgiving occurs in the formula 'thanks be to God'. Robinson (1964: 230) argues that this reflects the 'blessed be to God' formula in Jewish traditions. As we have discussed, thanksgiving and blessing cannot be strictly separated. In any case, the non-formulaic uses in 1 Cor. 10:30 and Col. 3:16 (cf. 2 Tim. 1:3) show that *eucharistia* and *charis* can both refer to acts of thanksgiving.

[72] See O'Brien (1977: 111), who also points to the frequent uses of the passive verbs in this introductory thanksgiving.

12:9).[73] This connection also emphasizes the work of God in spite of human limitations. More relevant for our passage is the connection between grace and gift in a context where certain gifts were being abused. In 1 Corinthians, grace is emphasized precisely to show that all gifts came from God. The juxtaposition of *charis* ('grace', 1:4) and *charisma* ('gift', 1:7) within this thanksgiving paragraph is therefore not coincidental, and the same connection can be found elsewhere in Paul (Rom. 12:6; cf. Eph. 4:7). In all these references, the role of God as the source of all goodness is emphasized, and it is because of this 'grace' that one is called to give thanks to God.

Grace as grounds for thanksgiving is also expressed in 2 Corinthians 4:15 where grace that is reaching 'more and more people' is expected to 'cause thanksgiving to overflow to the glory of God'.[74] Paul Barnett (1997: 245) is correct in noting that both grace and thanksgiving are to be understood 'vertically' since grace refers to God's action for his people and thanksgiving points to the appropriate response to such acts. Unique to this passage is the close relationship between grace and thanksgiving, as the increase of the manifestation of God's grace should lead to the increase of thanksgiving offered to God.

In its context, 2 Corinthians 4:13 begins with a quotation from Psalm 116:10, and in 2 Corinthians 4:14 the death and resurrection of Jesus are noted. This context is important for two reasons. First, grace and thanksgiving are again related to the mighty acts of God through his son Jesus Christ, through whom we have hope in the midst of suffering. Furthermore, the context points to Psalm 116, a psalm that is often overlooked in treatments of 2 Corinthians 4:15.[75]

---

[73] The connection between power and grace is not limited to the Pauline corpus. In Acts 6:8, for example, Stephen is described as one who is 'full of God's grace and power' and this is manifested by his 'wonders and miraculous signs among the people'. See also Luke 2:40; 4:22; Acts 13:43; 20:24; 20:32. Cf. Cambe 1963: 193–207.

[74] This is a difficult verse since it remains unclear (1) what exact words the prepositional phrase *dia tōn pleionōn* modifies, and (2) whether the verbs *pleonasasa* and *perissuesēi* are transitive. For our purpose, it is sufficient to say that the various possibilities will lead to the understanding of thanksgiving functioning either as the object (in a causative sense) or as the means in relationship to the increasing of grace. While syntactical analysis may not be able to provide a clear answer, many have argued for the understanding that 'grace . . . may cause thanksgiving to overflow . . .' This understanding of grace as grounds for thanksgiving is further supported by other passages in which both are connected. For a further discussion, see Plummer 1915: 135; Furnish 1984: 259–260; cf. Barnett 1997: 244–245.

[75] See, however, the insightful treatment in A. Hanson 1987: 51–53.

In Psalm 116, death (vv. 3–7) and deliverance (vv. 8–11) are mentioned. What follows is an offering of thanksgiving:

> How can I repay the LORD
>   for all his goodness to me?
> I will lift up the cup of salvation
>   and call on the name of the LORD.
> I will fulfil my vows to the LORD
>   in the presence of all his people . . .
> I will sacrifice a thank-offering to you
>   and call on the name of the LORD.
> I will fulfil my vows to the LORD
>   in the presence of all his people,
> in the courts of the house of the LORD –
>   in your midst, O Jerusalem.
>
> (Ps. 116:12–14, 17–19)

Grace is revealed through death and deliverance, and thanksgiving in the sense of public confession is offered. One can hardly think of a better explication of the relationship between Pauline thanksgiving and grace.

In the same epistle, the connection between grace and thanksgiving reappears in 2 Corinthians 9:11–15.[76] This passage that contains numerous references to thanksgiving culminates in yet another exclamation of thanksgiving: 'Thanks be to God for his indescribable gift!' (v. 15). This gift is the 'surpassing grace God has given you' noted in verse 14. As in 1 Corinthians 1, the connection between grace, gift and thanksgiving is made.[77] The connection between grace and thanksgiving is further established by the use of the same word (*charis*) in reference to both.[78] Further evidence of the play on the word *charis* is found when Paul begins and ends this wider section (2 Corinthians 8 – 9) with the word *charis*.[79] In 8:1, the word is used in the sense of 'grace', while 9:15 takes on the sense of 'thanksgiving'.

[76] Another possible reference to grace and thanksgiving can be found in 2 Cor. 8:16 where, in context (cf. 8:9), thanksgiving is offered in part because of grace received.

[77] In 1 Cor. 1, however, different words are used for both 'gift' (*charisma*; cf. 2 Cor. 9:15: *dōrea*) and 'giving thanks' (*eucharisteō*; cf. 2 Cor. 9:15: *charis*).

[78] The connection between grace and thanksgiving in 2 Cor. 9:14–15 is further established by the use of a different Greek word for thanksgiving. In 2 Cor. 9:11–12, the word *eucharistia* is used instead of *charis*.

[79] Barnett (1997: 448) further notes that this word *charis* 'has served to give an overarching unity to the whole, thus forming an "elaborate *inclusio*".'

In this section, the grace that is freely given by God becomes the motivation for our sharing of material gifts (cf. 8:9).[80]

The use of *charis* for thanksgiving elsewhere in Paul may also recall the grace of God that forms the basis of all thanksgiving.[81] This connection between grace and thanksgiving points again to the connection between thanksgiving and the mighty acts of God. In remembering these mighty acts, one is called to remember God and his son through whom salvation history reaches its climax. Pauline thanksgivings are therefore theocentric and christocentric acts of remembering.

When thanksgiving is grounded on salvation history, the call to give thanks is no longer understood primarily in psychological terms. In an age when spirituality is defined primarily through the lens of subjective sentimentalism, and, even more fundamentally, of postmodern epistemology, the Pauline call to thanksgiving as an act of remembering God through his mighty acts provides a much needed correction in our understanding of the development of our lives in the Spirit. As a covenant people, we are to look to God as the source of all power and goodness, and we need to 'practise' acts of remembering as we move our attention away from our 'self' as the criterion of truth to what God did for us through his beloved Son.

---

[80] The salvation-historical connection should again be noted since 2 Cor. 8 – 9 is not simply concerned with gift-sharing. The collection from among the Gentiles for the Jerusalem saints is to serve as a sign of the unity of the church (2 Cor. 8:13–15; cf. Rom. 15:25–27). Therefore, Paul's concern for the money signifies his concern for the future of the church as Jews and Gentiles become one body in Christ.

[81] Lohse (1971: 152), for example, has pointed to Col. 3:16 where the use of the word *charis* 'reminds the readers of *sola gratia*' although the connection is not explicit.

Chapter Four

A life of thanksgiving

Thanksgiving is grounded on history but it is not limited by the past. In Paul, thanksgiving is a call to conduct one's living in light of that which is to be remembered. This points to the pastoral concerns of the apostle as reflected in the passion of his epistles. Theological discussions are not provided to fulfil the curiosity of inquiring minds. Instead, they are aimed at changing lives. At the intersection of theology and ethics, Pauline thanksgiving functions as a link that bridges the gap between the two. While thanksgiving calls for the evocation of the past, it also aims at affecting the behaviour of the present generation. The traditional paradigm expressed by the connection between the 'indicative' and the 'imperative' provides a helpful lens as actual thanksgiving offered by Paul recounts the mighty acts of God through his Son while the Pauline call to thanksgiving frequently draws one's attention to the present age when thanksgiving can be expressed in concrete ways.

In covenantal terms, acts of remembering are not simply mental exercises. To remember God and what he did for us is to act in light of such affirmations. In remembering the past, we pledge to be faithful partners in the covenantal relationship. In confessing God as the Lord of all, we are called to live out this confession. In this chapter, the ethical context of the Pauline call to thanksgiving will be examined. The surprising places where one finds his call to thanksgiving can be understood only within the wider context of Paul's theological concerns.

To walk in him

In Old Testament covenantal traditions, the recounting of the past is followed by the presentation of covenantal stipulations as Israel is called to be a faithful covenant partner. As we have noted earlier, the Mosaic Torah is built around the memory of the mighty acts of God, and to observe these commandments is to live out this recognition. Laws and commandments are therefore not simply ways in which human relationships can be regulated within the setting of a society. They are the response to divine grace, and they reflect personal commitments to God.

In the context of the covenantal relationship, the most fundamental of all the commandments is to worship God and God alone. Immediately after God identifies himself as the one who brought Israel out of Egypt there came the affirmation of the one God: 'You shall have no other gods before me' (Exod. 20:3; Deut. 5:7). The other commandments that follow aim at guarding this central affirmation of the covenant. This is best expressed by Deuteronomy 6:4–5 where the affirmation of 'the LORD is one' is followed by the call to '[l]ove the LORD your God with all your heart and with all your soul and with all your strength'. To observe the commandments therefore is to love God and to be faithful to the one Lord.

Residing within this affirmation of the one God, one finds the definition of holiness. This holiness of God is explicitly expressed in the paradigmatic song of thanksgiving in Exodus 15 where Israel's deliverance points to the unique status of God:

'Who among the gods is like you, O LORD?
Who is like you – majestic in holiness, awesome in glory,
working wonders?
You stretched out your right hand
and the earth swallowed them.
In your unfailing love you will lead
the people you have redeemed.
In your strength you will guide them
to your holy dwelling.'

(vv. 11–13)[1]

Essential to the idea of holiness is the exclusive claim that God himself alone deserves to be worshipped. The covenant people of God, therefore, are to separate themselves from their neighbours: 'Be holy because

[1] The destruction of the enemies of God as proper content of thanksgiving can be understood only within the context of the holiness of God. In the Old Testament, God's holiness points to his unquestionable sovereignty that cannot be challenged. When the fall of the nations is noted, 'nationalism' is never the basis of thanksgiving. In the later history of the fall of Israel and Judah, one can see that it is the exalted name of the Lord that remains at the centre of praise and thanksgiving.

I, the LORD your God, am holy' (Lev. 19:2). The logic behind this statement is that since God separates his people from the nations by might and power, God's people are also called to separate themselves in acknowledgment of who God is and his acts on their behalf. When gratitude is understood as the proper response to the mighty acts of God, gratitude is expressed by the way the covenant people conduct their lives. Gratitude, therefore, does not simply point to the inner disposition of an individual but it changes his or her life and thereby affects the relationship between the subject and object of thanksgiving.[2]

In the New Testament, God revealed himself through his son Jesus Christ. As in ancient times, God's acts of deliverance create a holy people for himself: 'Once you were alienated from God and were enemies in your minds because of your evil behaviour. But now he has reconciled you by Christ's physical body through death to present you holy in his sight' (Col. 1:21–22).[3] The connection between God's act in Christ and Christian conduct is emphasized throughout the Pauline epistles.[4] Believers are called to participate in the death and resurrection of Christ. In Romans 6:5, for example, Paul states that we who have been 'united with him like this in his death' will 'also be united with him in his resurrection'. When we participate in Jesus' death, our old selves will be crucified. When we are raised with him, we have the power to live in him. Therefore, we can count ourselves 'dead to sin but alive to God in Christ Jesus' (6:11). In Paul, Christian living is not based on a new set of commandments but is anchored in the climactic events of salvation history (cf. Gal. 2:20; Col. 2:9–15; 3:1–4; Eph. 5:14).

To Paul, to participate in Christ's death and resurrection is to conduct one's life 'in him'. In Colossians 2:6–7, thanksgiving is mentioned alongside of this life in Christ:

> So then, just as you received Christ Jesus as Lord, continue to live in him, rooted and built up in him, strengthened in the faith as you were taught, and overflowing with thankfulness.

[2] The involvement of both the subject and the object in acts of thanksgiving departs from our modern usage that focuses on the inner state of the person on the receiving end of deeds of kindness. Reinhart (1989: 116) rightly notes that 'in English both "thanks" and "gratitude" belong to the domain of individual inner life and using them in a religious context mirrors our Western understanding of religion as interior and affective, as dispositional rather than operational'.

[3] Marital imagery may be at work here as the church is to be presented to Christ as a pure bride (cf. 2 Cor. 11:2; Eph. 5:25–26).

[4] Moule (1973: 484) makes this clear with this succinct sentence: 'The Christian gospel is, in any case, statement before it is exhortation.'

In these two verses one finds the explication of the earlier passage that asserts the superiority and the Lordship of Christ (Col. 1:15–20).[5] Since Christ is the Lord of all, no Christian existence is justified apart from him.[6] Within this confession of Christ as Lord,[7] Paul mentions the 'overflowing' of thanksgiving. Elsewhere in Paul, the word 'overflowing' points to the richness that accompanies the experience of the power of the gospel. James Dunn (1996: 142–143) notes that in Paul, 'overflowing' is connected with hope (Rom. 15:13), comfort (2 Cor. 1:5), grace (2 Cor. 4:15; 9:8), and love (Phil. 1:9; 1 Thess. 3:12), and that these characterize the experience of the believers. While one cannot deny the importance of subjective experience in relation to the gospel, these terms, as used by Paul, refer primarily to the objective work of Christ as salvation is accomplished through his death and resurrection. Therefore, in the same way as Christ's work generates hope, comfort, grace and love, Christ is also the source from which a genuine sense of thanksgiving flows.[8] In a striking way, thanksgiving provides the context in which believers can properly conduct themselves in Christ.[9] Ethical living is therefore connected to God's acts in Christ when thanksgiving is considered the proper response to such acts.

The phrase 'live in him' in Colossians 2:6 literally reads, 'walk in him', and it is often used in Paul to refer to the conduct of one's life.[10] Earlier in Colossians 1:10–12, one already encounters the mentioning

---

[5] The connection with Col. 1:15–20 is further established by the allusion to 1:19 in 2:9–10. Statements on the superiority of Christ therefore envelope the intervening material. W. Wilson (1997: 242), who sees Col. 2:6–7 as concluding the section that begins with chapter one, further points to the conceptual parallels between 1:3 and 2:6–7 as both affirm the Lordship of Christ in the context of the call to thanksgiving.

[6] The importance of these two verses is noted by Dunn (1996: 138) who considers this as 'a brief summary sentence of the main point to be made in the body of the letter'.

[7] The 'receiving' of Christ Jesus as Lord can be understood as 'receiving the tradition that affirms Jesus Christ as Lord' since the word can be used in a technical sense for the reception of traditions although the personal object of the verb may point to simply the reception of the Messiah himself. See Barth and Blanke 1994: 301.

[8] God as the ultimate subject is also supported by the context where one finds the three participles in passive voice ('rooted', 'built', 'strengthened').

[9] This unexpected allusion to thanksgiving may be partly responsible for the appearance of the various textual variants. Instead of 'with thanksgiving', some manuscripts have 'in him' or 'in it' (i.e., 'in faith') with or without the phrase 'with thanksgiving'. The reading 'with thanksgiving', however, receives strongest external support (e.g., ℵ*, 33, 81, 1739).

[10] See, for example, the call to 'live (lit: "walk") in the Spirit' in Gal. 5:16. Cf. Rom. 6:4; 8:4; 13:13; 14:15; 1 Cor. 7:17; 2 Cor. 4:2; 5:7; 12:18; Eph. 2:10; 4:1; 5:2, 8, 15; Phil. 3:17; Col. 4:5; 1 Thess. 2:12; 4:1, 12.

of thanksgiving in the context of Christian living. In 1:10, the purpose of Paul's prayer for knowledge is that (1) the Colossians 'may live a life worthy of the Lord' and (2) they 'may please him in every way'. The second phrase explains the first; to walk in a manner worthy of the Lord is to please him in all that one does. Following this verse are four participles that modify this call to lead a life that pleases God: 'bearing fruit', 'growing', 'being strengthened' and 'giving thanks'. All four serve to define what it means to 'live a life worthy of the Lord'.[11] To place thanksgiving together with these three verbs also places thanksgiving squarely within Pauline ethics. Thanksgiving becomes an essential part of the day to day living of the believers. To live a life worthy of the Lord is to live with the constant awareness of God's grace.

The connection between God's acts on our behalf and our response is reflected in the use of the first three participles. The first two may properly be understood as referring to the responsibility of Christians in their Christian walk: 'bearing fruit in every good work' and 'growing in the knowledge of God' (Col. 1:10). A few verses earlier, however, Paul notes that it is the gospel that is 'bearing fruit and growing' (v. 6). The gospel that centres on God's work in Jesus Christ is understood as the one that generates the good works of the believers. The third participle, 'being strengthened', is in the passive voice with God as the implied subject. In light of the use of these participles, acts of thanksgiving should also be understood as generated by the work of God.[12] Since thanksgiving is by nature an act of 'response', the prior acts of God are always assumed. As in Colossians 2:6–7, thanksgiving is to characterize the lives of believers, but God is the one who makes this life of thanksgiving possible.

Thanksgiving as a Pauline concern reflects the distinct emphases in Pauline ethics. For Paul, ethics is not defined simply by isolated acts that may or may not conform to an abstract set of rules. Paul is equally if not more concerned with the foundation that lies behind patterns of behaviour. First of all, ethical behaviour is generated by the power of God. An individual is expected to be fundamentally changed as he or she encounters the powerful gospel message that points to God's act in Christ. Pauline ethics is, there-

---

[11] See O'Brien 1977: 63. It is also worth noting that while life that is pleasing to the Lord is discussed in the thanksgiving paragraph, it is thanksgiving that makes this life possible.

[12] See the previous chapter on the work of God through human agency.

fore, concerned not simply with the definition of goodness and moral purity but also with the way an individual can do that which is pleasing to God. Secondly, Pauline ethics is grounded on salvation-historical events and not in universal ideals accessible to human reason. A precise theological paradigm provides the framework in which ethical discussion can take place. To compare Pauline ethics with other 'systems' without taking sufficient consideration of the theological premise will lead to misleading results.[13] Thirdly, this ethics is concerned with the building up and the maintenance of the covenantal relationship. In one sense, then, Paul is concerned with the centre of moral relationship and not simply negative ethics that focuses on the 'grey areas'.[14] Terms such as love, hope, faithfulness, trust and endurance, together with thanksgiving, in the Pauline epistles all point to Paul's concern for the relationship between God and his people. Corresponding to this vertical relationship is the relationship between individuals that is in turn determined by their relationship with the Creator.[15] With these clarifications on the fundamental aspects of Pauline ethics, individual emphases can now be discussed.

Anti-idol polemic

In the previous section, we have touched on the relationship between thanksgiving and Pauline ethics. To move ahead, we need to reiterate the central affirmation of the covenantal traditions and the ethical boundaries this affirmation delineates.

We have noted that the affirmation of God as the one Lord of all is central to Old Testament covenants. The Ten Commandments

[13] A recent attempt that takes the wider theological emphases into account in discussing the 'moral vision' in Paul can be found in Hays (1996: 19–36) who argues that images such as body of Christ, the cross and the new creation provide a helpful lens through which individual assertions can be appreciated.

[14] In modern discussion, one can point to 'virtue ethics' that focus on moral character and not simply issues that occupy the 'grey areas'. For a well-balanced discussion of the prospect of virtue ethics, see Kruschwitz and Roberts 1987.

[15] In Pauline thanksgiving, interpersonal relationships are also determined by one's gratitude to God himself. In response to God's grace, we are obliged to care for God's creation (cf. 2 Cor. 8 – 9). Vacek (2000: 117) correctly notes that '[s]ince God is still at work in creating, preserving, renewing, redeeming, judging, and the like, we can give a return gift to God by cooperating, to the degree we are able, in these activities of God (John 9:4; 1 Cor. 3:9; 2 Cor. 1:3–5, 2:14)'. On a more fundamental level, our love for others is grounded on God's love for us: 'Be imitators of God, therefore, as dearly loved children and live a life of love, just as Christ loved us and gave himself up for us' (Eph. 5:1–2).

open with the affirmation: 'I am the LORD your God, who brought you out of Egypt, out of the land of slavery' (Exod. 20:2; Deut. 5:6). Whether the covenant people can continue to make that assertion depends on their obedience to the commandment that follows: 'You shall have no other gods before me' (Exod. 20:3; Deut. 5:7). In concrete terms, the people of Israel are forbidden to make idols for themselves (Exod. 20:4; Deut. 5:8). The prohibition against idol-worship came at the beginning of the section that follows the Ten Commandments when details of God's commandments are presented (Exod. 20:23). Throughout the discussion of covenantal stipulations, this prohibition plays an important role (e.g., Exod. 23:24; 34:14, 17; Lev. 19:4; 26:1; Deut. 4:15–20; 6:14; 12:29–31; 13:1–18; 17:2–7).[16]

This prohibition is based on the relationship between God and his people.[17] José Faur (1978: 1) aptly notes that the 'Bible injunction against idolatry rests on two different premises: it violates the Covenant and it is useless'. In Deuteronomy 31:20, the future rebellion of Israel is discussed in these very terms: 'they will turn to other gods and worship them, rejecting me and breaking my covenant'. In the continuation of covenant traditions in the Old Testament, one continues to find warnings against idol-worship. At the occasion of the renewal of the covenant in Joshua 24, for example, a decision is called for as the people have to decide on their relationship with their covenantal partner: 'Throw away the gods your forefathers worshipped . . . But if serving the LORD seems undesirable to you, then choose for yourselves this day whom you will serve' (vv. 14–15). Again, in the prophets, the worship of false gods as 'their forefathers' did signifies the breaking of the covenant (e.g., Jer. 11:9–10). It is ironic, therefore, to find idol-worship taking place at the very time when Moses was on the mountain receiving the Torah from God (Exod. 32). It is precisely Israel's failure in the wilderness that is recalled in Joshua 24 and Jeremiah 11.

---

[16] We are indebted to Weinfeld (1990: 1) who has pointed to the influence of the Ten Commandments throughout the Mosaic Torah. Cf. Mettinger 1979: 15–29.

[17] Halbertal (1998: 161) has argued that 'the ban against idolatry is not universal, but is directed only towards Jews, since the prohibition against worshipping other gods is based upon the particularly historical relationship between Israel and God'. He further suggests that it is only in the rabbinic period that the ban against idolatry is universalized. Halbertal's observation is helpful but it needs to be considered in light of the focus on the covenantal relationship in the Old Testament. Moreover, the establishment of the covenantal relationship itself is to show the universal sovereignty of the God of Israel in the presence of all nations.

Within the context of covenantal relationship, it is clear that God alone deserves to be worshipped. God is a jealous God (Deut. 6:13–15) but Israel had 'abandoned the God who made [them]' as they 'made him jealous with their foreign gods and angered him with their detestable idols' (Deut. 32:15–16).[18] Idols were made so that God's people would have something visible in which to place their trust, something other than their God. In Deuteronomy 32:37, these idols are described as 'the rock they took refuge in'. This touches at the heart of the prohibition against idol-worship. When God chose Israel in the establishment of the covenantal relationship, Israel was expected to respond properly to this divine act of grace. To place trust in someone or something other than God himself is to deny the power and majesty that God had revealed through his mighty acts.[19]

In the Pauline epistles, the same prohibition against worshipping false gods is emphasized.[20] We have already noted that the covenantal affirmation of the one God is the basic presupposition of Pauline theology.[21] Unique aspects in Pauline discussion of idols can be detected as he addresses both Jewish and Gentile audiences. To the Gentiles, Paul understandably argues against the worship of other 'gods'[22] as they were so used to doing before their conversion. The contrast between the true God and idols is expressed in Galatians 4:8:

[18] For an understanding of God's jealousy within the wider use of marital metaphors, see the helpful treatment in Ortlund 1996: 25–45.

[19] In Isaiah, for example, anti-idol polemic is directed not so much at the spiritual infidelity of God's people. The focus is rather on the power of God who alone is able to deliver his people from among the nations because he is above all 'gods'. See Spykerboer 1976 and A. Wilson 1986.

[20] As in Isaiah (see the previous footnote), the powerlessness of the foreign gods and idols is also the focus of Second Temple anti-idol polemic. Nevertheless, one can still find discussions pointing to idolatry as the reason for Israel's suffering. See the helpful survey in Roth 1975: 21–47, and the specific treatments in Murphy 1988: 275–287 and Zeidman 1997: 125–144. In his recent study, Bauckham (1999: 10–12) further notes that in Second Temple material the uniqueness of the God of Israel lies in the affirmation that he is the only true God and sole creator and ruler of all things.

[21] Please refer to chapter two above. Paul here may also be indebted to traditions concerning Jesus when Jesus cites the first part of the Shema in his discussion of the greatest commandment: 'Hear, O Israel, the Lord our God, the Lord is one. Love the Lord your God with all your heart and with all your soul and with all your mind and with all your strength' (Mark 12:29–30; cf. Deut 6:4–5). Although explicit anti-idol polemic does not play an important role in the gospel material, allusions to idolatry can be found in a number of passages. For a further discussion, see Sandelin (1996: 412–420), who suggests that the lack of explicit anti-idol polemic in the gospels can be explained by the attempt of the churches to survive under Roman imperial rule during the second half of the first century.

[22] Consistent with the Septuagint (e.g. Ps. 115:4; Is. 10:11), the term 'idol' is used to describe false gods.

'Formerly, when you did not know God, you were slaves to those who by nature are not gods.'[23] Turning to the true God of Israel is therefore turning away from idols. In 1 Thessalonians 1:9, for example, Paul mentions the good report he heard concerning those who turned to Christ: 'They tell how you turned to God from idols to serve the living and true God.'[24]

In his arguments with Jewish legalists, Paul also brings up the subject of idolatry. In the same passage that we have noted (Gal. 4), Paul has turned his anti-idol polemic against those Gentile converts who are now bound by Jewish traditions. Before they were converted, they were slaves to idols. Now they are 'turning back to those weak and miserable principles' (4:9; cf. vv. 3–5). Jewish traditions, therefore, are now understood as idols that are worshipped by those who are bound by them.[25] The importance of Galatians 4 for our discussion is the simple fact that, in Paul, anything that takes away the glory and sufficiency of Christ is understood as idolatry. In a more general way, for Paul 'false teachings' are defined as those which fail to affirm this Christocentric emphasis.[26] This confirms our understanding that the 'all-inclusiveness of Jesus Christ was the conviction that determined Paul's thinking and practices' (Moule 1987: 50).

Thanksgiving is a call to focus solely on God and his Son, while idolatry is the failure to do so. This contrast between thanksgiving and idolatry is made explicit in Ephesians 5:3–5, a passage that should be quoted in full:

---

[23] The phrase, 'those who are not gods', is often used to refer to idols in the Septuagint (e.g., Is. 37:18–19; Jer. 2:11–28). Elsewhere Paul refers to idols as 'nothing at all' since 'there is no God but one' (1 Cor. 8:4; cf. 10:19).

[24] In Second Temple Jewish traditions, Gentiles are often characterized by their worship of idols. In Wisdom of Solomon, one finds this description of the Gentiles: 'they worship even the most hateful animals, which are worse than all others when judged by their lack of intelligence' (15:18 NRSV). This is true of other Jewish works. Chesnutt (1995: 100), for example, notes that the 'most fundamental ground of distinction in *Joseph and Aseneth* between Jew and Gentile is that the former is a worshipper of God and the latter an idolater'. See also the discussion in Grant 1986: 45–53 and J. J. Collins 1997: 209–213. Meeks (1993: 68) further points to the fact that both Jewish and Pauline vice lists depart from their pagan counterparts in emphasizing the sin of idolatry.

[25] See the helpful study by Calvert (1993: 222–237), who further points out that the reference to Abraham in context (Gal. 3:29) should be highlighted, especially when Abraham is depicted as the 'archetypal anti-idolater' in Second Temple Jewish traditions.

[26] Col. 2:8 illustrates this point: 'See to it that no-one takes you captive through hollow and deceptive philosophy, which depends on human tradition and the basic principles of this world rather than on Christ.'

> But among you there must not be even a hint of sexual immo-
> rality, or of any kind of impurity, or of greed, because these
> are improper for God's holy people. Nor should there be
> obscenity, foolish talk or coarse joking, which are out of
> place, but rather thanksgiving. For of this you can be sure:
> No immoral, impure or greedy person – such a man is an
> idolater – has any inheritance in the kingdom of Christ and
> of God.

The most striking aspect of this passage is the contrast[27] that Paul
sets up. He begins by listing vices that are improper for God's
people. Then three more are mentioned, pointing to various unacceptable acts.[28] After this list, when the readers expect Paul to
provide a counter list of virtues, a call to offer thanksgiving to God
is issued instead. This contrast demands an explanation. A number
of church fathers have suggested that the word *eucharistia* should be
translated as 'gratifying', thus providing a natural contrast to the
list that includes unacceptable speech. This translation is unlikely in
light of the way Paul uses the term elsewhere.[29] A more plausible
explanation has been provided by modern scholars who suggest that
'[t]ongues which are habituated to the praise of God should not
readily lend themselves to language which dishonours His name'
(Bruce 1961: 103; cf. O'Brien 1977: 59). This note is helpful but it
focuses too narrowly on thanksgiving as a verbal act and thus fails
to account fully for the contrast between thanksgiving and sexual
impurity. The ethical import of thanksgiving needs to be further
developed.

A more fundamental explanation of this contrast should begin
with the fact that thanksgiving is to be understood primarily as an
acknowledgment of God as the Lord of all. To commit a variety of
sins, sins that are not limited to those of a verbal nature, is to fail to

---

[27] Note the use of the phrase *alla mallon* in pointing to the strong contrast.

[28] The exact nature of the vices listed is subject to debate. In light of the list in Col.
3:5 ('sexual immorality, impurity, lust, evil desires and greed'), one is justified to understand the three vices in Eph. 3:5 as moving from the more specific external acts to the
general internal desires of the heart, although it should also be noted that sexual
immorality can be used as a metaphor for unfaithfulness to God. The second group
refers to the use of impious speech. In light of the previous list, however, sexual references cannot be excluded.

[29] It seems that some fathers have read *eucharitia* for *eucharistia*, thus leading to
the understanding of the term as 'gracious speech'. There is, however, no textual
basis for this reading. For a further discussion, see M. Barth 1974: 562; and Best
1998: 479.

live up to such a commitment.[30] Therefore, instead of the various vices, Paul calls his audience to lead a life that centres around God the creator. This contrast between thanksgiving and the vices clearly reveals the ethical nature of acts of thanksgiving; thanksgiving is what characterizes 'God's holy people' (Eph. 5:3; cf. 1 Thess. 4:3–8).

In verse 5 of this passage, the mentioning of the 'idolater' further extends the contrast. Although the use of the singular neutral pronoun implies that the word points primarily to greed, it is possible that all three terms were referred to, especially since in essence the three cannot be separated when they refer to three different levels of sinfulness.[31] As one or more of the vices are linked to idolatry, thanksgiving serves as a contrast to idolatry. This surprising contrast is supported by other details in this passage. First, a number of the 'vices' have been tradi-tionally connected with acts of idolatry. As in this passage, greed is connected to idolatry in both the Old Testament and in Second Temple Jewish traditions.[32] Sexual immorality, the issue that lies behind several of these vices, is also connected with idolatry. In Wisdom of Solomon 14, for example, in a context where idols were considered as 'snares for human souls' (v. 11), the author further notes that 'the idea of making idols was the beginning of fornication' (v. 12 NRSV).[33]

Second, as it has been suggested concerning the two vice lists of Colossians 3:5 and 8,[34] the list in Ephesians 5 may also reflect tradi-tions that point back to the Ten Commandments.[35] If this is the case, the relationship between the affirmation of the one God and the various commandments is again made.

Third, the phrase 'among you there must not even be a hint of' (NIV), which is literally 'let it not be mentioned among you', could be a refer-

---

[30] Clement of Alexandria provides a succinct statement on the Pauline understand-ing of thanksgiving: 'And he who gives thanks does not occupy his time in pleasures' (*Pedagogus* 2.1 [*ANF* 2:240])

[31] See the discussion in note 28 above. Even in terms of Hellenistic Greek usage, it is not impossible that the pronoun refers to all three ideas previously mentioned. See M. Barth 1974: 2.563–564; Best 1998: 481. Cf. O'Brien 1999: 362.

[32] E.g., *T. Judah* 19.1; and *Sirach* 31:6–7. The parallel passage in Col. 3:5 also iden-tifies greed as idolatry. See also the discussion in Rosner 1999: 37–48.

[33] O'Brien 1999: 359 notes that in Paul, one 'who surrenders to sexual immorality indicates ultimately that he or she has broken from God'. Cf. Rom. 1:24–27; 1 Cor. 5:1–2; 6:12–20; 7:2; 10:7–8; 2 Cor. 12:21; Gal. 5:19; 1 Thess. 4:3.

[34] Scholars have disagreed over the exact relationship between Eph. 5:3–5 and Col. 3:5–7 although the similarities between the two cannot be denied. One can argue that Eph. 5 is dependent on Col. 3, or that they are both dependent upon prior traditions (or vice lists). If Pauline authorship is affirmed for both, the issue ceases to be an urgent one. For a comparison of the two passages, see Lincoln 1990: 319–320.

[35] See, for example, Hartman 1987: 240.

ence to anti-idol passages in the Old Testament. Ernest Best (1998: 477), for example, has suggested that this phrase may reflect a number of Old Testament passages that forbid the naming of false gods (e.g., Exod. 23:13; Hos. 2:17; Zech. 13:2). If this is the case, references to idolatry permeate the entire passage. In this anti-idol passage, the antidote that Paul highlights is thanksgiving.[36] Moving beyond remembering the past, this call to thanksgiving is focused on the present as Paul calls believers to lead a God/Christ-centred life in all that they do and say. In short, it is to do 'what pleases the Lord' (Eph. 5:10).

Thanksgiving by its very nature is anti-idol polemic. Romans 1:18–32 provides a definition of what idolatry is. Idolaters 'exchanged the glory of the immortal God for images made to look like mortal man and birds and animals and reptiles' (v. 23). This verse alludes to Psalm 106:20, a verse that in turn points back to the worship of the golden calf at Sinai (Exod. 32:1–34).[37] In doing so, they believe the ultimate lie: 'They exchanged the truth of God for a lie, and worshipped and served created things rather than the Creator' (v. 25). This verse that alludes to Isaiah 44:19–20 is important for a number of reasons. First, it defines idolatry not by the precise objects being worshipped but by the one who demands sole glory. Any act of allegiance that attracts one's attention away from God and his glory is idolatry. Second, it defines idolatry as deception (cf. v. 18). Objects that claim to offer hope and security to those who worship them constitute ultimate deception. Third, this verse touches on the central claim of Old Testament covenantal traditions.[38] God is recognized as the creator of all, and the covenantal relationship is built on this acknowledgment. Idolatry therefore can be understood as the fundamental act of betrayal.

As in Ephesians 5, the contrast between thanksgiving and idolatry is explicitly stated. In Romans 1:21, the act of idolatry is equated

---

[36] The importance of thanksgiving is again highlighted later in the chapter when Paul calls believers always to give thanks to God for everything (Eph. 5:20). This passage will be further examined below.

[37] Fitzmyer 1993: 283 further points to Deut. 4:15–18; Jer. 2:11; and Wisdom of Solomon 11:15.

[38] Although the Gentiles are the primary target of this passage, Israel is not exempted. This explains the Old Testament allusions found here. Furthermore, as Rom. 5:12–14 makes clear, Israel has not been able to escape the charges made against the Gentiles. Directed specifically to the Jews, Paul also accused them of bragging about the law but dishonouring God in the process (2:23). In a sense, then, the Torah has become their idol. On a more general level, idolatry understood in a narrow sense as the worship of images seems to have continued through the Second Temple period. See Porton 1988: 243; and Schiffman 1994: 374–377.

97

with the failure to glorify God as God and to give thanks to him. To thank God is to give him the glory that only he deserves, and the failure to give thanks reflects one's refusal to submit to God's authority. In his lectures on Romans, Martin Luther (1959: 26) provides a succinct statement on this connection between ingratitude and idolatry:

> See, then, how great an evil ingratitude is: it produces a love of vanity, and this results in blindness, and blindness in idolatry, and idolatry brings about a whole whirlpool of vices.

Thanksgiving, therefore, is not an isolated act of gratitude. It is to be lived out as a life of worship. In thanksgiving, the affirmation of God as the Lord of all becomes a discipline that needs to be practised.

Thanksgiving offering

Any distraction from the work of God is considered as idolatry. On the flip side, one is called to devote one's entire life in response to God's grace and his mighty acts. It is expected, therefore, to find sacrificial metaphors applied to a life of thanksgiving as one seeks to offer one's entire self to live a God-centred life.

In the Old Testament, the thanksgiving sacrifice is one of the three 'fellowship offerings' mentioned in Leviticus 7:11–21 (cf. 22:29–30). This sacrifice is to be offered with the acknowledgment of God's act of deliverance. In the Psalms, one reads about the offer of thanks in response to the experience of God's power:

> Then they cried to the LORD in their trouble,
>   and he saved them from their distress
> He sent forth his word and healed them;
>   he rescued them from the grave.
> Let them give thanks to the LORD for his unfailing love
>   and his wonderful deeds for men.
> Let them sacrifice thank-offerings
>   and tell of his works with songs of joy.
>   (Ps. 107:19–22)

In offering this sacrifice of thanksgiving, the past is recalled, allowing the individual to find hope in the present. As a communal sacrifice, this offering will be presented as a public act:

> I will sacrifice a thank-offering to you . . .
> I will fulfil my vows to the LORD
>   in the presence of all his people.
>
> (Ps. 116:17–18)

While specific acts of deliverance are frequently grounds for thanks-giving, some psalms reflect a more general context. In Psalm 100, for example, the psalmist points to Israel's past when God elected his own people:

> Know that the LORD is God.
>   It is he who made us, and we are his;
>   we are his people, the sheep of his pasture.
>
> (v. 3)[39]

The significance of this sacrifice is confirmed by references in the Psalms as well as in the prophets (e.g., Jer. 33:11; Amos 4:5). Even in the Psalms, however, one can detect that the confession of the mighty acts of God is becoming the focus taking the place of the sacrificial victim.[40] Psalm 69:30–31, for example, notes:

> I will praise God's name in song
>   and glorify him with thanksgiving.
> This will please the LORD more than an ox,
>   more than a bull with its horns and hoofs.

Thanksgiving through words and deeds is emphasized as the cultic practices are transformed in the worship life of the people.

This development also signifies the beginning of the spiritualiza-tion of sacrifices in general.[41] While Psalm 69 reflects the idea that thanksgiving and praise are better than sacrifice itself, other psalms

[39] The title of Ps. 100 further points to the use of this psalm in the context of thanks-giving offering.

[40] See Gese 1981: 129–134 for a further discussion of the theological development of the thank offering in the Old Testament. He suggests that thank offering 'consti-tuted the cultic basis for the main bulk of the Psalms' (131). He also notes the impor-tance of thank offering in private worship: 'The official post-exilic cult, with its sharp separation between priests and laity on the basis of a far-reaching concept of holiness, become more and more the concern of the priests, while private worship was largely determined by the thank offering' (131).

[41] This is best illustrated in Philo where, among other sacrifices, the Passover sacri-fice is considered as a thank offering (*De sacrificiis Abelis et Caini* 62). Cf. LaPorte 1983: 56.

note that thanksgiving itself is the proper sacrifice. In Psalm 141:2, for example, prayer itself is understood as a sacrifice:

May my prayer be set before you like incense;
may the lifting up of my hands be like the evening sacrifice.
(cf. Hos 4:2)

In the Second Temple period, this development continues and finds its expression in various forms. Obedience and purity of soul become acceptable sacrifices to God.[42] This reflects the wider theological development in Second Temple Jewish traditions: (1) the ethical life of Israel is emphasized together with the observances of the Torah; and (2) the focus on individual piety.[43] In Philo, for example, not only should individual acts of kindness be considered as sacrifices to God, the entire person should be dedicated to God (e.g., *De decalogo* 108; *De sacrificiis Abelis et Caini* 109).[44]

In the New Testament, Christ is the ultimate sacrifice and all we should and can do is to respond to this climactic act that fulfils all sacrifices. Everett Ferguson (1980: 1163) rightly notes: 'Since atoning sacrifice was effected by Christ, Christian sacrifices were seen largely as thank offering or else as enabling one to share in the sacrifice of Christ.' This is made explicit in Hebrews 13:15, a passage that points to the sacrifice of praise and thanksgiving in response to God's act through Christ: 'Through Jesus, therefore, let us continually offer to God a sacrifice of praise – the fruit of lips that confess his name.' The author goes on to note the ethical focus of this sacrifice: 'And do not forget to do good and to share with others, for with such sacrifices God is pleased' (13:16).

For Paul, the connection between Christ's sacrifice and the presentation of believers as sacrifice can be found in Ephesians 5:25–27:

. . . Christ loved the church and gave himself up for her to make her holy, cleansing her by the washing with water through the

[42] For a further discussion of the spiritualization of sacrifices, see also Ferguson 1980: 1157.

[43] Both can be traced back to the diminishing role of the Temple cult that begins with the fall of the Jerusalem temple in 586 BC. Even after the Second Temple was established, competing voices can still be heard. The case of the Qumran community, in their opposition to the cultic practices of the Jerusalem priests, provides the best example (cf. 1QS 9.4–5).

[44] In Philo, the entire universe itself is to be consecrated to God (*Quis rerum divinarum heres sit* 200). See the discussion in LaPorte 1983: 45–47.

word, and to present her to himself as a radiant church,
without stain or wrinkle or any other blemish, but holy and
blameless.

Terms like 'present' and 'without . . . blemish' are cultic terms used in
the context of sacrifice.[45] The death of Christ purifies the believers so
that they might become an acceptable sacrifice to God (cf. 2 Cor.
5:21; Col. 1:22).[46]

While Christ is the subject in Ephesians 5:25–27, Christians are
also called to offer themselves as sacrifices. In Romans 12:1, Christian
are called to offer their lives as sacrifices as they live out their conviction: 'Therefore, I urge you, brothers, in view of God's mercy, to offer
your bodies as living sacrifices, holy and pleasing to God – which is
your spiritual worship.' This passage is significant to our discussion
of Christian life as thanksgiving offering in a number of ways. First,
the connection between God's work in Christ and Christian behaviour is made. The phrase 'in view of God's mercy' points back to
Christ's death and resurrection. More importantly, this verse connects the first half of Romans that describes God's grace through
Christ with the remaining chapters that focus on the outliving of the
gospel message.[47] As in Ephesians 5, the connection between Christ's
sacrifice and believers' living sacrifice cannot be missed.

Second, the phrase 'pleasing to God' finds its parallel in the following verse where the same adjective is used to describe 'the will of
God'. The ethical implications of the gospel message are noted as the
transformation of believers is to be worked out in their following the
will of God.[48]

---

[45] Some (e.g., O'Brien 1999: 425) have interpreted these terms as part of the marital
metaphor where the spotless virgin is said to be presented as the perfect bride. In light
of the reference to Christ's death and the lack of marital metaphor in Col. 1:22, the
Old Testament sacrificial background should not be ignored. Cf. Exod. 29:1; Lev. 1:3,
10; 4:3; 5:15; Luke 2:22–23; Rom. 12:1. The word 'present' is frequently used in a cultic
context in extra-biblical material.

[46] While this paragraph seems to point to the end times, the present aspect of
Christ's sanctifying work cannot be denied.

[47] The word 'therefore' should also be noted. Moo (1996: 748) rightly states:
'"Therefore" must be given its full weight: Paul wants to show that the exhortations of
12:1 – 15:13 are built firmly on the theology of chaps. 1 – 11.' The connection between
offering ourselves and Christ's act on our behalf can also be seen in Rom. 6:4–14.

[48] In Paul, 'the will of God' is frequently used to refer to the sanctification of God's
people. See, for example, the definition provided in 1 Thess. 4:3: 'It is God's will that
you should be sanctified: that you should avoid sexual immorality.' Of particular
importance is 1 Thess. 5:18 where thanksgiving itself is understood to be 'the will of
God'. These two verses will be discussed in greater detail in the next section.

Third, in the context of the wider argument of Romans, this sacrifice is to take the place of Old Testament cultic sacrifices. These sacrifices are not simply democratized in that every believer can now have direct participation in them. More importantly, the living sacrifices in Romans 12 point to the dedication of the entire person to the will of God. In light of the work of Christ, nothing short of a complete surrender of one's will and desires is required of those who had experienced the power of the gospel. The continuity with Old Testament traditions can still be felt, however, since the entire people of God is called to offer this 'sacrifice'.[49]

Significantly, in the call to true worship in Romans 12, Paul calls believers to reverse the false worship described in Romans 1.[50] Instead of worshipping 'created things rather than the Creator' (Rom. 1:25), Paul calls us to be involved in 'spiritual worship' (12:1). Instead of degrading our 'bodies' (1:24), we are called to offer our 'bodies' to God (12:1). Instead of 'sexual impurity' (1:24), we are called to offer the sacrifice that is 'holy' (12:1). Once given over to a 'depraved mind' (1:28), the 'mind' will now be renewed (12:2). Once being 'filled with every kind of wickedness' (1:29), we are called not to 'conform any longer to the pattern of this world' (12:2). If Romans 1 describes the ingratitude (cf. 1:21) that characterizes those who refuse to worship him, Romans 12 calls us to offer all of ourselves 'as living sacrifices' (12:1) to him who deserves all praise and thanksgiving.

In Romans 12, therefore, believers are urged to offer themselves as living sacrifices in grateful response to God's mighty acts through the death and resurrection of Christ. This 'sacrifice' is to be worked out in our daily lives, as is made clear in Romans 12:2 and the remainder of the epistle. The call to 'spiritual worship' therefore should be understood in the same way. David Peterson (1993: 69) has rightly reminded us that the phrase should not be understood primarily in a Hellenistic sense that focuses on the interiorization of worship. Instead, the Jewish context should be noted where 'the movement was towards a development of the ethical implications of ritual worship'. In response to God's grace, believers are not simply called to offer verbal acts of thanksgiving. Instead, we are to live a life that

---

[49] The corporate aspect is reflected by the use of the plural for 'bodies' but singular for 'sacrifice' (NIV has 'sacrifices' for the singular Greek word) in Rom. 12:1.

[50] The general reversal of Rom. 1 in Rom. 12 has been noted by many. See, for example, the discussion in Hooker 1985: 4. The connection between thanksgiving and living sacrifices as the appropriate response is often missed, however.

reflects our recognition of this debt and our acceptance of the obligation that comes with the reception of God's gift.[51]

This understanding of Christian life as (thanksgiving) sacrifice is also assumed in other Pauline passages. In Ephesians 5:1–2, for example, one finds a passage that reflects a similar understanding, although it is God's work in Christ that is explicitly identified in cultic terms: 'Be imitators of God, therefore, as dearly loved children and live a life of love, just as Christ loved us and gave himself up for us as a fragrant offering and sacrifice to God.' The logic behind this passage is similar to that of Romans 12. In response to what God did for us, we should act accordingly. Gratitude is again described in terms of the way Christians act out their convictions.[52] Finally, 2 Corinthians 5:15 best summarizes our discussion thus far: 'And he died for all, that those who live should no longer live for themselves but for him who died for them and was raised again.'[53]

In all circumstances

The understanding of our lives as 'living sacrifice' leads naturally to a discussion of the Pauline call to give thanks in all circumstances. A notable parallel to Romans 12 can be found in 1 Thessalonians 5:18 where Paul exhorts believers to live a life of thanksgiving: 'give thanks in all circumstances, for this is God's will for you in Christ Jesus'. As in Romans 12, the will of God is mentioned.[54] In the case of Romans 12, Paul calls us to present our bodies as living sacrifices. While the metaphor of living sacrifice points to the devotion of the entire

---

[51] In his anthropological study of reciprocity in various cultures, van Wees (1998: 26) points to the focus on verbal expressions in modern conceptions of thanksgiving: 'Our verbal displays of gratitude, it would seem, are shallow substitute for a deeper sense of obligation and greater concern to reciprocate which characterizes other cultures; they are an index, perhaps of the comparatively small role played by gifts and favours in keeping together the fabric of our society.' For a further discussion of the nature of gratitude as being open to the transformative nature of the gift, see L. Hyde 1983: 40–55.

[52] The passage that follows (Eph. 5:3–5) is treated above. The fact that one finds an explicit discussion of moral acts together with thanksgiving in the passage that follows 5:1–2 confirms our understanding of the connection between God's act and ours within the context of sacrifice.

[53] In discussing Christian life as living sacrifice, one should also point to 1 Cor. 3:16 where believers are described as the temple of God (cf. 2 Cor. 6:16).

[54] The parallels are not limited to Rom. 12:1 and 1 Thess. 5:18. As R. F. Collins (1998: 411) has pointed out, the exhortations of 1 Thess. 5:12–22 are also comparable to that of Rom. 12:9–18.

person, the phrase 'in all circumstances'[55] also points to the same vision from which no aspect of life is excluded. The call to the church to give thanks in all circumstances stands in contrast with 'the occasional cultic celebration of ancient Israel' (Shedd 1987: 143).

In 1 Thessalonians 5, this will of God is expressed in terms of thanksgiving.[56] To further define what this will is, one may wish to refer back to the same epistle in which the content of this will of God is explicitly emphasized: 'It is God's will that you should be sanctified' (1 Thess. 4:3). The connection between 1 Thessalonians 4:3 and 5:18 is further established by the fact that this construction ('It is God's will'/'for this is God's will') appears only in these two places in the Pauline epistles.[57] If we read 1 Thessalonians 5:18 in light of 4:3, to give thanks is to be holy. While on a linguistic level these two cannot be equated,[58] on a theological level the relationship between the two cannot be denied. As we have discussed in the earlier chapters, to give thanks is to set our focus solely on God. For Paul, to give thanks 'in all circumstances' is not a call for us to remain in a certain emotional state all the time.[59] It is a call to lead a God-centred life. To 'give thanks in all circumstances' is to live under the Lordship of Christ in all that we do (cf. 4:1–2).

This same emphasis on thanksgiving is made in Ephesians 5:19–20: 'Sing and make music in your heart to the Lord, always giving thanks to God the Father for everything, in the name of our Lord Jesus

---

[55] The phrase literally reads 'in all', and it is used in connection with the call to thanksgiving only here in this passage. Elsewhere in Paul the phrase points to an emphasis on inclusiveness or comprehensiveness (e.g., 1 Cor. 1:5; 2 Cor. 6:4; Phil. 4:12).

[56] Commentators remain divided as to whether the phrase ('for this is God's will for you in Christ Jesus') refers to all three preceding phrases ('Be joyful always; pray continually; give thanks in all circumstances') or to thanksgiving alone. Our interpretation will not be affected by this disagreement. See O'Brien 1977: 58; and Malherbe 2000: 330.

[57] Malherbe (2000: 330) further notes that while 1 Thess. 4:3 introduces the first paraenesis, 5:18 introduces the last. According to this reading, 'the two references to God's will would form the two brackets of an *inclusio* that encompasses all the paraenesis contained in chaps. 4 and 5'. If one considers 5:18 as pointing backward, the function of 4:3 and 5:18 as brackets to the intervening material becomes even more apparent. For the connections between 1 Thess. 4:1–12 and 5:12–22, see also R. F. Collins 1998: 398–414.

[58] It is better to see 'the will of God' as a general category that contains a number of subcategories.

[59] Even the call to be 'joyful' in its immediate context (1 Thess. 5:16) should not be understood in a purely psychological sense. In Rom. 5:3, for example, to 'rejoice in our sufferings' is to understand the purpose of suffering in light of the wider plan of God. In cases where 'joy' is to be understood to refer to a certain emotional state, its relationship with thanksgiving need not be taken in a parallel sense (cf. Col. 1:11).

Christ.' A slightly different phrase is used ('for everything') but the same point is made.[60] Added to this is the temporal aspect as believers are to give thanks 'always'[61] as Paul himself has demonstrated elsewhere.[62] Not to be missed is the evocation of the Lordship of Jesus Christ. Again, the act of thanksgiving is to be carried out with reference to the authority of Jesus. Furthermore, the main clause to which this subordinate clause is attached is also worth noting: the act of thanksgiving is to qualify and express what it means to be 'filled with the Spirit' (5:18).

The ethical focus on this call of thanksgiving becomes even clearer in the Colossian parallel to Ephesians 5:20: 'And whatever you do, whether in word or deed, do it all in the name of the Lord Jesus, giving thanks to God the Father through him' (Col. 3:17). All things are to be done in light of the confession of the Lordship of Christ, and this confession is expressed in thanksgiving. The precise sense of this call to thanksgiving is expressed by 1 Corinthians 10:31: 'So whether you eat or drink or whatever you do, do it all for the glory of God.' As in Colossians 3:17, all possible acts are included in this Pauline injunction. The phrase, 'do it all in the name of the Lord Jesus, giving thanks to God', is, however, replaced by a reference to the glory of God.

The question that is often brought to these verses can now be addressed: 'Is it possible to thank him for the evil events themselves?' (Best 1998: 514). This question itself reflects a misunderstanding of the Pauline call to thanksgiving. We are not asked to be elated over the news of tragedies. We are, however, called to focus on God and

[60] The phrase literally reads 'for all', and it can be understood as referring to things or persons. In its context, the neuter sense should be retained. See M. Barth 1974: 2.584; and Best 1998: 513.

[61] Some have limited this to times of corporate worship. Best (1998: 513), for example, notes: '"All times" are all those occasions when worship is offered.' This is correct when worship is understood as extending to everyday Christian living. The Colossian parallel discussed below will make this clear.

[62] In Paul, thanksgiving prayers are offered 'always' or 'continually' (Rom. 1:9; 1 Cor. 1:4; Phil. 1:4; Col. 1:3; 1 Thess. 1:2–3; 2:13; 2 Thess. 1:3; 2:13; Philem. 4). O'Brien (1977: 21) has noted that 'to speak of prayer by this and similar terms was part and parcel of the style of ancient letters'. In light of our discussion, however, the theological emphasis on thanksgiving as the constant consciousness of the Lordship of Christ should also be noted. Perhaps 1 Cor. 7:35 provides the best paraphrase of this emphasis as Paul's exhortation is provided so that believers 'may live in a right way in undivided devotion to the Lord'. Aus (1973: 436) further points to the use of Deut. 6:5 ('Love the LORD your God with all your heart and with all your soul and with all your strength') in Rabbinic material to explain why God's people should always thank/bless their Lord.

God alone in spite of all that can happen to us and around us. Rather than being obsessed with the well-being of our own selves, acts of thanksgiving force us to worship the one who deserves all glory and honour. In the face of evil, our responsibility is to be faithful to him who is the Lord of all. To give thanks in all circumstances is, therefore, to challenge the power of Satan as we participate in the cosmic struggle, anticipating the consummation of the eschatological victory that is rooted in the cross and the empty tomb.[63]

This understanding of the relationship between Pauline thanksgiving and the reality of suffering is affirmed by Philippians 4:6–7, another passage that calls us to give thanks in all circumstances:

> Do not be anxious about anything, but in everything, by prayer and petition, with thanksgiving, present your requests to God. And the peace of God, which transcends all understanding, will guard your hearts and your minds in Christ Jesus.

As is the case in Ephesians and Colossians, Paul here is also writing from prison. His call to thanksgiving should not be understood as a naïve dismissal of the power of evil. In spite of the presence of evil, believers are called again to focus on God. Scholars[64] have pointed to Paul's use of the gospel traditions as contained in Matthew 6:25–34 (par. Luke 12:22–32). In Matthew 6, Jesus said: 'Do not worry about your life, what you will eat or drink; or about your body, what you will wear' (v. 25). Jesus provided two reasons for this call. First, the people of God do not have to be concerned with their future because God is ultimately the one who is taking care of us (vv. 26–31). On a more fundamental level, Jesus provides yet another reason: 'seek first his kingdom and his righteousness, and all these things will be given to you as well' (v. 33). We should not worry about our well-being because our attention should be focused on God.

If we can trust that Paul is a faithful interpreter of the words of Jesus, Matthew 6:25–34 has to be considered in our interpretation of Philippians 4:6–7. On the surface, it may seem surprising to mention thanksgiving in his discussion of ways to avoid being anxious. When

---

[63] This is quite the opposite of the claim that thanksgiving reflects a passive stance toward injustice and evil. Cf. Vacek (2000: 111) who argues: 'Trying to give thanks for everything would blind us to genuine evils such as disease and disasters, sin and suffering.'

[64] E.g., O'Brien 1991a: 22; Fee 1995: 408–409.

thanksgiving is understood as God-centredness, however, its appearance in this context is no longer out of place. As in Matthew 6, two reasons are implied when thanksgiving is mentioned. Thanksgiving provides the proper theological grounding for 'prayer and petition' as it looks back to the mighty acts of God and therefore provides the confidence that indeed he is in control and will continue to be the faithful creator and Lord.[65] More importantly, to give thanks is to 'seek first his kingdom and his righteousness'. Understood in this way, the following sentence can now be appreciated: the powerful peace of God is able to keep our eyes on Jesus Christ (Phil. 4:7). Instead of giving his audience the comfort that all their desires will be answered, Paul focuses on Jesus, the centre of all worship. Thanksgiving is not simply focused on the confidence of God's provision. Thanksgiving points one towards God himself, and once again Paul reminds us that our eyes should be fixed on Jesus himself.

This is not to say that petition is not an important element in Pauline thought. While thanksgiving points to the sovereignty and power of God the creator, petition builds on this confession through intercession for God's creation. As Philippians 4:6–7 makes clear, thanksgiving is to provide the perspective through which petitions can be offered. Our concerns should be determined by our confession. Instead of reflecting our own desires, petitions should centre on God and his kingdom as we set our hearts and our minds on Jesus Christ. This lesson is demonstrated by the model Paul has provided for us as he intercedes for the churches in the introductory thanksgivings. In Colossians 1:3–14, for example, petition follows thanksgiving as Paul asks God for more evidence of the grace that he has seen in the Colossian believers.[66] This connection is made clear by the phrase 'For this reason' (Col. 1:9) as Paul builds upon his remembrance of God's grace. The fact that the gospel produces fruit (1:6) leads Paul to ask for God's continued empowerment when believers are called to participate in the ministry of 'bearing fruit' (1:10).

Pauline thanksgiving by its very own nature leads to petition. In Paul, therefore, thanksgiving does not reflect a sense of complacency or passive quietism that is controlled by the memory of the past. Pauline thanksgiving points to an active and living God who will continue to work among his people. With the recognition of the

---

[65] Contrary to popular belief, here thanksgiving is not just one element in Christian prayer. Thanksgiving is the reason why prayer is possible.

[66] See the discussion in O'Brien 1977: 82–100; and Carson 1992: 100.

sovereignty of God, we can also present all our daily needs to God since he is the Lord of all. The call to offer thanksgiving in all circumstances is therefore a call to submit all under the Lordship of Christ.

Redefinition of the structure of authority

The Pauline call to thanksgiving as a way of life is frequently understood as an abstract and vague exhortation. In at least one place, however, the call to thanksgiving appears in the context of specific ethical exhortation. In Colossians 3:18 – 4:1, one finds the presentation of the 'household rules'[67] as the relationships between wives and husbands, children and parents,[68] and slaves and masters are discussed. It is surprising, however, that immediately before and after this section one finds the Pauline call to thanksgiving:

> Let the peace of Christ rule in your hearts, since as members of one body you were called to peace. And be thankful. Let the word of Christ dwell in you richly as you teach and admonish one another with all wisdom, and as you sing psalms, hymns and spiritual songs with gratitude in your hearts to God. And whatever you do, whether in word or deed, do it all in the name of the Lord Jesus, giving thanks to God the Father through him. (Col. 3:15–17)

> Devote yourselves to prayer, being watchful and thankful. (Col. 4:2)

Reading the Colossian household rules in its context, two questions immediately come to mind. First, in a letter that affirms the supreme authority of Christ, one who is depicted as 'before all things' (Col. 1:17) and 'the head of the body, the church' (1:18), one wonders why Paul includes a treatment of human relationships that seems to affirm the authority of certain persons in their positions of power. The second question is concerned with the immediate context. The function of the calls to thanksgiving that envelop the Colossian house-

---

[67] In this chapter, the term 'household rules/codes' is used to refer to the various presentations of the relationship between members of the household. The existence of a universal type, however, is not assumed.

[68] We are following Barth and Blanke (1994: 443) in taking the plural 'fathers' as referring to both parents (cf. Heb. 11:23).

hold rules demands further examination. When the two questions are considered together, one is forced to deal with the relationship between authority and the Pauline understanding of thanksgiving.

Before getting to the heart of the matter, the form of the household rules should be briefly noted. Examples of household rules can be found in the Pauline epistles (Eph. 5:22 – 6:9; Col. 3:18 – 4:1; 1 Tim. 5:1 – 6:2; Titus 2:2–10) and elsewhere in the New Testament (1 Pet. 2:18 – 3:7). The Pauline discussion of church order is also understood to be based on such household rules (e.g., 1 Tim. 2:8 – 3:13). These household rules are also being identified as forming the structure of a number of passages although the explicit forms did not appear,[69] and they survive in the early Christian literature (e.g., *Didache* 4.9–11; *Barnabas* 19.5–7; *1 Clements* 21.6–9).

Various attempts have been made to identify the background of these household codes.[70] Martin Dibelius (1953: 46–50), for example, points to Hellenistic Stoic philosophy,[71] but the differences in content and setting call for significant qualifications.[72] Others point to Hellenistic Jewish sources (e.g., Lohse 1971: 154–157)[73] while noting modifications made by Paul and other early Christian writers.[74] For

---

[69] Examples include Matt. 19 – 20 (Carter 1994) and 1 John 2:12–13 (see Rengstorf 1953: 133–134).

[70] Still useful is the survey in Crouch 1972. For a more recent treatment, see Balch 1988: 25–50.

[71] Many have pointed to phrases such as 'it is fitting' and 'it pleases' that appear frequently in Stoic material. The basis for these Hellenistic discussions can be found in Aristotle where the management of the household is considered as the foundation of the constitution of the polis. It is in Aristotle that one finds the three sets of relationship discussed:

> The parts of household management will correspond to the parts of which the household itself is constituted. A complete household consists of slaves and freemen. But every subject of inquiry should first be examined in its simplest elements; and the primary and simplest elements of the household are the connexion of master and slave, that of the husband and wife, and that of parents and children. We must accordingly consider each of these connexions, examining the nature of each and the qualities it ought to possess. (*Politics* 1.1253b [Barker 1958: 8]. Cf. Plato, *Republic* 4.433–434.)

[72] It should also be recognized that Stoic literature reflects the wider Hellenistic culture and therefore elements in household rules may not be unique to the Stoic school.

[73] See, for example, Philo, *De decalogo* 165–167. Crouch (1972) further argues that Greek teachings were transformed in synagogue teachings. Jewish forms of the household codes provided the added element of reciprocity in the discussion of the relationship between various groups.

[74] The influence of the Old Testament has also been noted. See, for example, Grant 1940: 1–17 and Gnilka 1980: 185–186, that point to the connection between the Ten Commandments and the Christian household rules.

those who emphasize the distinct Christian elements, household rules were considered as a Christian invention (e.g., Schröder 1959). The failure to reach a consensus points to the fact that there is no universal household code from which different authors drew. Nevertheless, the use of traditional material cannot be denied in light of similarities between the various codes. The use of household rules also reminds us of the importance of the 'household' in the development of early Christianity.[75]

The debate concerning the source of the Colossian household rules should yield to a study of this passage within its literary context. As mentioned above, the Lordship of Christ is firmly established in exalted discourse concerning the supremacy of Christ in Colossians 1:15–20. The significance of the supremacy and sufficiency of Christ can be seen throughout this epistle. In 2:3, Paul states that in Christ 'are hidden all the treasures of wisdom and knowledge'. This is the main argument against the Colossian heresy as it challenges the sufficiency of the gospel of Christ. This is explicitly noted in 2:8 as the false teaching 'depends on human tradition and the basic principles of this world rather than on Christ'. Repeating the essence of 1:15–20, Paul states that 'in Christ all the fulness of the Deity lives in bodily form' (2:9). Moving to the second half of the epistle, the same point is being emphasized. In 3:1, Christ is described as 'seated at the right hand of God'. This leads to the ethical exhortation that calls us to do all in the name of our 'Lord' (3:17). Throughout this epistle, then, the supreme status and absolute authority of Christ is maintained.

In light of the affirmation of Christ's authority, the presence of the household rules is indeed surprising since the basis of many of such Hellenistic codes is the idea of submission to human authorities.[76] Because of the uncertainty of the precise 'model' that Paul is using in the construction of his own version of the household rules, a detailed

---

[75] See, for example, the discussion in Malherbe 1983: 60–91.

[76] See, for example, the representative statement in Aristotle's *Politics* 1.1254a (Barker 1958: 12) on the relationship between masters and slaves within the household: 'Ruling and being ruled [which is the relation of master and slave] not only belongs to the category of things necessary, but also to that of things expedient; and there are species in which a distinction is already marked, immediately at birth, between those of its members who are intended for being ruled and those who are intended to rule.' For a further discussion on the issue of authority and subordination in Greco-Roman household codes, see Balch 1981: 23–80. Balch's understanding of early Christian household codes as primarily functioning as defence against charges of social insubordination requires significant qualification, however.

redactional study would not be possible. Nevertheless, distinctive emphasis in the Colossian code can still be felt.

Frequently noted are the distinctively 'Christian' phrases that can be found in this code. These phrases do not simply 'Christianize' the code, however. They point to the redefinition of the power structure in light of the previous discussion in Colossians 1 – 2. In this household code, the Lordship of Christ is emphatically asserted through these 'insertions'. The submission of the wives is qualified by the phrase 'as is fitting in the Lord' (3:18). The duty of the children has its grounding in that which 'pleases the Lord' (3:20). Slaves serve their human master with 'reverence for the Lord' (3:22) as they serve 'as working for the Lord' (3:23). They will be rewarded by the 'Lord' (3:24) since 'it is the Lord Christ' that they are serving (3:24). Likewise, those who are masters need to be reminded that they 'also have a Lord in heaven' (4:1).[77] No matter how one comes down on the source-critical issue, the emphasis on the Lordship of Christ cannot be denied.

While household codes typically affirm the 'lordship' of those who are in positions of power, the Colossian code strikingly departs from them by asserting the unique Lordship of Christ. This emphasis on the Lordship of Christ is after all a continuation of the arguments presented in the preceding chapters of Colossians. The focus on the Lordship of Christ is reflected from a simple word count. In Colossians 1:1 – 3:17, the word 'Lord' (*kyrios*) appears six times. In the household code that occupies only nine verses, however, one finds the same word appearing eight times. What this illustrates is that Paul's focus on the supreme authority of Christ did not stop when he discusses the life of the household. More importantly, the commonly accepted way of life is being challenged as the power of those who lord over their subjects is being relativized when the confession of the universal Lordship of Christ is made. Instead of affirming the accepted values of the world, this code reaches to the root of the structure of society in an attempt to question the power and authority of those who claim to be in control.

In 'rewriting' the household code, Paul is able to show the practical outworking of the Lordship claim of Christ. Not only is the code

---

[77] In this verse, the NIV has 'master' to translate the word (*kyrios*) that was otherwise translated as 'Lord'. While in context 'master' is an appropriate rendering, the rhetorical force of the repeated mentioning of the 'Lord' in this section is lost through this translation.

saturated with references to the Lordship of Christ, the power relationships are also qualified in various ways. First of all, wives and
children are given moral voice as they are able to do that which is
fitting in and pleasing to the Lord (Col. 3:18, 20). As people without
voices in the ancient world, the recognition that they should also be
considered as moral agents is to be heard.[78] The created order is
maintained, but women and children are no longer considered as
inferior beings who require the mediation of their 'powerful' counter-
part in their approach to God.[79] In the discussion of the role of the
slaves, the plausibility of 'inheritance' is striking when slaves in the
ancient world were characterized by their being possessed by their
masters. Again, their vertical relationship with God relativizes the
power of their human masters.

On the other side of the three sets of relationships, the duty of the
dominant partners is emphasized. Husbands were called to love their
wives, parents to not discourage their children, and masters to be just
and fair.[80] The conclusion of this code applies to all three sets of relationships: 'because you know that you also have a Master [lit: 'Lord']
in heaven'.

The repeated appearances of the term 'Lord', the address to
women, children and slaves as moral agents, and the mentioning of
the duties of the dominant members all point to the Pauline understanding of the supreme authority of Christ that can be played out
in everyday living. The first question that we raised at the beginning
of this section can now be answered: the presence of the household
rules in this epistle that focuses on God does not point to inconsis-
tency in the theology of Paul.[81] Through the redefinition of the struc-

[78] Most household codes do not address women and children directly, although
elsewhere ethical exhortations were directed to these groups (cf. Balch 1981: 97). For
the social and political implications of the inclusion of women, children and slaves, see
also Laub 1986: 249–271.

[79] It should be noted that our argument for the redefinition of the power structure
in the Colossian household code does not resolve the issue of the women's role in
church and family. In this passage, at least, Paul does not move away from his other
statements concerning the creation order. On the other hand, the ultimate authority of
Christ is repeatedly noted and this emphasis forces one to question whether the term
'authority' is appropriate in the discussion of the relative roles of men and women.

[80] The term 'fair' (*isotēs*) in 4:1 can be translated as 'equal'. This would be considered a radical challenge to the system of slavery. Nevertheless, in light of its parallel
with the word 'right' (*dikaiosynē*), it seems best to understand the term as referring to
'equity' instead. In light of Eph. 6:9, Stählin (1965: 355) is probably correct in his explication of the verse: 'Both masters and slaves are to be guided by the same principles.'

[81] For a survey of other attempts at reconciling the Pauline gospel with the existence
of the household rules, see the survey in Motyer 1989: 33–48. Motyer's own conclu-

ture of power, Paul shows how the Lordship claim of Christ affects our understanding of human relationships.

This leads us to address the second question concerning the immediate context of the Colossian household code. The connections between Colossians 3:15–17 and the household code that follows is made through a number of parallel themes. First, the reference to 'one body' (3:15) elsewhere in Paul points to the unity among the different groups of believers within the church.[82] The household code that follows deals with relationships between diverse groups that were divided according to the commonly accepted set of criteria. The Pauline call to be of 'one body' naturally leads to a concrete discussion of the diversity within society and also the church. The Colossian household code should therefore be read in light of Colossians 3:15.

A more explicit connection can be found in Colossians 3:17: 'And whatever you do, whether in word or deed, do it all in the name of the Lord Jesus.' Allusions to this verse appear only a few verses later in 3:23 when Paul addresses the slaves: 'Whatever you do, work at it with all your heart, as working for the Lord, not for men.' The reappearance of the general exhortation of 3:17 in the household code shows that the discussion of household relationships is to be considered a concrete manifestation of the principles stated just before the presentation of the code.[83]

Now that we have established the connection between Colossians 3:15–17 and the household code, the significance of the thanksgiving

---

sion points to the distinction between the 'already' and the 'not yet' in Pauline theology in explaining the implementation of an ethic that is controlled by the limitations of the 'not yet'. In the context of Colossians, however, to see the household code as a compromise fails to appreciate the focus on the power of the gospel that is emphasized throughout the epistle. The subversive element in the household code should not be ignored when the gospel message challenges the assumptions and practices of the world.

[82] See, for example, Rom. 12:4–5; 1 Cor. 10:17; 12:12–31; Eph. 2:15–16. The factor that distinguishes between members of the one body may differ, but the emphasis is always on the unity of the church despite obvious diversity. In the immediate context of Col. 3:15, the concern for unity is also explicitly noted: 'And over all these virtues put on love, which binds them all together in perfect unity' (3:14; cf. v. 11).

[83] Nash (1989: 46) has further argued that the 'slaves' mentioned in the Colossian household code are to serve as a model for all Christians. He points to the 'repetition of the inheritance theme from 1:12' as well as the 'general nature of the statement in 3:24' ('It is the Lord Christ you are serving') and concludes: 'The specific instruction to the slaves would have functioned in an exemplary way similar to that of the Haustafel as a whole.' Whether Nash is correct in focusing solely on the exhortations to the slaves or not, his analysis again highlights the issue of Lordship as the focus of the Colossian household code. All believers are called to submit as slaves to the Lordship of Christ.

theme in 3:15–17 should be reiterated. In 3:15, while exhorting believers to be 'of one body', the theme of thanksgiving is again noted: 'And be thankful.' Instead of simply 'an afterthought' (Dunn 1996: 235), this phrase introduces one of the main focuses of this passage. In 3:16, the act of praising God again is to be done 'with gratitude in your hearts to God'. Finally, in 3:17, every act is to be carried out while 'giving thanks to God the Father through him'. In these three verses that describe peace, acts of praise and the Christian life in general, thanksgiving is behind them. The peace of God points to the salvation that was accomplished on the cross through which reconciliation is made possible.[84] Acts of praise are to be performed in response to the salvation proclaimed through the 'word of Christ' (3:16).[85] The Christian life is likewise to be a response to the death and resurrection of Christ.[86] In all three, God's climactic act in history is remembered; and in all three, thanksgiving is the appropriate response. This response is sustained through the various acts that characterize the believers. In yet another form, therefore, the Pauline call to give thanks 'in all circumstances' finds its expression.

The call to thanksgiving as a response is the call to live in light of the sovereignty of God and his Son. In acts of thanksgiving, the power and authority of God and his Son are recognized. In Colossians 3:15–17, it is precisely the Lordship claim of Christ that is emphasized. The all-inclusive command in 3:17 points to Jesus as 'Lord'. This connection between thanksgiving and the Lordship of

---

[84] In the Old Testament, the concept of peace frequently points to the end of the period of judgment when God acts again on behalf of his people. See, for example, Is. 52:7 on the proclamation of the good news:

> How beautiful on the mountains
> are the feet of those who bring good news,
> who proclaim peace,
> who bring good tidings,
> who proclaim salvation,
> who say to Zion,
> 'Your God reigns!'

In Colossians, the use of the term 'peace' in 1:20 describes the fulfilment of such a vision in Christ: 'and through him to reconcile to himself all things, whether things on earth or things in heaven, by making peace through his blood, shed on the cross'.

[85] In light of Col. 1:5–6 where 'the word of truth' is identified as 'the gospel that has come to you', the 'word of Christ' in 3:16 should not be understood as referring to individual sayings of Jesus but to the gospel message as a whole.

[86] In Colossians, the death and resurrection of Christ provide the foundation for the lives of the believers (cf. Col. 2:20 – 3:9, 12–14). To 'do it all in the name of the Lord Jesus' therefore points to the outworking of the centre of the gospel message.

Christ reminds one of the earlier passage in Colossians 2:6–7: 'So then, just as you received Christ Jesus as Lord, continue to live in him, rooted and built up in him, strengthened in the faith as you were taught, and overflowing with thankfulness.' Through these two passages, the Pauline argument continues as the Lordship of Christ is to intrude into every aspect of the life of the people of God.

The connection between the Pauline call to thanksgiving in Colossians 3:15–17 and the household code now becomes clear. In thanksgiving, we affirm the Lordship of Christ. In the household code, this affirmation is expressed in more specific terms with the numerous references to 'the Lord'. While the household code is preceded by a call to thanksgiving, it also ended with a similar call (4:2).[87] The ethical imperative embedded in the call to thanksgiving is clear and through this call Paul articulates the obligation that the Christocentric gospel carries.[88]

This reading of Colossians 3 – 4 is confirmed by passages in an epistle that expresses many of the similar themes found in Colossians. As in Colossians, the household code in Ephesians is also preceded by a call to thanksgiving: 'Sing and make music in your heart to the Lord, always giving thanks to God the Father for everything, in the name of our Lord Jesus Christ' (Eph. 5:19–20). In Colossians 3:17, the phrase 'in the name of the Lord' modifies all acts, 'whether in word or deed'. In Ephesians 5:20, however, the phrase is used to modify 'giving thanks'.[89] Taken together, these two

---

[87] This verse will be discussed in greater detail in the next chapter. The connection between Col. 3:15–17 and 4:2 has been noted by some (e.g., Lähnemann 1971: 56) but the function of these two passages in framing the discussion of household relationship is often missed.

[88] Our discussion has shown how the Colossian household code fits in the argument of the epistle. Standhartinger's (2000: 129–130) statement that this code is 'barely contextualized in the letter' and that one can detect 'the lack of continuity between the household code and its context within the epistle' should therefore be qualified. Lincoln's (1999: 93–112) earlier treatment in the same journal provides a better reading as he points to the significance of the calls to thanksgiving in Col. 3:15–17 and 4:1. His use of Wisdom traditions to explain the connection between thanksgiving and the domestic duties of the Christian household is, however, unnecessary in light of Paul's use of the wider covenantal traditions elsewhere in connection with the call to live a life of thanksgiving.

[89] This close comparison of the two epistles is based on the assumption that the two epistles share a special relationship. As noted above, the issue of the authorship of these two epistles should not be excluded in the discussion of this literary relationship. For a helpful discussion from the perspective of those who affirm Pauline authorship for both, see the recent treatment in O'Brien 1999: 8–21.

verses point to the close relationship between behaviour and thanksgiving. When believers give thanks to the Lord, all that they do will be done 'in the name of the Lord'.

In our comparison of the words that precede the household codes in Colossians and Ephesians, an apparent difference in wordings can be located in the verse that comes between the call to thanksgiving in Ephesians 5:19–20 and the household code in 5:22 – 6:9. In Ephesians 5:21, that which is implicit in the Colossian call to thanksgiving is now explicitly stated: 'Submit to one another out of reverence for Christ'. This emphasis on submission to the Lordship of Christ is central to our understanding of the Pauline call to thanksgiving; this verse clarifies both the call to thanksgiving that precedes and the discussion of household relationships that follows.

In short, one can argue that if the Lordship of Christ is at the centre of the Pauline gospel, both the existence of the specific form of the Colossian household code and the context within which it is situated can be understood. Moreover, it is precisely Paul's emphasis on the supremacy and sufficiency of Christ that prompted him to focus on the life of thanksgiving.[90]

Covenantal relationship

To conclude our discussion on the life of thanksgiving with the household code may give a false impression that Pauline thanksgiving is to be understood primarily in the sense of 'duty'. In Paul, moral imperatives are grounded on the active and ongoing relationship with God.[91] It has long been noted that expressions of gratitude should not simply be understood as a repayment of favours. Even the appropriate temporal distance between the reception of the gift and the return of the favours has been discussed. If the favour is not acknowledged after a period of time, the relationship between the giver and the recipient will be impaired. If, on the other hand, the favour is immediately 'repaid', such an act may indicate a lack of interest in the

---

[90] It is by no accident, therefore, that the Pauline call to thanksgiving is most extensively discussed in an epistle that is also characterized by its emphasis on the supremacy of Christ.

[91] M. Martin (1996: 165) has rightly noted that the focus on obligation in discussions of gratitude often results in a neglect of gratitude among equals. In our discussion of thanksgiving within the covenantal framework, the 'relationship' between the Creator and the created beings should also be noted. While this relationship is not one between 'equals', one needs to move beyond duty language when one comes to an examination of this relationship.

further development of the relationship.[92] For our discussion, the point is simply that genuine gratitude fosters a relationship that will be strengthened both by the memory of the gift and the response offered.

In the Pauline call to thanksgiving, we are not asked simply to be courteous in response to a gift. We are called to build up a relationship with our God to whom we owe all that we have. This is well illustrated in a verse within the introductory thanksgiving of 1 Corinthians: 'God, who has called you into fellowship with his Son Jesus Christ our Lord, is faithful' (1:9). In remembering the gracious act of God, we can be assured that God is a faithful God; and faithfulness points to God's unfailing loving relationship with his covenant people. In giving his Son to us, a word of 'thanks' is not the only goal of this divine act. We are called to have 'fellowship' with his Son, who is also our 'Lord'. When fellowship is understood as 'participation', we are called to enter into the life of Christ. A similar point is made in Colossians 2:7, where one finds the phrase 'overflowing with thankfulness' being used to modify the exhortation of verse 6: 'continue to live in him'. The goal of a life of thanksgiving is then to bridge the separation between the giver and the recipients who are believers in Christ.

As a relational term, gratitude can be compared to the virtue of love. Mike Martin (1996), for example, suggests that gratitude 'is an enabling virtue, one that sustains love between partners who cherish their shared history and identity'.[93] In a loving relationship, as in a life of thanksgiving, the giver is valued beyond the gifts that are presented. The Pauline statement that 'Christ's love compels us' (2 Cor. 5:14) points to a relationship built on the memory of God's act through his Son, and the verse that follows serves well as a definition of the life of thanksgiving: 'And he died for all, that those who live should no longer live for themselves but for him who died for them and was raised again' (2 Cor. 5:15). Moreover, when a life of thanksgiving is understood as a way to respond to the immeasurable grace of God, the Pauline reference to 'the continuing debt to love one

---

[92] Here, McConnell's (1993: 52) comment is worth noting: 'The promptness of a response . . . may indicate that the recipient does not want the sort of relationship with the benefactor that gratitude engenders and instead prefers a "tit-for-tat" contractual relationship that can be concluded with a payoff.'

[93] Milton (1983: 11) goes even a step further in noting the connections between the two: 'Love, like gratitude, is not a separate value but is an attitude toward reality. In this respect – and it is an important one – love and gratitude are the same thing.'

another' (Rom. 13:8) naturally reminds one of the need to respond to God's love by loving those around us.[94]

This leads us to move beyond the focus on the vertical relationship between the divine giver and the human recipients to the horizontal relationship among the recipients as they reflect on the gift of grace. In Paul, the basis of community is the grace of God, while gratitude also acquires a significance in the upbuilding of the people of God. In Colossians 3:12, for example, thanks are offered because of the participation of the Colossians in the wider people of God. More explicitly, in Philemon, Paul gives thanks for Philemon's experience of God's grace that is reflected in his love for the people of God: 'I always thank my God as I remember you in my prayers, because I hear about your faith in the Lord Jesus and your love for all the saints' (v. 4). This thanksgiving that calls to mind the significance of God as the basis of a new set of relationships allows Paul to continue arguing for a new understanding of Philemon's relationship with his slave. In verse 16, Philemon is asked to treat Onesimus 'no longer as a slave, but better than a slave, as a dear brother'.[95] This horizontal relationship is, therefore, not simply one limited to the human sphere. Through the transformation that accompanies the experience of God's grace, believers, as the corporate people of God, can now build up their relationship with God in a new way.[96]

---

[94] To love others can be a way to express our gratitude to God. Vacek (2000: 105–116) has rightly pointed to the importance of the grateful use of gifts: 'Gratitude includes not only reception and response but also grateful use of the gift . . . Were we to misuse or abuse the gift, we would be showing disregard or even contempt for the donor, not gratitude.' The Pauline call to 'love one another' should therefore be understood as a grateful response to the love that God has shown through the giving of his Son.

[95] In discussing the new relationship that is to be developed between Philemon and Onesimus, the public nature of this epistle should also be noted. The emphasis on community is best reflected by Paul's address at the beginning of the epistle: 'To Philemon our dear friend and fellow-worker, to Apphia our sister, to Archippus our fellow-solider and to the church that meets in your home' (vv. 1–2). First, more than one person is addressed. Second, the 'church' is explicitly mentioned as the recipient of this letter. Furthermore, appellations such as 'fellow-worker' and 'fellow-soldier' point to their roles in the church. The relationship between Philemon and Onesimus, therefore, has implications for the entire community. For a further discussion, see S. Winter 1987: 1.

[96] As the people of God, believers are called to respond not simply as individuals but also as a community. This aspect that focuses on the people of God as a community of thanksgiving also finds its roots in the covenantal traditions of Israel. When the covenant is established between God and his people, it is not to an individual but to the entire community that the covenant finds its meaning. In the covenant renewal of Joshua 24, for example, the entire people gathered together and proclaimed their loyalty to their God. In acts of remembering, the tribes of Israel were united as they face the future knowing that God is on their side.

Chapter Five

Thanksgiving and the future

A strict separation between the past, present and future cannot be found in the Pauline emphasis on thanksgiving. This is well illustrated by the numerous passages that cannot be placed neatly within just one category. To examine the theme of thanksgiving using these temporal markers does, however, highlight the historical distance between the ancient texts and the modern readers. This is particularly true as we come to this chapter. In modern usage, thanksgiving is most often taken as a way to understand the past. The way a deep sense of thanksgiving affects the behaviour of an individual is also understandable, although the Pauline understanding of thanksgiving encompasses much more than what the English word 'gratitude' may evoke. It is unusual, however, to expect thanksgiving to be offered in reference to an act that lies in the distant future.

In colloquial usage, one does occasionally hear a 'thank-you' uttered when an act is expected to be fulfilled in the near future. In biblical traditions, acts of thanksgiving that anticipate the future acts of God reflect the acceptance of a set of beliefs. They point to an understanding of who God is and his relationship with his people. Moreover, they are frequently offered even when the immediate circumstances do not necessarily encourage the belief that the arrival of God's 'gift' or 'grace' is imminent. To understand this aspect of the Pauline call to thanksgiving for acts that are yet to be accomplished, we need to return to the Old Testament text.

Faithful and powerful God

In chapter two above, we have shown that the future is an essential component in biblical covenantal traditions. What needs to be emphasized is the fact that at the heart of the Old Testament covenant is the set of promises that point beyond the present condition. Some have even gone as far as to affirm that it is this aspect that shapes Old Testament covenantal traditions, if not the entire Old

Testament.[1] What is not debatable is the importance of the temporal framework within which the relationship between God and Israel is articulated, and it is the future that provides meaning and goal to this relationship. Behind the progression of the different covenants is the affirmation of the sovereignty of God, the Lord of history. It is also this expectation of the complete manifestation of the sovereignty of God that becomes the most visible object of biblical hope.[2]

In this vision of the future, one finds the affirmation of the God of Israel as the faithful and powerful God. His faithfulness sustains the covenantal history, and his power enables him to fulfil his own promises. God's faithfulness is manifested in his continuing presence with his people, a presence that endures beyond our present existence.[3] God's power is well established from the time of creation when he revealed himself to be the supreme Lord who is in control.[4]

It is in this context that we should situate Old Testament eschatological songs of praise and thanksgiving. In Isaiah 52:9–10, for example, the people of God were called to celebrate God's eschatological deliverance:

> Burst into songs of joy together,
> you ruins of Jerusalem,
> for the LORD has comforted his people,
> he has redeemed Jerusalem.

[1] See, for example, the extensive treatment of Kaiser (1978: 69), who asserts, against the claims of the majority of critical scholars, the possibility of locating a unifying theme that ties together the Old Testament blocks of material: 'The OT does possess its own canonical inner unity which binds together the various emphases and longitudinal themes. This is not a hidden inner unity. It lies open and ready for all: The Promise of God.'

[2] The vision in Is. 40:10 expresses this point well: 'See, the Sovereign LORD comes with power, and his arm rules for him.' Similarly, in Zech. 14:9, one reads: 'The LORD will be king over the whole earth. On that day there will be one LORD, and his name the only name.'

[3] Although the temporal aspect is not apparent, the pervasive presence of the faithful God is described already in Psalm 139:

> If I go up to the heavens, you are there;
> if I make my bed in the depths, you are there.
> If I rise on the wings of the dawn,
> if I settle on the far side of the sea,
> even there your hand will guide me,
> your right hand will hold me fast.

(vv. 8–10)

[4] For a discussion on creation as the manifestation of power, see ch. 3 above.

This passage is important for two reasons. First, the future salvation of God is described as if it had already happened. Second, the confidence of God's action is expressed in songs and not simply in creedal statements. With songs, biblical authors call the people of God to share in this confidence in their God.

The grounds for this confidence in God's deliverance are expressed in other songs of thanksgiving. In Jeremiah 33:11, in the context of the promise of restoration, 'those who bring thank-offerings to the house of the LORD' sing to their Lord:

> 'Give thanks to the LORD Almighty,
>   for the LORD is good;
>   his love endures for ever.'

The word translated as 'love' (*hesed*) is one that is typically used in describing the covenantal faithfulness of God.[5] The temporal marker, 'for ever', also points in the same direction in anticipation of the time when God 'will restore the fortunes of the land as they were before' (v. 11).[6]

Another kind of eschatological song that celebrates God's faithfulness can be found in the Old Testament where the author describes how thanksgiving will be offered in the future when God's salvation is realized. In Isaiah 25:9, at the time when God wipes away the tears of his people (v. 8), they will say:

> Surely this is our God;
>   we trusted in him, and he saved us.

---

[5] See the discussion in Sakenfeld 1985.

[6] This song belongs to the worship life of the community. In Psalm 118, one finds a similar call that brackets this eschatological song:

> Give thanks to the LORD, for he is good;
>   his love endures for ever.
>
> (vv. 1, 29)

The object of worship is the one who can be trusted:

> It is better to take refuge in the LORD
>   than to trust in man.
> It is better to take refuge in the LORD
>   than to trust in princes.
>
> (v. 8)

Significantly, it is this song that appears in all four accounts of Jesus' entry into Jerusalem (Matt. 21:9; Mark 11:9–10; Luke 19:38; John 12:13) to accomplish the final act of deliverance fulfilling the covenantal hope of Israel.

This is the LORD, we trusted in him,
  let us rejoice and be glad in his salvation.

The confidence is here expressed through the description of the thanksgiving song that will be offered to Israel's deliverer.[7] The setting of this song is the eschatological banquet that will take place when God fulfils his covenantal promises to Israel. God is honoured for his faithfulness:

[F]or in perfect faithfulness
  you have done marvellous things,
    things planned long ago.

(Is. 25:1)

The model used to describe the future is drawn from the feast that celebrates God's covenantal relationship with his people (cf. Exod. 24).[8]
  Thanksgiving prayer offered for future acts is not limited to acts of the distant future. The prayer of Jonah betrays the same understanding when thanksgiving is offered to God in anticipation of God's imminent deliverance:

Those who cling to worthless idols
  forfeit the grace that could be theirs.
But I, with a song of thanksgiving,
  will sacrifice to you.
What I have vowed I will make good.
  Salvation comes from the LORD.

(Jonah 2:8–9)

What is unusual is the specific context of this song of thanksgiving.[9] By mentioning the 'grace' that was forsaken by those who did not rely

---

[7] This way of expressing confidence in God can be found throughout the first part of Isaiah (e.g., Is. 12:1, 4; 26:1; 27:2). Nitzan (1994: 175) further points to the importance of these prophetic statements in the formulation of the eschatological poetry in the Qumran scrolls.

[8] Gese (1981: 133) points to the fact that this feast is celebrated with all the nations at the end times and 'this transforms the feast into the thank offering of the entire spiritual community of God'. Not only is the covenantal feast important in the shaping of the expressions of the future, the paradigmatic Song of Moses in Exod. 15 also plays a significant role in the formulation of eschatological victory songs as Nitzan (1994: 203) has suggested. Moreover, the Song of Moses itself also points to the future when God will accomplish what he began during the sea-crossing event (cf. Exod. 15:13–18).

[9] Stuart (1987: 471) calls this 'an overly specific psalm, useless except to Jonah!'

on God, Jonah points to God's gracious act as the foundation of his conviction that salvation is imminent. Although not an eschatological song, this song belongs to those that affirm that God will act in the future, basing that affirmation on an appropriate understanding of God's faithfulness.

Jonah's song/prayer points to the second reason for giving thanks to God: confidence in the power of God. Needless to say, this cannot be separated from the affirmation of the faithfulness of God since God's faithfulness is often shown through the manifestation of his power. Jonah's prayer does, however, point to another type of thanksgiving prayer/song in which God is called to exercise his power by delivering his people (or an individual) from immediate danger. It is this trust in the power of the faithful God that binds the eschatological songs with other songs that refer to the future but do not emphasize the eschatological moment to which the covenantal promises point.

The numerous lament psalms in the Old Testament should first be noted.[10] Frequently appearing in these psalms is a cry for help that is immediately followed by a note of thanksgiving.[11] In Psalm 28, for example, the psalmist begins with this plea:

> To you I call, O LORD my Rock;
>   do not turn a deaf ear to me.
> For if you remain silent,
>   I will be like those who have gone down to the pit.
> Hear my cry for mercy
>   as I call to you for help,
> as I lift up my hands
>   towards your Most Holy Place.
>
> (vv. 1–2)

[10] The generic identification of some of these psalms is subject to dispute (e.g., Pss. 61, 77, 94). Some have considered a number of them as 'thanksgiving psalms' and therefore suggest that the petition embedded within these psalms has already been fulfilled. Nevertheless, the change of tone remains a problem in those psalms that clearly reflect wishes that are yet to be fulfilled. Furthermore, the frequency of the appearance of such thanksgiving sections in the midst of prayers of desperation cannot be ignored. For a further discussion of these psalms, see Westermann 1981: 79–81; and Miller 1994: 187–190.

[11] Frost (1958: 382–383) points to selected psalms (e.g., Ps. 86) and suggests that thanksgiving and praise in some of the lament psalms reflect the function of thanksgiving as making strong assertions. Frost is certainly correct in noting the use of thanksgiving in such a way. The wider theological foundation upon which the equation between assertion and thanksgiving can be made needs to be further explored.

In the second section of this psalm, the psalmist offers thanks for the manifestation of God's power as if it had already happened:

> Praise be to the LORD,
>> for he has heard my cry for mercy.
> The LORD is my strength and my shield;
>> my heart trusts in him, and I am helped.
> My heart leaps for joy
>> and I will give thanks to him in song.
> The LORD is the strength of his people,
>> a fortress of salvation for his anointed one.
>
> (vv. 6–8)

Neither the setting of the psalm nor the nature of the suffering that the psalmist is experiencing are clear. What is certain is the confidence of the psalmist that indeed God is both able and willing to answer the prayer uttered.[12]

In these lament psalms, thanksgiving is not just an afterthought reflecting the wish of the psalmist. Thanksgiving is the result of the experience of God's faithfulness and power, and the continued cry to the Lord reflects a willingness to continue to trust him. In Psalm 40, this point is illustrated by a different arrangement of the psalm. Instead of concluding the psalm with a note of confidence, this psalm begins with thanksgiving that points to the trust the psalmist has in God:

> I waited patiently for the LORD;
>> he turned to me and heard my cry.
> He lifted me out of the slimy pit,
>> out of the mud and mire;
> he set my feet on a rock
>> and gave me a firm place to stand.
> He put a new song in my mouth,
>> a hymn of praise to our God.
>
> (vv. 1–3)

---

[12] Some have suggested a liturgical setting in which the prayer uttered is responded to by a priest when assurance is offered. The individual can then give thanks to God for responding through the mediation of the priest. Whether this liturgical context provides the best way to interpret the text is subject to dispute. What is clear is that these prayers of help have been transformed into creedal statements that affirm the goodness of God. For a further discussion of the formal aspects of this psalm, see Craigie 1983: 236–237.

It is on this basis that the psalmist can begin recounting the 'troubles without number' that surround him (v. 12), and the psalm ends with a cry of help: 'O my God, do not delay' (v. 17).

Outside of the Psalms,[13] one also finds similar thanksgiving prayers elsewhere in the Old Testament. A striking example can be found in 2 Chronicles 20:21 in which the victory song was sung before the battle itself:

> After consulting the people, Jehoshaphat appointed men to sing to the LORD and to praise him for the splendour of his holiness as they went out at the head of the army, saying:
>
> > 'Give thanks to the LORD,
> > for his love endures for ever.'

As in the other thanksgiving songs that we have discussed, this victory song is based on the confidence that God will act on behalf of his people. What is unique, as Patrick Miller (1994: 183) has noted, is that this assurance comes directly from the mouth of the Lord: 'Do not be afraid or discouraged because of this vast army. For the battle is not yours, but God's' (20:15).

While the condition of an individual may be the focus of some of the psalms discussed above, the concern for the entire people of God is not missing. In Psalm 85, for example, remembering God's goodness leads directly to petition for God's continued grace toward his people:

> You showed favour to your land, O LORD;
> you restored the fortunes of Jacob.
> You forgave the iniquity of your people . . .
> Restore us again, O God our Saviour,
> and put away your displeasure toward us.
>
> (vv. 1–2, 4)

The psalm ends with the confident assertion that God will indeed act on behalf of his people, and this assertion is described as though it is already taking place (vv. 10–13).

---

[13] Confidence in God as expressed through verbal acts of thanksgiving is not limited to the lament psalms. Although the thanksgiving word-group is absent, the beloved Ps. 23 can also be understood in a similar way. In this psalm, God's provision in the future is stated as a present reality (v. 5) and God's covenantal faithfulness is again noted (v. 6).

This leads us back to the eschatological songs of thanksgiving that we have noted at the beginning of this section. When the distant future is referred to, the faithfulness of God is emphasized alongside the assertion of his sovereign power (cf. Ps. 98). As in the lament psalms, eschatological songs of thanksgiving point to the certainty that God will act as he did in the past.[14] It is within this context that certain Pauline statements should be examined. Before examining these statements, however, the distinct focus on the future in some of the Pauline introductory thanksgivings should first be considered. This will allow us to place other eschatological statements of thanksgiving in the wider context of Pauline theology.

Bridging the past and the future

In the words of André Ridouard and Jacques Guillet (1967: 526), 'Thanksgiving carries biblical history and prolongs it in eschatological hope.' In looking back at the gracious acts of the faithful God in history, thanksgiving points forward to God's continued involvement with his people. This aspect is well illustrated in the Pauline introductory thanksgiving paragraphs.

The existence of 'eschatological climaxes' in a number of the Pauline introductory thanksgivings is first noted by Paul Schubert (1939: 30–31) who highlights the literary functions of these eschatological statements. Some, such as Peter O'Brien (1975: 148 and 1977: 268), have suggested that this reflects the importance of the parousia in the mind of Paul. Others (e.g., Von der Osten-Sacken 1977: 176–199; Roberts 1986: 30) point to the importance of these references for the development of Paul's argument in the respective epistles. M. C. Dippenaar (1994: 147–188) further suggests that this reflects the way Paul extends the Hellenistic epistolary situation to accommodate the early Christian affirmation of the dawn of the eschatological era. Yet to be explored is the obvious connection between acts of thanksgiving and the expected fulfilment of all covenantal promises.

Without 'reading through' the introductory thanksgivings to search for hidden secondary concerns, the mere existence of the

---

[14] These eschatological songs of thanksgiving can also be found in Second Temple Jewish literature. See, in particular, the numerous victory songs contained in the Qumran War Scrolls (1QM 13.12–16; 18.6–14) and the discussion in Nitzan 1994: 206–207.

'eschatological climaxes' in Paul's thanksgiving reports/prayers needs to be highlighted. In 1 Corinthians 1,[15] Paul's thanksgiving begins with God's grace: 'I always thank God for you because of his grace given you in Christ Jesus' (v. 4). The reference to the eschaton appears in the section that follows where Paul mentions the anticipation of 'our Lord Jesus Christ to be revealed' (v. 7). This eschatological focus continues in verse 8: 'He will keep you strong to the end, so that you will be blameless on the day of our Lord Jesus Christ.' For Paul, acts of remembrance naturally lead to confidence in God's[16] future actions.[17]

As in the Old Testament, the faithfulness of God forms the basis of any confidence that the people of God may have. In 1 Corinthians 1, the faithfulness of God is explicitly noted immediately after the eschatological statement: 'God, who has called you into fellowship with his Son Jesus Christ our Lord, is faithful' (v. 9). In biblical traditions, the faithfulness of God is not understood as an abstract virtue but is manifested in God's dealings with his covenantal partner. In Deuteronomy 7:8–9, for example, the past is recounted together with the affirmation of God's faithfulness that points to the future:

> But it was because the LORD loved you and kept the oath he swore to your forefathers that he brought you out with a mighty hand and redeemed you from the land of slavery, from the power of Pharaoh king of Egypt. Know therefore that the LORD your God is God; he is the faithful God, keeping his covenant of love to a thousand generations of those who love him and keep his commands.

[15] In the case of Rom. 1, it is not clear whether an eschatological statement can be identified. One can argue that Jesus' mediatorial role (v. 8) is being fulfilled when Jews and Gentiles accept the good news (vv. 16–17; cf. Is. 50:7–8; 51:4–5). The entire work can be understood as the affirmation of the sufficiency of the cross in accomplishing cosmic reconciliation. The absence of any explicit reference to the parousia may then be an intentional way of drawing attention to the unique outworking of the power of the gospel in the present age.

[16] The exact antecedent of the relative pronoun in verse 8 (translated 'he' in the NIV) is debatable. In light of the flow of the thanksgiving prayer, it seems best to see God as the subject especially when it is his covenantal faithfulness that is being emphasized (cf. 2 Cor. 1:21). For a further discussion, see O'Brien 1977: 127.

[17] Many have pointed to the eschatological references in 1 Cor. 1 as reflecting an attempt to correct the 'over-realized eschatology' of the Corinthians (e.g., Fee 1987: 36; M. Mitchell 1993: 195). This contextual reading is helpful, but the prevalence of this motif in other Pauline thanksgivings needs to be considered also.

Both the past and the future are understood within the context of the covenant. As in Deuteronomy 7, Paul links the past with the future and this is possible because of who God is. In the recounting of the history of God's mighty acts, Pauline thanksgiving becomes the vehicle through which the confidence of God's deliverance in the future is expressed.[18]

The same connection between the past and the future can be found in Philippians 1. After describing the blessings in the past, Paul makes the following affirmation: 'he who began a good work in you will carry it on to completion until the day of Christ Jesus' (v. 6).[19] The 'good work' may point to the Philippians' partnership in the gospel ministry (e.g., Hawthorne 1983: 121), but more plausible is the reading that understands Paul as referring back to the acceptance of the gospel and its power that prompts the Philippians to participate in Paul's ministry (R. Martin 1959: 61; Fee 1995: 85).[20] When the cross event and its impact are remembered, one is assured that the same God will be able to accomplish his goal when Jesus himself returns.[21]

This eschatological emphasis reappears in the prayer report that follows where a reference to the 'day of Christ' is made (Phil. 1:10).[22]

---

[18] Both 'thanksgiving' and 'faithfulness' can be understood as 'conjunctions' linking the future with the past. In the Old Testament, the 'faithfulness' of God is frequently evoked when the future is open to question, and this character of God cannot be separated from his covenantal promises:

> The LORD is faithful to all his promises
> and loving toward all he has made.
>
> (Ps. 145:13)

In Paul, covenantal promises are fulfilled with the coming of the Messiah (Gal. 4:4–5), and upon the same foundation the expectation of his return is built (1 Thess. 5:24).

[19] The exact syntactic function of this statement within the complex sentence remains unclear. O'Brien's (1977: 26) understanding of this statement as one that provides yet another ground for Paul's thanksgiving is sufficient for our purpose. Because of the nature of this affirmation, one is also justified in seeing this as the ultimate grounds for Pauline thanksgiving, here as elsewhere in his epistles.

[20] Phil. 2:13 ('for it is God who works in you to will and to act according to his good purpose') supports this reading. See also Gal. 3:3 where the reference to the 'beginning' refers to the time when believers accepted the Holy Spirit.

[21] The Old Testament 'day of the Lord' now becomes 'day of Christ Jesus'. The significance of God's work through his Son is emphasized, and the return of Jesus signifies the consummation of all promises.

[22] Prayer reports are frequently connected with introductory thanksgivings in Paul (Rom. 1:9–10; Eph. 1:16–23; Col. 1:9–14; 1 Thess. 1:11–12; Philem. 4, 6). This also supports our reading when an act of remembering God's grace has an inherent future character to it. Remembrance calls for a response, and the past provides the basis upon which the future can be built.

This prayer report mentions the fruits of the spirit that come from Jesus Christ himself (v. 11; cf. 3:9) and it points to the future when Christians may be presented as 'pure and blameless' (v. 10). The notion of 'faithfulness' is embodied in Jesus Christ himself who is referred to once again in this passage. In him, Christians can live a new life, and in him we can place our hope.[23]

In 1 Thessalonians 1, Paul again points to the future hope of the people of God in the report he had received:

> They tell how you turned to God from idols to serve the living and true God, and to wait for his Son from heaven, whom he raised from the dead – Jesus, who rescues us from the coming wrath. (1 Thess. 1:9–10)

God's act of deliverance is repeatedly mentioned in this thanksgiving paragraph. Divine election is noted (v. 4) together with the power of the gospel message (v. 5). In 1:9–10, the connection between the past and the future is located in the person of Jesus. This resurrected Christ is the one who will deliver his people from the judgment at the end of times (cf. 5:9). The way Jesus' resurrection is emphasized in the context of the expectation of the final deliverance is noteworthy. With this reference to the resurrection, Paul is pointing both to the past and to the future. Christ's resurrection in the past guarantees the future resurrection of believers as Paul himself argues later in the same epistle: 'We believe that Jesus died and rose again and so we believe that God will bring with Jesus those who have fallen asleep in him' (1 Thess. 4:14).[24]

The subject of Jesus' return dominates 2 Thessalonians 1:3–12. Jesus' return is explicitly mentioned in verses 7 and 10. When he returns, those who obey will be blessed (vv. 7, 10) while those who disobey will be punished (vv. 6, 8–9). Thanksgiving is offered to God

---

[23] For a further discussion of this passage that points to Christian living in light of the future, see the final section of this chapter.

[24] Malherbe (2000: 121–122) further points to Rom. 8:11; 1 Cor. 15:20–57; and 2 Cor. 4:14. He also notes the emphasis on the role of God in these two verses: 'the summary begins with a reminder that the readers had converted to God from idols, not the traditional order, from idols to God (Acts 14:15). "God" is then repeated and further characterized as living and true, Jesus is described in his relationship to God and as the object of God's action in his resurrection, and the last item in the summary speaks of God's wrath. God is the one who acts, from creation to eschatological judgment' (132). This point is important especially when thanksgiving is directed to God, the covenantal partner who will remain faithful to the end. For a further discussion of the parallels between 1 Thess. 1:9–10 and the missionary speeches in Acts, see Wilckens 1974: 81–91; and Wenham 1988: 53–55.

because of the evidence of their faithfulness to the gospel in the midst of suffering (vv. 3–4). The faithfulness of the believers rests not simply on the foundation of the gospel but also on the hope that it generates when the just God will be fully revealed in the future. The connection between the thanksgiving proper in verses 3–4 and its further elaboration in verses 5–10 is established by the theme of perseverance and endurance (v. 4),[25] through which the present condition of the believers can be situated within the wider temporal framework. This temporal framework allows the present to be understood in light of both the past and the future.

This exact point is made explicit later in the text when the connection between the past and the present is established within the context of thanksgiving:

> But we ought always to thank God for you, brothers loved by the Lord, because from the beginning God chose you to be saved through the sanctifying work of the Spirit and through belief in the truth. He called you to this through our gospel, that you might share in the glory of our Lord Jesus Christ. So then, brothers, stand firm and hold to the teachings we passed on to you, whether by word of mouth or by letter. (2 Thess. 2:13–15)

This passage has often been considered as a summary of Paul's gospel (e.g., O'Brien 1977: 184). As in the introductory thanksgiving, a similar formula is used ('we ought always to thank God for you').[26] Both aim at encouraging believers to be faithful to the gospel. What this passage contributes to our understanding of 1 Thessalonians 1:3–10 is the explicit connection between the past and the future. This connection rests on the understanding of God as the faithful God who will complete what he began[27] to do: the God who called his people is

---

[25] The theme of faithfulness is also present. Although the word *pistis* in verse 4 should probably be understood as referring to faith, the way Paul discusses the outworking of faith in this context comes close to the idea of faithfulness.

[26] Aus (1973: 432–438) has shown that this formula is not unusual in apocalyptic texts when the subject of suffering is being dealt with. Moreover, the reappearance of the stem *axios* in 1 Thess. 1:5 and 11 points to the unique significance of this formula that ties the various sections together.

[27] The phrase 'from the beginning' is based on a problematic textual tradition, and external evidence alone cannot settle the issue. In the context of this verse, and in light of the parallels elsewhere (e.g., Eph. 1:4; cf. 1 Cor. 2:7), it seems best to see this as referring to the act of election from the beginning of times. See the discussion in Wanamaker 1990: 266; cf. Malherbe 2000: 436. For a further discussion of Paul's concept of election within the context of thanksgiving, see also our discussion in ch. 3 above.

the one who will continue to lead them into the glory of his Son.[28] The inner logic of 1 Thessalonians 1:3–10 is articulated in 2 Thessalonians 2:13–15: we are called to be faithful because God himself is faithful.

From the examples that we have presented, it is clear that eschatology plays an important part in Pauline introductory thanksgivings. Whenever the future is referred to, God's acts in history are also remembered. When the future cannot be separated from what God did in the past, the role of thanksgiving becomes clearer. Thanksgiving evokes the past but it also transcends history. In the covenantal relationship between God and his people, the past points forward to the future. It is not surprising, therefore, that one finds references to the future within Pauline introductory thanksgivings.

While the connection between the past and the future is emphasized in Paul, it can be traced back to the words of Jesus. In this context, the Lord's Supper should again be mentioned.[29] In the Old Testament, the Passover not only points back to God's act of deliverance but also looks forward to a time when the people enter the Promised Land. In the New Testament, the Lord's Supper also points to the future by way of looking back at the cross. In the Synoptic accounts, Jesus himself points to the messianic banquet when the power of the cross will be fully realized (Matt. 26:29; Mark 14:25; Luke 22:16). In the Pauline account, this eschatological emphasis comes through Paul's own comment: 'For whenever you eat this bread and drink this cup, you proclaim the Lord's death until he comes' (1 Cor. 11:26). To 'remember' Jesus' death is to place our hope in the one who conquered death. With the cross and the empty tomb, the rest of history is simply the working out of the implications of these events.[30] To remember Jesus' death and to offer thanks for this climactic act of history is, therefore, to look forward to his return.

Future as grounds for thanksgiving

In the previous section, we have discussed how the past and the future are linked together in a number of Pauline introductory thanksgiving

---

[28] The emphasis on glory also connects this passage with the introductory thanksgiving (cf. 2 Thess. 1:8–10, 12). Paul's emphasis on the placement of the time of glory at the end of history may be intended to provide a correction to those who thought that 'the day of the Lord has already come' (2 Thess. 2:2).

[29] Various issues related to the Lord's Supper have been dealt with already in ch. 3 above. In this context, only the eschatological overtones will be noted.

[30] For a further discussion of the Lord's Supper as an essentially eschatological institution, see Wainwright 1981; Farrow 1999, and 2000: 199–215.

paragraphs. In those instances, remembering the past leads to the anticipation of the future. Thanksgiving can then be understood as providing a way to think in covenantal terms. In this section, a number of passages in which Paul directly gives thanks for the future will be examined. Not only is the future noted in the context of thanksgiving, in these passages the future becomes the grounds for thanksgiving, and these remind one of the eschatological songs of thanksgiving that were discussed at the beginning of this chapter.

In Romans 7, one finds Paul lamenting his inability to find favour with God by his attempt to be obedient to the law. At the end of the lament, a note of hope is sounded: 'Thanks be to God – through Jesus Christ our Lord' (Rom. 7:25a).[31] While this statement can be read as referring simply to the past event when salvation was accomplished through the death and resurrection of Jesus, this verse seems also to point to the future. The second part of the verse that follows portrays a situation that can be improved: 'So then, I myself in my mind am a slave to God's law, but in the sinful nature a slave to the law of sin' (7:25b). This sentence does not invalidate the note of thanksgiving. It does, however, reflect the reality of the present state of affairs when we all await the final victory.

This leads us to the more difficult question concerning the material that precedes Romans 7:25. The question as to the exact identity of the 'I' in Romans 7:14–24 does complicate the issue at hand, although the future reference is not lost in either interpretation.[32] If the 'I' represents the state of a believer, 7:25a naturally refers to the final victory that is yet to come. If Romans 7:14–24 describes non-believers, Romans 7:25a would still point to the deliverance from sin that lies in the future. While a detailed analysis would distract us from our present discussion,[33] the continuation of the Christian struggle is affirmed both in 7:14 and 7:25b,[34] and the hope for the final victory never fades throughout the Pauline corpus. This hope continues to be emphasized in Romans 8: 'Not only so, but we ourselves, who have the firstfruits of the Spirit, groan

[31] Several readings can be found in textual traditions for the phrase 'thanks be to God'. Most would agree that our present reading best explains the existence of others. See Fitzmyer 1993: 476–477; Metzger 1994: 455.

[32] See Moo 1996: 466–467.

[33] For a further discussion, see the helpful survey in Lambrecht 1992. See also Seifrid 1992: 313–333 for the reading of this passage as referring to Christian existence in general.

[34] See also the future tense of the verb in 7:24 ('Who will rescue me from this body of death?'). Cf. Rom. 11:26.

inwardly as we wait eagerly for our adoption as sons, the redemption of our bodies' (v. 23).[35]

Robert Banks (1978: 34–42) points to the parallel in 1 Corinthians 15:57 in support of an eschatological reading of Romans 7:25a. One finds in both (1) expression of thanks to God; (2) deliverance/victory; and (3) the mediation of Jesus Christ 'our Lord'.[36] The contexts of Romans 7 and 1 Corinthians 15 are also comparable. References to sin, death, and law are found in both: 'In both we find the idea of "sin" gaining "power" through the "law" leading to "death" of the "body", either in close proximity or directly implied by the immediate context' (Banks 1978:37). Reading in light of 1 Corinthians 15:57,[37] Banks concludes that Romans 7:25a is an expression of eschatological thanks for ultimate deliverance from the body that is destined to experience death as a result of sin.

While Banks may be accused of reading too much into Romans 7:25a, the parallels with 1 Corinthians 15:57 do at least point to the eschatological nature of this text. The fact that 1 Corinthians 15:57 is not foreign to Paul's argument in Romans 7 is shown by Paul's continuing argument in Romans 8. In Romans 8:11, for example, Paul is operating within the same thought world that produced 1 Corinthians 15:57: 'And if the Spirit of him who raised Jesus from the dead is living in you, he who raised Christ from the dead will also give life to your mortal bodies through his Spirit, who lives in you.'[38]

In Romans 7:25a, therefore, we find an example of an eschatological note of thanksgiving in Paul. Paul gives thanks for that which will happen in the future. From Romans 8:11, Paul makes it clear that his confidence in the future rests on what God did through his Son (cf. Rom. 8:3). More explicit is Romans 8:32: 'He who did not spare his

---

[35] As Gebauer (1989: 138–139) has suggested, Rom. 7:25a also functions to introduce Rom. 8. In Rom. 8:1–4, the certainty of the victory is grounded on the work of God through his Son.

[36] In Rom. 7:25a, the phrase 'through Jesus Christ our Lord' seems to modify the act of thanksgiving. If that is the case, the phrase in 1 Cor. 15:57 should be understood in the same way. It is possible, however, to argue that the mediation of Christ is the grounds for thanksgiving. In 1 Cor. 15:57, therefore, it is the 'victory' that the phrase modifies. The two cannot be separated, however, since the act of thanksgiving is possible precisely because of what God has done through his Son (see, e.g., Thiselton 2000: 1303).

[37] Banks (1978: 37) also points to Rom. 6:17 that contains an expression of thanksgiving to God. The parallels in form and content that one finds in 1 Cor. 15:57, however, are missing.

[38] For a further discussion of Paul's argument in 1 Cor. 15 and its thematic ties with Rom. 8, see Harris 1983: 162–165.

own Son, but gave him up for us all – how will he not also, along with him, graciously give us all things?' As in the Old Testament eschatological songs of thanksgiving, Paul points to the faithful God who will not forget the covenantal promises he made to his people.

Our discussion of Romans 7:25a naturally leads us to 1 Corinthians 15:57. In this passage, a clear eschatological cry of thanksgiving is made: 'But thanks be to God! He gives us the victory through our Lord Jesus Christ.' The basis of this hope undoubtedly rests on the resurrection of Jesus. Paul's discussion begins with the kerygma: 'that Christ died for our sins . . . that he was buried, that he was raised on the third day . . .' (15:3–4). His resurrection, understood as 'the firstfruits of those who have fallen asleep', provides hope for the believers (15:20; cf. 15:23).[39] Because the enemy has been destroyed (15:26–27), Paul looks forward to the day when 'the dead will be raised imperishable, and we will be changed' (1 Cor. 15:52). In the present time, however, one's confidence in God's victory and experience of God's grace makes this thanksgiving possible.[40] The God who raised Jesus will also raise the believers at the end of times.[41]

Significantly, this Pauline thanksgiving for the future act of God is situated in a context where an Old Testament eschatological song of thanksgiving is explicitly quoted:

When the perishable has been clothed with the imperishable, and the mortal with immortality, then the saying that is written will come true: 'Death has been swallowed up in victory.' (1 Cor. 15:54)

Here, one finds the quotation from Isaiah 25:8. Immediately following this verse, one finds an eschatological song of thanksgiving (Is.

[39] Elsewhere in Paul, the imagery of the 'firstborn' is used to describe the power of Jesus' resurrection for the believers (Col. 1:15, 18).

[40] The participle (translated as 'He gives us') is in the present tense which may denote the certainty and present state of God's work (cf. Conzelmann 1975: 293; Thiselton 2000: 1304). One should be careful, however, not to read too much into the temporal reference of Greek tenses.

[41] This connection is made elsewhere in Paul. In 2 Cor. 4:14, for example, one reads: 'because we know that the one who raised the Lord Jesus from the dead will also raise us with Jesus and present us with you in his presence' (cf. Rom. 8:11; 1 Cor. 6:14). Barnett's (1997: 242 n.20) comment concerning 2 Cor. 4 may also be relevant in our discussion of 1 Cor. 15: 'Paul is preoccupied, not with the Parousia of Christ (unmentioned in 2 Cor.), but with resurrection.' While one should not suggest that Paul is unconcerned with the end of times, his vision of the future arises from and is shaped by his emphasis on Christ, his death and his resurrection.

25:9) in which the ultimate salvific act of God is described as an accomplished act.[42] As in Paul, the certainty of Isaiah's affirmation relies on the knowledge of who God is and what he has done for his people:

> I will exalt you and praise your name,
> for in perfect faithfulness
>   you have done marvellous things,
>   things planned long ago.

(Is. 25:1)

In addition, one also finds an implicit reference here to the resurrection to be understood as the manifestation of God's power (cf. Is. 25:10–12).[43] Both Isaiah and 1 Corinthians provide the context in which the confident affirmations of God's faithfulness and sovereign power can be made. It is no surprise, then, that an eschatological note of thanksgiving can be found in both.[44] This thanksgiving note in 1 Corinthians 15:57 forms an appropriate conclusion to the long chapter on the power of the resurrection of Christ.

In light of the Old Testament eschatological songs of thanksgiving discussed above, Paul's comments in Romans 7 and 1 Corinthians 15 can be appreciated. Since God is the God of history, he is therefore also in control of the future. In the struggle to describe the tension between the 'already' and 'not yet', the certainty of God's action in the future acquires a new significance. While the Old Testament authors can point to the future by looking at the past acts of God, Paul is able to look back at the climactic 'eschatological' event in the

---

[42] See the discussion at the beginning of this chapter.

[43] Harrelson (1990: 149–159) points to two traditions behind Old Testament conceptions of life after death: (1) the presence of God beyond death; and (2) the public manifestations of the power of the sovereign Lord in history. Both ideas are reflected in Is. 25. One obvious difference between Is. 25 and 1 Cor. 15 should also be noted, however. In Isaiah 25, the victory over death is set in a context where the fate of the nation of Israel is at stake. In Paul, however, the people of God is defined by one's relationship with the 'last Adam' (1 Cor. 15:45).

[44] The two are also connected by the word 'victory' (1 Cor. 15:54 [Is. 25:8]; 15:57). While the word 'victory' is missing in the Hebrew text, it does appear in some versions of the LXX (Aquila and Theodotion). Here, the quotation from Hos. 13:14 in 1 Cor. 15:55 should also be noted. In this quotation, the word 'victory' again appears. This word does not appear, however, in either the Hebrew text or the LXX. In both quotations, one can then argue that Paul has inserted the word 'victory' and their connections with 1 Cor. 15:57 are, therefore, undoubtedly intentional. Furthermore, the context suggests that one might also consider Hos. 13:14 as an eschatological affirmation.

cross and the empty tomb while pointing to the future which is understood primarily as the unfolding of God's work in Christ. On a vertical plane, the reality of the incarnation through which the presence of God can be felt also destroys any neat definition of 'eschatology' embedded in the Pauline corpus. Old Testament eschatological traditions are thus both affirmed and transformed. God is the same faithful and powerful covenantal partner who is able to fulfil his own promises. On the other hand, the 'future' is already present through the mediation of Jesus Christ: 'Therefore, if anyone is in Christ, he is a new creation; the old has gone, the new has come' (2 Cor. 5:17).

Noting the complexity of Pauline eschatology will prepare us to examine one more passage in the Pauline corpus. In Philippians 4, in the midst of a number of seemingly loosely connected phrases, is a reference to the eschatological presence of the Lord and a call to thanksgiving:

> Rejoice in the Lord always. I will say it again: Rejoice! Let your gentleness be evident to all. The Lord is near. Do not be anxious about anything, but in everything, by prayer and petition, with thanksgiving, present your requests to God. And the peace of God, which transcends all understanding, will guard your hearts and your minds in Christ Jesus. (vv. 4–7)

Unlike Romans 7:25a and 1 Corinthians 15:57, this is not an eschatological cry of thanksgiving. As in the other two passages, one finds a connection between thanksgiving and the affirmation of the presence of God, but the precise relationship between the two here is not clear. First, the exact meaning of the phrase, 'The Lord is near', needs to be determined. Second, the function of this phrase within its context also calls for further discussion.

The reference to the proximity of the presence of God can be understood in spatial or in temporal terms. Pointing to verses such as Psalm 145:18 ('The Lord is near to all who call on him'),[45] some have argued that Paul is referring to the presence of God among his people in the present times of need. Noting the support of Calvin and others, Allan Chapple (1992: 149–165) has provided a recent defence of this reading. He concludes that in Philippians 4:5, 'Paul is using the language, not of Christian eschatology, but of biblical piety' (160). While one cannot deny the importance of the Psalms in the

---

[45] See also Pss. 34:18; 119:151.

Pauline epistles, one wonders whether the source text alone should determine the meaning of the phrase in Philippians 4. Moreover, others have pointed to apocalyptic material as providing the background for this Pauline phrase.[46]

The context in Philippians should provide the primary framework for interpretation. In its immediate context, the expectation of the Lord's return is noted: 'But our citizenship is in heaven. And we eagerly await a Saviour from there, the Lord Jesus Christ' (Phil. 3:20). More importantly, the dichotomy that has been set up is foreign to the mind of Paul. As we have already noted, the expectation of Christ's return is grounded on the presence of God in the earthly life of Jesus (cf. Phil. 2:6–8). Without separating the 'already' and the 'not yet', one wonders if both senses are present in Philippians. Assuming that Paul is aware of the gospel traditions,[47] the prayer that Jesus himself taught may be worth noting for our discussion of Philippians 4. In both, one finds a call not to be anxious about our needs (cf. Matt. 6:8; Luke 11:9–10); and in both the way one should pray is noted.[48] In the Lord's Prayer, the present experience of God's grace merges with the expectation of God's presence in the future.[49] While we are not suggesting that Philippians 4 is dependent upon the Lord's Prayer, what we find in the gospels does provide a way to transcend the present/future dichotomy as we experience the eschatological presence of God.

The second problem in the text lies in the relationship between the phrase, 'The Lord is near', and its immediate context. The phrase may be understood as modifying the preceding call to rejoice. It can also modify that which follows. Modern commentators have increasingly preferred to see the phrase as modifying both.[50] The presence of God, both in the present and in the future, forms the basis for rejoicing. This

---

[46] Fee (1995: 407–408), for example, points to the phrase, 'the day of the LORD is near', in Zeph. 1:7, 14. This phrase is used by Paul in Rom. 13:12 in reference to the future return of the Lord.

[47] Gospel traditions should not be understood as limited to their respective local 'communities'. The understanding of early traditions concerning Jesus as belonging to the wider church is established by the essays in Bauckham 1998.

[48] The parallel is strengthened by our understanding of thanksgiving as 'God-centredness'. In ch. 4, we have already noted the connection between Matt. 6:25–34 and Phil. 4:6–7.

[49] One does not have to adopt a thorough eschatological reading of the Lord's Prayer to affirm this point. The petitions, 'your kingdom come, your will be done on earth as it is in heaven', call upon God to allow his people to have a taste of heaven in the midst of mundane existence.

[50] See, for example, the discussion in O'Brien 1991b: 490; and Fee 1995: 407.

presence also provides assurance that the believers have no need to be anxious.

The way not to be anxious is through prayer and petition. Prayer and petition are accompanied by thanksgiving.[51] In acts of thanksgiving, God's presence through his Son is recalled. In an eschatological sense, this call to give thanks reminds one of Paul's own thanksgivings in Romans 7:25a and 1 Corinthians 15:57. Believers are to pray with the same certainty that God is in control of the future. It is this certainty that allows us not to be anxious. The ambiguity of the phrase, 'The Lord is near', is then translated into the double functions of the call to thanksgiving. Remembering what God has done for us, we can continue to trust him who is the Lord of the future.

Acts of giving thanks for the future move beyond modern conceptions of thanksgiving that focus on the past. We have shown that eschatological songs of thanksgiving can already be found in the Old Testament. In the New Testament, evidence outside of the Pauline corpus will also support our reading of the several Pauline statements. In Hebrews 13:6, the author expresses confidence in God's power and faithfulness by citing Psalm 118:6–7. As noted above,[52] this psalm can be considered as an eschatological song of thanksgiving in which the faithfulness of God is emphasized:

> Give thanks to the LORD, for he is good;
>   his love endures for ever.
>   (Ps. 118:1, 29; cf. Jer. 33:11)

A clearer non-Pauline example of an eschatological song of thanksgiving can be found in the Apocalypse. In chapter 11, thanksgiving is offered by the twenty-four elders:

> 'We give thanks to you, Lord God Almighty,
>   the One who is and who was,
> because you have taken your great power
>   and have begun to reign.
> The nations were angry;
>   and your wrath has come.
> The time has come for judging the dead,
>   and for rewarding your servants the prophets

---

[51] For a further discussion of the call to thanksgiving 'in everything', see ch. 4 above.

[52] As noted in footnote 6 above, this is also the psalm that was used in all four gospel accounts of Jesus' triumphal entry into Jerusalem.

and your saints and those who reverence your name,
   both small and great –
and for destroying those who destroy the earth.'
                                    (Rev. 11:17–18)

In this hymn, the final victory is described as an accomplished event. This thanksgiving song accompanies the song of victory that appears in 11:15:

'The kingdom of the world has become
   the kingdom of our Lord and
   of his Christ,
   and he will reign for ever and ever.'

Taken together, one again finds confidence in God as he fights for his own people. At stake is the question that faces the suffering people of God: Who is in control of history? John provides an unequivocal answer through apocalyptic narratives together with an eschatological song of thanksgiving.

For Paul, as he addresses believers who are also struggling spiritually and/or physically, eschatological thanksgiving notes point to the certainty of God's power and covenantal faithfulness.

In light of the future

Pauline references to the future are not only concerned with the faithfulness of God. The loyalty of the covenant people is also described in reference to the future. While affirming that God will fulfil his promises, Paul also calls the believers to live in light of the future eschatological events.

We have already noted that some of the Pauline introductory thanksgivings contain references to the future. We have shown that in remembering what God did for us, we have confidence that God will be able to continue to accomplish what he promised. In some of these thanksgiving paragraphs, Paul also encourages his audience to live lives worthy of these promises. This, after all, is to live a life that puts God at the very centre.[53]

---

[53] Here, the present life once again becomes the focus. In Pauline theology, eschatology is never only about the future. The future is mentioned because of its potential impact on the believers. Through acts of thanksgiving, the past affects the present lives of the believers. Similarly, the power of the vision of the future can be felt in the present time. All this is possible because of who God is and the way he reveals himself in covenantal history.

In the thanksgiving paragraph in Philippians 1, Paul expresses confidence in God who will complete the good work that he began in the lives of the believers (v. 6). In addition, he is also concerned with the present lives of the believers as they prepare themselves for the future:

> And this is my prayer: that your love may abound more and more in knowledge and depth of insight, so that you may be able to discern what is best and may be pure and blameless until the day of Christ. (vv. 1:9–10)

This prayer that follows the thanksgiving proper reflects Paul's concern for the church. To present the church as blameless at the time of the Lord's return is a theme that reappears in the Pauline epistles.[54] To 'discern what is best' prepares the believers for their ultimate purpose of being 'pure and blameless' in the presence of Christ. The 'day of Christ' alludes to the Old Testament 'day of the LORD' and points to the Christocentric gospel that is yet to be consummated in the return of God's Son. The prepositional phrase, 'until the day of Christ', should not be read simply in a temporal sense.[55] In context, Paul is emphasizing sanctified living as one looks forward to the day when all will be held accountable for their deeds.[56] In thanksgiving, the present and future acts of God are evoked. This calls for a proper response.

A similar point is made in the introductory thanksgiving in 2 Thessalonians. In our previous discussion, we noted the emphasis on eschatology in 1:3–10. The perseverance of the saints is mentioned alongside the focus on God's own faithfulness. In the prayer report that follows, the call to live a life in view of the end of times is noted (1:11–12). This theme continues in the thanksgiving section in 2:13–15 where believers are called to continue to stand firm.

The connection between eschatology and ethics can be found throughout the Pauline corpus.[57] Its appearance in the introductory

---

[54] Referring to passages such as 1 Thess. 2:19; 3:9–11; 5:23; Rom. 15:16; 2 Cor. 1:14; 11:2; and Phil. 2:16, Wiles (1974: 4–5) points to the priestly duties of the apostle Paul.

[55] The preposition often used to denote the temporal sense of 'until' is *achri*, one that is used in precisely this way in Phil. 1:6. Here, the preposition *eis* denotes direction and purpose. A better translation would then be 'in light of' or 'towards'.

[56] This, however, is not to suggest that our work will earn us favour on the day of judgment. The verse that follows (Phil. 1:11) makes it clear that 'fruits of righteousness' ultimately come from Jesus Christ himself.

[57] See the discussion in the dissertation of Rogahn (1975) and the work of Lohse (1991: 41–43, 125).

paragraphs is consistent with Paul's emphasis elsewhere. A more explicit expression of the relationship between thanksgiving and eschatology in the context of exhortation for the present lives of believers can be found in two Pauline passages. In the previous section, we have discussed the eschatological note of thanksgiving in 1 Corinthians 15:57. Immediately following this thanksgiving is a verse that points to the appropriate behaviour for those who look forward to the final resurrection:

Therefore, my dear brothers, stand firm. Let nothing move you. Always give yourselves fully to the work of the Lord, because you know that your labour in the Lord is not in vain. (1 Cor. 15:58)

The connection between the preceding thanksgiving is made clear by the preposition *oun* ('therefore'). This verse therefore functions as the implication of the anticipation of the final victory. Believers are called to stand firm and be faithful to their faithful God. The justification lies in the fact that the work will not be done 'in vain'. This phrase points back to the beginning of the chapter where Paul reminded the Corinthians to 'hold firmly to the word' so that they shall not have 'believed in vain' (1 Cor. 15:2; cf. 15:14). The reason that their belief and labour will not be in vain is described in detail in the intervening material. It is the power of Jesus' resurrection and its effect on the future of the believers that produces ultimate meaning in the lives of the believers.[58] The certainty that is reflected in this eschatological thanksgiving should also be the anchor of one's mind and heart.

We should now return to a verse that we have noted in our discussion of the Colossian household rules.[59] While the household rules are preceded by a sustained call to thanksgiving, what follows is also a call to prayer with thanksgiving: 'Devote yourselves to prayer, being watchful and thankful' (Col. 4:2). In the New Testament, the word

---

[58] For a discussion of hope and the generation of meaning, see the recent discussion of Bauckham and Hart (1999: 26–71) who argue that Christian eschatology, properly understood, will be able to provide the metanarrative within which meaning can be found. This metanarrative is functional precisely because it transcends the existence of any one individual. This metanarrative does not provide a way to escape present reality, however. Precisely because it shows how the world can be different, it demands believers to act and behave in a different way in their present lives.

[59] See ch. 4 above.

'watchful'[60] is frequently used in context when the day of the Lord is referred to (e.g., 1 Thess. 5:6; Rev. 3:3; 16:15; cf. 1 Cor. 16:13). The word is also used together with 'prayer' in other eschatological discussions. In Luke 21:36, for example, one reads: 'Be always on the watch, and pray that you may be able to escape all that is about to happen, and that you may be able to stand before the Son of Man.'

While the verse can be interpreted in a non-eschatological sense, the use of the verb ('being watchful') together with the call to pray point in a different direction.[61] In its context, the emphasis on eschatological concerns can also be felt.[62] This interpretation is further supported and nuanced by the close parallels in Ephesians 6 after the presentation of the household code: 'And pray in the Spirit on all occasions with all kinds of prayers and requests. With this in mind, be alert and always keep on praying for all the saints' (v. 18). While a different verb is being used, the idea of wakefulness/watchfulness is again present in the context of prayer. In its own context, the eschatological struggle between God and Satan is emphasized. Interpretations of this verse often again reflect the false dichotomy that may have existed in our interpretation of Pauline thought. To Paul, the eschatological age is already present, and we are called to be alert constantly in anticipation of our Lord's return.[63] To be watchful, therefore, is to continue to live in light of what God has done for us in the past and what he will accomplish in the future. In Ephesians 6, the vertical plane takes precedence over the temporal plane as we are called to struggle 'against the spiritual forces of evil in the heavenly realm' (v. 12).[64] The consummation of this struggle, however, can be realized only when the temporal plane is also in view.

---

[60] The participial form should be taken as modifying the main clause ('continue to pray') and not as an independent command. Cf. Lohse 1971: 164.

[61] See Oepke 1964: 338; and O'Brien 1982: 237. Dunn (1996: 262) further suggests that this eschatological use may reflect an awareness of the Jesus tradition.

[62] Dunn (1996: 262) points to the following terms/phrases in Col. 4:2–5: to keep awake, the mystery of Christ, to reveal, *dei* (appearing twice), and buying up opportune time (*kairos*).

[63] Lövestam (1963: 76) has rightly pointed to the significance of Col. 1:12–14 where the dawn of the eschatological era is noted within the context of thanksgiving.

[64] In the Garden of Gethsemane, the call to be 'watchful' in prayer is of a similar nature (Mark 14:38; Matt. 26:41). The disciples are called to be vigilant at an eschatological moment when the critical war between God and Satan is to take place. The term 'eschatological' in this context refers primarily to the vertical plane, but this war will affect the temporal scene once and for all.

If our reading of Ephesians 6 is correct, Colossians 4:2 should also be understood within the same framework. To be watchful is to be aware of the present struggle between God and Satan. It is also to anticipate the time when the final victory is achieved.[65] In Colossians 4:2, therefore, we are called to be faithful to God.[66] The mentioning of thanksgiving is therefore appropriate; it adds to the eschatological reading of the verse. In thanksgiving, we remember God's mighty acts as we look forward to the continued manifestation of his own faithfulness.

In the wider context of Colossians 4:2, this anticipation is explicitly mentioned. In Colossians 3:1–4, Christ becomes the paradigm for Christian living:

> Since, then, you have been raised with Christ, set your hearts on things above, where Christ is seated at the right hand of God. Set your minds on things above, not on earthly things. For you died, and your life is now hidden with Christ in God. When Christ, who is your life, appears, then you also will appear with him in glory.

The concern for Christian living is set within an eschatological framework. Not only is the death and resurrection of Christ remembered, his anticipated return also forms the basis of Pauline ethics. Christian existence is defined by the past as well as the future. Within this paradigm, therefore, Christian living is by definition 'eschatological'.

This passage from Colossians 3 also serves to explain the importance of the future in Pauline thanksgiving. In Paul's Christocentric gospel, acts of remembrance cannot be separated from acts of anticipation. To live 'in Christ' is also to live in light of his return.[67] Similarly, the conception of the future can be found only in Christ himself.[68] Focusing solely on Christ, one cannot separate the empty tomb from the cross. In the same way, Christ's

---

[65] The role of prayer in this context is to be highlighted. As Lövestam (1963: 76–77) has noted, prayer is a condition, an expression and a means for wakefulness.

[66] Faithfulness is implied in the use of the word *proskartereō* (literally, 'to continue to').

[67] See also Rom. 6:5; 8:11; 1 Cor. 6:14; 15:20; Phil. 3:20–21; 1 Thess. 4:16–17.

[68] In discussing the basis of Pauline ethics, R. Longenecker (1985: 89) is correct in noting that one's 'eschatological hope is based on what one thinks of Christ Jesus, not *vice versa*'.

return cannot be separated from the past. If thanksgiving is understood as God-centredness and Christ-centredness, the future cannot be denied its place in this confession of God's nature and deeds.[69]

---

[69] One is reminded of a passage in the rabbinic literature: 'In time to come all offerings will come to an end, but the thanksgiving-offering will never come to an end. All forms of prayer will come to an end, but the thanksgiving-prayer will never come to an end' (*Pesiqta* 9.12 [Neusner 1987: 151]).

Chapter Six

Ingratitude

Warning against ingratitude is necessarily implied in the Pauline call to thanksgiving. When thanksgiving is understood as God-centredness, the failure to offer thanks reflects a refusal to acknowledge God as the sovereign Lord and Creator. In biblical traditions, the failure to give thanks for what God has done for his people has crystallized into a distinct form, and this form finds its root in the exodus traditions.

Rejection of the mighty acts of God

God's deliverance of his people from Egypt forms the foundation of the history of the covenant people. As we have shown, in this event God's sovereignty and power were revealed. In response, the people of God were called to remember God and his mighty deeds. Immediately after the Sinai covenant was established, however, Israel started to 'forget' her God. In the exodus narrative, this is symbolized by the constant 'murmuring' of God's people.[1]

In Exodus 15 – 17, one finds a description of the 'murmuring' of the people against the God who delivered them from Egypt.[2] Immediately after the Song of Moses in which God was honoured as Israel's Saviour, the people displayed their distrust of their deliverer when they were not able to find water: 'So the people grumbled against Moses, saying "What are we to drink?"' (Exod. 15:24). This question begins a pattern where the guidance of God and his servant

---

[1] In the Pentateuch, the rebellion of Israel is portrayed by the use of various images and episodes. The golden calf episode (Exod. 32), for example, should be noted alongside the 'murmuring' of the people. As we shall see, this golden calf episode also comes to be understood as part of the people's murmuring against their God.

[2] The rebellious nature of the people is noted already in passages that precede the account of the exodus event. See, for example, Exod. 2:14; 5:20–21; 6:9; 14:10–12.

Moses is doubted.[3] In Exodus 17 (cf. Num. 20), the issue of the lack of drinking water reappears when the people 'quarrelled with Moses' (v. 2). In this episode, the murmuring is understood as directed against the Lord: 'the Israelites quarrelled and . . . they tested the LORD saying, "Is the LORD among us or not?"' (v. 7). The root of this murmuring is now made clear. The murmuring reflects the people's distrust of the presence and power of God.

In the account of the provision of manna and quail (Exod. 16:1–35), the power of the Lord is also directly questioned by 'the whole community' of Israel (16:2). In the version in Numbers 11, this grumbling is explicitly identified as a rejection of their God (v. 20). This murmuring becomes a defining characteristic of Israel's response to God and his servants. The climax of this distrust of their God came when they reacted to the report of the spies (Num. 13).[4] Because of their murmuring, punishment was now issued against those who failed to honour God as their sovereign Lord:

> The LORD said to Moses, 'How long will these people treat me with contempt? How long will they refuse to believe in me, in spite of all the miraculous signs I have performed among them? I will strike them down with a plague and destroy them, but I will make you into a nation greater and stronger than they.' (Num. 14:11–12)

Their complaint reflects their rejection of all that God had done for them. The intercession of Moses failed to stop Yahweh from punishing Israel. The lives of the people were spared, but they would no longer be able to see the Promised Land (Num. 14:23). As in other murmuring accounts, the murmuring of Israel is here understood as an active rebellion against her God (cf. Num. 14:9).[5]

---

[3] Critical scholarship has suggested that this negative portrayal of Israel originated from a much later period of time (e.g., Tunyogi 1962: 385–390; Coats 1968: 53; De Vries 1968: 51–58). One does not have to resort to the critical paradigm to explain this portrayal of Israel in Exod. 15, however. The pattern of questioning Yahweh's sovereignty is emphasized throughout the Pentateuch; this forms one of the distinct characteristics of this national epic of Israel.

[4] In Num. 14:4, Israel's distrust is articulated through the expression of regret of their leaving Egypt. As Budd (1984: 155) has noted, '"return to Egypt" is an important symbol in the OT of apostasy and alienation from Yahweh (Deut. 17:16; Hos. 7:11; Is. 30:1–7; 31:1–3; Jer. 2:18, 36; Ezek. 17:15)'.

[5] For linguistic support of this point, see Coats 1968: 7–59. See also the comment in Deut. 9:7: 'Remember this and never forget how you provoked the LORD your God to anger in the desert. From the day you left Egypt until you arrived here, you have been rebellious against the LORD' (cf. 9:24).

To murmur against God is to deny the exodus event. In the deliverance of his people, God's loving-kindness (*hesed*) is revealed. In the eyes of the wandering people, however, God's deliverance becomes a sign of betrayal: 'The LORD hates us; so he brought us out of Egypt to deliver us into the hands of the Amorites to destroy us' (Deut. 1:27). If love and hatred are understood as covenantal terms, Israel has rejected the very basis of the exodus event when God forms a people for himself.

Beyond the Pentateuch,[6] the connection between murmuring and the failure to remain faithful to the covenant is also made. In Psalm 78, for example, the forefathers of the people of God are described as

> a stubborn and rebellious generation,
> whose hearts were not loyal to God,
> whose spirits were not faithful to him.
>
> (v. 8)

What follows is a catalogue of the mighty acts of God on behalf of his people:

> He did miracles in the sight of their fathers
> in the land of Egypt, in the region of Zoan.
> He divided the sea and led them through;
> he made the water stand firm like a wall.
> He guided them with the cloud by day
> and with light from the fire all night.
> He split the rocks in the desert
> and gave them water as abundant as the seas.
>
> (Ps. 78:12–15)

In spite of all these, the people 'continued to sin against him, rebelling in the desert against the Most High' (v. 17), 'they willfully put God to test' (v. 18), 'they spoke against God' (v. 19), 'they did not believe in God or trust in his deliverance' (v. 22), and 'they kept on sinning' (v. 32). These acts against their God are understood as failure to remain loyal to their covenant partner:

---

[6] The specific word for murmuring (*lûn*) appears only in Exod. 15 – 17; Num. 14 – 17 and Josh. 9. The murmuring motif is referred to in various other ways throughout the Old Testament (e.g., 'to rebel', 'to speak against').

> their hearts were not loyal to him,
> they were not faithful to his covenant.
>
> (v. 37; cf. v. 57)

Their murmuring is therefore understood not as an isolated instance of the weakness of the will; when situated in the covenantal context, their rebellious acts reflect their unwillingness to acknowledge God's deliverance and faithfulness.

The same understanding can be found in Ezekiel 20. The exodus event is again presented, together with the accounts of Israel's rebellion (vv. 10–20). In this passage, however, Israel's murmuring or rebellion is extended to included her entire history. They rebelled against Yahweh even in Egypt (cf. Ezek. 23:3), and their rebellion continued beyond their possession of the Promised Land (cf. Ezek. 2:3–8).[7] In reference to the future, the Lord proclaimed the time when Israel will be brought back under the control of the covenantal agreement:

> As I judged your fathers in the desert of the land of Egypt, so I will judge you, declares the Sovereign LORD. I will take note of you as you pass under my rod, and I will bring you into the bond of the covenant. (Ezek. 20:36–37)

Israel's murmuring is therefore understood as breaking the covenantal bond. Instead of giving honour to the God who brought them out of Egypt, they have rejected him and they have ignored the covenant that was established.

The Song of Moses of Exodus 15 provides the way Israel should be responding to the God's deliverance. 'He is my God, and I will

---

[7] In Ezek. 20:30, Israel's rebellious acts are described as forming a pattern that recurs throughout her relationship with her God. Comparable is the argument presented in Is. 1 where the rebellious nature is expressed through the father-child relationship:

> 'I reared children and brought them up,
> but they have rebelled against me.'
>
> (v. 2)

This rebellion continues up to the time of the exile:

> Why do you persist in rebellion?
> Your whole head is injured,
> your whole heart afflicted.
>
> (v. 5)

praise him', (Exod. 15:2) is the acknowledgment expected from the people of God. In this act of praise and thanksgiving, two points were made. First, the mighty acts of God are to be remembered and recounted (vv. 4–10). Secondly, the sovereignty of their God is to be recognized:

> 'Who among the gods is like you, O LORD?
> Who is like you –
> majestic in holiness,
> awesome in glory,
> working wonders?'

(v. 11)

In the murmuring traditions in the Old Testament, Israel was precisely accused of forgetting her God and of worshipping idols and false gods. In exploring ingratitude within the covenantal contexts, these are the two aspects that require further examination.

Forgetting their Lord and worshipping idols

In the previous chapters, we have established that thanksgiving is to be understood as placing God at the centre, a place that only God himself deserves to occupy. We have also discussed the importance of remembering as one looks to the past while placing one's trust in God who is also in control of the future. In the present, we are called to worship God and God alone. To forget and to worship idols are therefore expressions of ingratitude. When God's people murmured in the wilderness, they were indeed accused of forgetting their Lord and worshipping other gods.

Within the Pentateuch, the murmuring of Israel is already considered as the failure to remember God and his covenant. In Deuteronomy 32:18, Israel is accused of rejecting her Saviour:

> You deserted the Rock, who fathered you;
> you forgot the God who gave you birth.[8]

---

[8] Their failure to remember now becomes an event that Israel is called to 'remember' as they look back at their relationship with their covenant partner. See, for instance, Deut. 9:7: 'Remember this and never forget how you provoked the LORD your God to anger in the desert. From the day you left Egypt until you arrived here, you have been rebellious against the LORD.'

This theme of not remembering continues in later writers. In a psalm already noted above, the mighty acts of God are remembered along-side Israel's lack of memory:[9]

> How often they rebelled against him in the desert
>   and grieved him in the wasteland!
> Again and again they put God to the test;
>   they vexed the Holy One of Israel.
> They did not remember his power –
>   the day he redeemed them from the oppressor,
> the day he displayed his miraculous signs in Egypt,
>   his wonders in the region of Zoan.
>
> (Ps. 78: 40–43)

Similarly, after the mighty acts of God are remembered in Psalm 106, one reads: 'But they soon forgot what he had done' (v. 13). Beyond the Psalms, in descriptions of God's provision in the desert, a similar note is sounded:

> When I fed them, they were satisfied;
>   when they were satisfied, they became proud;
>   then they forgot me.
>
> (Hos. 13:6; cf. Neh. 9:16–17; Is. 17:10)

In covenantal terms, to forget is to reject their Lord and deliverer. It is also an act of forsaking the covenant with their God (cf. Prov. 2:17). While remembering leads to worship and thanksgiving, forgetting leads to the breaking of the covenant:

> But remember the LORD your God, for it is he who gives you the ability to produce wealth, and so confirms his covenant, which he swore to your forefathers, as it is today.
> If you ever forget the LORD your God and follow other gods and worship and bow down to them, I testify against you today that you will surely be destroyed. (Deut. 8:18–19)

This points us to the connection between forgetting and worshipping false gods. In the same book, Moses warned the people 'not to forget

---

[9] As Childs (1962: 49) has observed, the appearance of this motif in the Psalms signifies another stage when the 'forgetfulness' of Israel is engraved into the cultic memory of Israel.

the covenant of the LORD' and not to make 'an idol' (Deut. 4:23; cf. 12:16; 2 Kgs. 17:38). In biblical traditions, there is no neutral ground between worshipping the one God and following other false gods. To forget God and his mighty deeds is to claim allegiance to other powers. In Jeremiah 13:25, the accusations against the people are presented precisely in terms of forgetting and idolatry: 'you have forgotten me and trusted in false gods' (cf. 18:15).

As a paradigmatic event in the history of Israel, the murmuring in the wilderness also comes to be associated with idolatry. In 1 Samuel 8:8, the word of the Lord reminds Israel of her past: 'As they have done from the day I brought them up out of Egypt until this day, forsaking me and serving other gods, so they are doing to you.'[10] This points to the episodes when the wilderness generation made and worshipped idols. Together with their murmuring, these constitute the rebellion of the people as they rejected their God. In Deuteronomy 9, the golden calf episode (vv. 8–21) is followed by the mentioning of the various incidents when Israel murmured against her Lord (v. 22). All these are considered as rebellious acts against God (vv. 7, 23). Moreover, in Ezekiel 20:16, all the instances of rebellion point to the fact that 'their hearts were devoted to their idols'.

The way murmuring and idolatry are tied together in describing the rebellion of the people is best illustrated in Psalm 106. The account of the wicked deeds of the wilderness generation begins with the note that 'they did not remember your [God's] many kindnesses' (v. 7). After the sea-crossing account, their forgetfulness is once again noted (v. 13). This is then followed by the account of Israel's murmuring against Moses and Aaron (vv. 16–18). Then, the golden calf episode is noted (vv. 19–23). After this incident of idolatry, Israel's murmuring is again mentioned' (vv. 24–27). This is followed by an account of her worshipping of Baal of Peor (vv. 28–31). Not surprisingly, Israel's murmuring is again noted (vv. 32–33) followed by incidents of idolatry (vv. 34–39). The pattern is clear. Israel's past is characterized by murmuring and idolatry. These were the responses God's people offered when confronted by the mighty acts God performed on their behalf.

Both murmuring and idolatry point to the fact that Israel's God had been forgotten. As responses to God's salvific acts, these point to Israel as an ungrateful people. In his *Dialogue with Trypho*, Justin

---

[10] Phrases such as 'forsaking me/God' and 'serving other gods' recall the language of Deuteronomy. See McCarter 1980: 157.

Martyr shows his familiarity with Old Testament covenantal history when he states that 'such have ever been your [the Jews'] practices: at one time you made a calf, and always you have shown yourselves ungrateful' (102 [*ANF* 1:250]).[11]

Throughout the discussions of Israel's forgetting and acts of idolatry, the unfailing love and faithfulness of God is constantly emphasized. In Psalm 106, for example, the recitation of Israel's evil deeds ends with a note of hope and comfort:

> Many times he [God] delivered them,
> but they were bent on rebellion
> and they wasted away in their sin.
> But he took note of their distress
> when he heard their cry;
> for their sake he remembered his covenant
> and out of his great love he relented.
>
> (Ps. 106:43–45)

Although Israel had forgotten her deliverer, God did not forget his people. This refrain reappears in various psalms that note Israel's failure.[12] Both the faithless acts of the people of God and the nature of God as a gracious covenant partner thus became ingrained in the cultic life of Israel.

---

[11] This statement should be read in its historical and literary contexts. The fact that believers are often ungrateful to our Lord and Saviour should prevent us from understanding this statement in an anti-Jewish sense as though they were the only people who had ever been ungrateful to their creator. The ungrateful nature of the wilderness generation should nevertheless be emphasized (cf. *Dialogue with Trypho* 19, 27). Other early Christian authors have also characterized Israel as an ungrateful people. See, for example, Tertullian's description of God's mercy in spite of Israel's ingratitude: 'And so He [God] gathered together a people for Himself, and fostered them with many liberal distributions of His bounty, and, after so often finding them most ungrateful, ever exhorted them to repentance and sent out the voices of the universal company of the prophets to prophesy' (*On Repentance* 2 [*ANF* 3:657]).

[12] The emphasis on God's faithfulness functions literally as a 'refrain' in Ps. 107, a thanksgiving psalm in which the faithfulness of God is contrasted with the sins of Israel. This psalm begins with this call:

> Give thanks to the LORD, for he is good;
> his love endures for ever.
>
> (v. 1)

Throughout the psalm one finds the recurrences of the phrase:

> Let them give thanks to the LORD for his unfailing love
> and his wonderful deeds for men.
>
> (vv. 8, 15, 21, 31).

Beyond the psalms, the prayer in Nehemiah 9 reflects a similar emphasis.[13] After noting the way God's people 'failed to remember the miracles you [God] performed among them' (v. 17), God's loving-kindness is evoked: 'But in your great mercy you did not put an end to them or abandon them, for you are a gracious and merciful God' (v. 31).[14] This can be traced back to the emphasis in Deuteronomy (e.g., ch. 32) where one finds the cycle of judgment and restoration.[15] Behind this cycle is the affirmation of the God of Israel as one who cares for his own people. Human failure and divine grace both point to the arrival of the one through whom the cycle can be broken.

'Do not grumble, as some of them did'

As Israel sinned against God by not remembering his mighty acts, Pauline churches are called to learn from Israel's past. In 1 Corinthians 10, Paul begins by alluding to the wilderness experience of Israel (vv. 1–5). This is followed by an explicit warning:

> Now these things occurred as examples to keep us from setting our hearts on evil things as they did. Do not be idolaters, as some of them were; as it is written: 'The people sat down to eat and drink and got up to indulge in pagan revelry.' We should not commit sexual immorality, as some of them did – and in one day twenty-three thousand of them died. We should not test the Lord, as some of them did – and were killed by snakes. And do not grumble, as some of them did – and were killed by the destroying angel. (1 Cor. 10:6–10)

In this passage, Paul alludes to four events. The first, with the quotation from Exodus 32:6, points to Israel's worship of the golden calf after the sea-crossing event. The second refers to the Baal Peor incident when Israel became involved with the Moabite women and worshipped their gods (Num. 25:1–9). The third refers to Numbers

---

[13] For the relationship between Neh. 9 and the Psalms, see Fensham 1981: 35–51.

[14] Sakenfeld (1985: 49) notes the way the history of Israel's rebellion came to be understood as manifestations of God's mercy and faithfulness. In Neh. 9, the people once again called upon their Lord to show his mercy in delivering his people from slavery (v. 37).

[15] Williamson (1985: 31) further points to Judg. 2:11–23 and 2 Kgs. 17. He notes that this reflects the existence of a broader traditio-historical context that holds this view of history.

21:4–9 where 'the people grew impatient on the way' and 'spoke against God and against Moses' (v. 5). The fourth evokes the murmuring tradition, but the exact incident to which Paul was referring remains unclear. Some have pointed to the Korah narrative (Num. 16) where one finds thousands killed.[16] Others have argued that Paul had Numbers 14 in mind, an account in which the murmuring motif played an important role.[17] Some have suggested that the allusion is more general in nature.[18]

Beyond the exact identification of the events behind the four references, two questions have further troubled modern commentators. First, the exact combination of the four events demands an explanation. Second, the function of these allusions to events in the wilderness journey in the context of 1 Corinthians also requires further discussion.

To answer the first question, many have pointed to the power of the Old Testament text in the moulding of Paul's argument here. Noting the explicit quotation in 1 Corinthians 10:7, Wayne Meeks (1982: 64–78) argues that 1 Corinthians 10:1–10 is a midrash on Exodus 32:6. The phrase 'to eat and to drink' leads to the discussion of the spiritual food in verses 1–4 while 'rose up to play'[19] is reflected in the discussion of the vices in verses 6–10. G. Collier (1994: 55–76) adds Numbers 11 to the textual basis of the midrash. Resisting the application of the label 'midrash', Brian Rosner (1992: 171–178) points to the significance of Numbers 14 and Deuteronomy 32 where the jealousy of God is emphasized. While these provide valuable insights into the sources of Paul's thinking, the reason why precisely these four events are recalled remains unclear.

Corresponding to these suggestions are the ones concerning the function of the four examples in Paul's argument. Some have suggested that Paul uses these examples to combat division within the church of Corinth;[20] others suggest that Paul uses the wilderness

---

[16] See, for example, M. Mitchell (1993: 139–140), who points to Josephus and Philo where the incident is described as a 'sedition'.

[17] See, for example, Fee (1987: 457–458), who further notes that the phrase in verse 5 ('scattered over the desert') alludes to Num. 14:37.

[18] See Thiselton (2000: 743), who points to the use of scriptural patterns elsewhere in 1 Corinthians.

[19] To clarify the meaning of the phrase, the NIV has 'got up to indulge in revelry'. This is justified by the fact that the phrase 'to play' can acquire a sexual connotation in the Old Testament (e.g., Gen. 26:8; 39:14).

[20] M. Mitchell (1993: 140) points to Philo, Josephus and later Rabbinic traditions and argues that these examples from Israel's past 'were regarded as examples of factionalism'.

examples to warn the Corinthians not to disobey the servants of God.[21] Without denying the plausibility of these hypotheses, the wider context in which these four examples are placed should also be noted.

In 1 Corinthians 10:14, Paul concludes the discussion of verses 1–13 with this exhortation: 'Therefore, my dear friends, flee from idolatry.' This conclusion clarifies the point of the previous discussion. The lesson that the Corinthians were to learn from the wilderness experience of Israel was to be faithful to the one and true God who delivered her from slavery in Egypt.[22] This focus on idolatry is recognized by many,[23] but the relationship between idolatry and the four examples requires further elaboration. If idolatry is to be defined as the failure to worship the true God, the other three examples can also be understood within this broader category. The reference to sexual immorality in Numbers 25 is explicitly linked to idolatry (vv. 2–3).[24] In the third example, Israel's distrust of their deliverer is yet another example of idolatry. The same can be said of the fourth example concerning the murmuring of God's people. The lack of clear reference to any one event may be deliberate as murmuring characterizes Israel's response to God's mighty acts.[25] As we have noted, both idolatry and murmuring point to Israel's failure to remember her God and his powerful deeds. Instead of giving him glory, they became the ungrateful people.

When Paul cites the four examples, he is concerned with the wider problems that lie behind the church in Corinth. In discussing the problem of idolatry, he is not simply listing yet another 'problem' of the church. Idolatry is understood as the root of the 'sins' believers are committing. Sexual immorality, division within the church,

[21] See, for example, Fee 1987: 457–458.

[22] Levenson (1989: 30–36) has made it clear that the exodus event signifies not 'liberation' but the transfer of ownership. Israel is no longer considered the slave of Pharaoh and the Egyptians. Now they are to submit to their master who is the Lord of all. See Lev. 25:55: '. . . for the Israelites belong to me as servants. They are my servants, whom I brought out of Egypt. I am the LORD your God.'

[23] The fact that only the first example is supported by an explicit quotation is also noteworthy. The least we can say is that this is a point emphasized by Paul.

[24] For the connection between idolatry and sexual immorality in the Old Testament discussion of the ingratitude of God's people, see also Ezek. 16:17: 'You also took the fine jewellery I gave you, the jewellery made of my gold and silver, and you made for yourself male idols and engaged in prostitution with them.'

[25] This may explain the repetition that one finds when the grumbling of Israel is mentioned twice. If this explanation is acceptable, the destruction by the angel can then be understood as the result of the pattern of disobedience.

disobedience to the apostolic teachings, the misuse of freedom, and even the involvement in pagan temples all point to the failure to acknowledge God as their Lord and master. Moreover, by alluding to the murmuring traditions, this act of idolatry also points to the inability of Israel to remember what God had done for her through the death and resurrection of Christ.[26]

This interpretation that affirms the unique ties between the general reference to idolatry and that to murmuring can be supported by noting the verbs used in Paul's commands in relation to the four examples. In both the first ('do not be idolaters') and the fourth ('do not grumble'), one finds the use of the second person imperative form of the respective verbs. In the second ('we should not commit sexual immorality') and the third ('we should not test the Lord'), however, the first person subjunctive form of the verbs is used. The first and the fourth can be understood as providing the general framework within which Paul expresses specific commands relating to the behaviour of the Corinthian believers.[27] Again, the inclusive nature of idolatry and murmuring can be seen.

We are again reminded of Old Testament passages where we find the account of Israel's disobedience in terms of their failure to provide the proper response to God's acts of covenantal love. Psalm 106, a psalm that Paul has alluded to elsewhere in his epistles,[28] needs to be highlighted. As noted above,[29] this psalm presents the history of the faithless Israel in terms of idolatry and constant murmuring. As in 1 Corinthians 10, this recounting of history serves as a reminder of the sins of the contemporary generation.[30] More importantly, examples Paul uses resemble those listed in Psalm 106. In this psalm, the golden calf incident is noted in verses 19–23 and the Baal Peor incident in verses 28–31. The murmuring of Israel is noted in various

---

[26] Immediately following 1 Cor. 10, one finds a discussion of the remembrance of Christ's death (1 Cor. 11; cf. 10:16) and the significance of Christ's resurrection (1 Cor. 15). One should not assume that Paul is simply discussing the various topics without any framework to provide structure to the flow of his argument.

[27] S. Porter (1989: 329–330) has noted the importance of this shift of moods. He points out how the use of the present subjunctive lays emphasis on the specific commands Paul is giving in this epistle that tackles various issues of 'morality'.

[28] The use of Ps. 106 will be discussed in our examination of Rom. 1 in the next section.

[29] See a discussion of this psalm in the previous section.

[30] Ps. 106:6:

We have sinned, even as our fathers did;
we have done wrong and acted wickedly.

sections of this psalm. In verse 14, it is noted that 'in the wasteland they put God to the test'.[31] Furthermore, both murmuring events in Numbers 14 and 16 appear in this psalm (cf. vv. 16–18, 24–27).[32]

While we are not attempting to establish a strict literary relationship between Psalm 106 and 1 Corinthians 10, the function of the events mentioned in this psalm helps us to gain a better understanding of Paul's use of the four examples. In both, idolatry and murmuring characterize the sins of the fathers, and in both, these events point to how the mighty acts of God had been forgotten. In Psalm 106, Israel 'soon forgot what he [God] had done' (v. 13). Likewise in 1 Corinthians, the acts of the believers can be understood as their forgetting what God had done through his Son Jesus Christ. The conclusion of 1 Corinthians 10:1–13 should again be noted, together with the mentioning of the cup of thanksgiving:[33]

> Therefore, my dear friends, flee from idolatry. I speak to sensible people; judge for yourselves what I say. Is not the cup of thanksgiving for which we give thanks a participation in the blood of Christ? (1 Cor. 10:14–16)

Immediately following the call to flee idolatry is a reminder that we ought to give thanks to God for what Christ did on the cross. This note to thank or bless God should not surprise us because the failure to give thanks is in and of itself idolatry.[34]

We can now begin to appreciate the point of the four examples Paul cites. Using the history of Israel, Paul is warning us not to be an ungrateful people. To be ungrateful is not simply a state of harmless absent-mindedness. It is the failure to acknowledge God as the creator and Lord of all. As such, ingratitude led to a host of sins that plagued the Corinthian church. It is this ingratitude that Paul warns us of

---

[31] In Ps. 106, this is most likely a reference back to Num. 11. The connection with 1 Cor. 10:9 can also be established through the use of the testing motif. One can argue that Paul is drawing the testing motif from Num. 11 while the reference to the snake points to Num. 25.

[32] The failure to determine the exact event behind 1 Cor. 10:10 can thus be explained by the fact that both Num. 14 and 16 play an active role in the murmuring traditions of Israel.

[33] The 'cup of thanksgiving' in the NIV is literally 'the cup of blessing'. In ch. 1 above, we have already established the close connection between blessing and acts of thanksgiving.

[34] One should, of course, note that the subject of participation in pagan feasts is in the mind of Paul. This also leads Paul to mention the participation in the meal that remembers Christ's death.

through the four examples taken from the time immediately after God's manifestation of his power and authority in the exodus event.

In light of this evocation of the history of Israel, Paul's warnings elsewhere against murmuring can also be understood. In Philippians 2:14–15, for example, one reads:

> Do everything without complaining or arguing, so that you may become blameless and pure, children of God without fault in a crooked and depraved generation, in which you shine like stars in the universe.

Old Testament allusions in this passage have long been recognized.[35] First, the phrase 'without complaining' naturally points to the Old Testament murmuring traditions.[36] The sentence that follows, 'blameless and pure, children of God without fault in a crooked and depraved generation', recalls the description of Israel in her rebellion in the wilderness in the LXX version of Deuteronomy 32:5: 'blameworthy children, a crooked and perverse generation'.[37] Furthermore, the reference to the 'stars' recalls Daniel 12:3 in the context of the eschatological vision.[38] Together with the references to the wilderness generation, this brief passage points to the journey from the wilderness into the Promised Land.

Most commentators have understood the reference to 'complaining' in the narrowest sense and therefore wonder whether the complaining is directed against God or other human beings. Based on the evidence provided in the epistle, some draw the conclusion that Paul's reference to 'complaining' should be limited to the level of interpersonal relationships.[39] One could note, however, that Israel's com-

---

[35] See, for example, the discussion in O'Brien 1991b: 290–294; and Fee 1995: 242.

[36] In the Pauline corpus, the noun *gongusmos* together with its verbal form *gonguzō* only appear in this passage and 1 Cor. 10. This word-group is frequently used in the LXX to describe the murmuring of Israel in the wilderness journey.

[37] In Phil. 2, however, the term 'children' is now applied to the believers, and the 'crooked and depraved generation' refers to the wider society in which the Christians are to serve as witnesses.

[38] Fee (1995: 242) has further pointed to the LXX where a reference to the words of God is made. This would also explain the next phrase in Phil. 2:16 where 'the word of life' is referred to.

[39] Hawthorne (1983: 101), for example, concludes: 'One should not imagine that the Christians at Philippi, like Israel in the wilderness . . . were grumbling against God or doubting his promises . . . Rather, as has been shown, the Philippians were doing things that generated both inward and outward feelings of unfriendliness toward one another.'

plaint against her leaders has also been considered as a sin against their God. More importantly, in the context of murmuring traditions, complaining should not be reduced to the level of disagreement. To murmur is to distrust God and to refuse to acknowledge his Lordship. In Philippians 2, therefore, the call not to 'complain' is a call to honour God as the true Lord and master.

This reading is supported and also nuanced by two observations. On the formal level, the parallel elsewhere in the Pauline material should first be noted. 'Do everything without complaining' finds its close parallel in Colossians 3:17: 'And whatever you do, whether in word or deed, do it all in the name of the Lord Jesus, giving thanks to God the Father through him.'[40] This verse states the prohibitive command in a positive way. Not to complain is to do all things in the name of the Lord Jesus with thanksgiving.

In its immediate context, this is also the focus of Paul's argument. Drawing on the example of Christ, believers are called to be obedient.[41] The phrase, 'fear and trembling', confirms this reading as it points to the way to live in the presence of the living God.[42] This, however, is not separated from Paul's discussion of the relationship among the Philippian believers (Phil. 2:1–4). To live in harmony is an expression of being obedient to Christ. A reference to the life of the church is, after all, an essential element in Paul's call to 'do everything without complaining', as the additional phrase, 'or arguing', indicates. Nevertheless, this call cannot be limited to this horizontal plane. We are called to live in harmony precisely because of what God has done for us through his one and only Son. Unlike the faithless Israel, we are called to be faithful people who remember God's grace in all that we do.

'They neither glorified him as God nor gave thanks to him'

We have already shown the connection between murmuring and idolatry. In this section, the explicit identification of idolatry as ingratitude

[40] For an examination of this and other related passages, see our discussion in ch. 4 above.

[41] This obedience is likely in reference to Christ and not to Paul himself (cf. 2 Cor. 10:5–6). Cf. Fee 1995: 232–233.

[42] Contra Hawthorne 1983: 99–100. In view of the saturation of Old Testament language in Phil. 2, this phrase should also be understood with the Old Testament usage in mind (e.g., Exod. 15:16). See also Col. 3:22 and our discussion in ch. 4 above.

in the Pauline epistles will be further explored. This identification will further help us in our appreciation of the Pauline emphasis on thanksgiving.

While the Pauline passages mentioned above are mainly addressed to the people of God, Paul's argument in Romans 1 aims at a wider audience:

> For although they knew God, they neither glorified him as God nor gave thanks to him, but their thinking became futile and their foolish hearts were darkened. Although they claimed to be wise, they became fools and exchanged the glory of the immortal God for images made to look like mortal man and birds and animals and reptiles. (Rom. 1:21–23)

The reference behind the third person plural pronoun 'they' has long been a subject of debate. Based on the flow of the argument, many have argued that the 'they' refers specifically to Gentiles.[43] Others, pointing to the Jewish material in Romans 1:18–32,[44] have questioned this narrow identification.[45] Incorporating the insights of these discussions, one can suggest that Romans 1:18–32 does have Gentiles as its focus, but it also serves as a general statement preparing for Paul's argument that follows.[46]

---

[43] See, for example, Fitzmyer 1993: 270; and Moo 1996: 93. Others, such as Hays (1989: 93–94), while maintaining a Gentile target, see Rom. 1 as a 'rhetorical trap' as the Jews will in turn be accused of disobeying their God (Rom. 2:1 – 3:20).

[44] These include both Hellenistic Jewish polemic against the Gentiles (e.g., Wisdom 12 – 14) and biblical material that contains accusations against Israel herself (e.g., Ps. 106).

[45] See E. P. Sanders 1983: 123–136; and Garlington 1990: 145. Others, such as Räisänen (1983: 97–109), point to the differences between Rom. 1 and 2, and question the consistency of Paul's rhetoric as it is applied to the Gentiles. A similar reading is presented by C. Porter (1994: 210–228) who notices the apparent tension but he does not conclude that Paul is inconsistent. According to Porter, 'Rom 1.18–32 is a self-contained discourse similar to that used in Hellenistic Judaism in order to establish, maintain and strengthen a well-defined boundary and distance between the Jewish community and the Gentiles' (215). In Rom. 2, however, Paul 'refutes both the content of the discourse and the practice of using such discourses' (215). In light the use of similar language, themes and source text elsewhere in the Pauline corpus, this reading of Rom. 1 requires further support. Furthermore, the apparent tension can be partly explained if Rom. 1 is understood as a general statement from which the remaining argument flows.

[46] Seifrid (2000: 50) has, for example, suggested that the issue is not ethnicity but idolatry in general. He also notes that the strict distinction between Jews and Gentiles is precisely the point that Paul is arguing against in his epistle to the Romans.

What is beyond dispute is the point of this passage that is placed at the beginning of Paul's epistle to the Romans. The fact that human beings fail to give glory to God is linked with their failure to give him thanks.[47] This is based on the portrayal of God as a beneficent God who has revealed himself in more than one way.[48] What immediately follows contains an allusion to idolatry. The word 'futile' is often used in the LXX in reference to idolatry.[49] Explicit reference to idols appears in verse 23. In this verse, we once again find an allusion to Psalm 106, a psalm that we have discussed in connection with 1 Corinthians 10:

> At Horeb they made a calf
> and worshipped an idol cast from metal.
> They exchanged their Glory
> for an image of a bull, which eats grass.
> They forgot the God who saved them,
> who had done great things in Egypt,
> miracles in the land of Ham
> and awesome deeds by the Red Sea.
>
> (Ps. 106:19–22)

In a number of ways, these few verses provide the context for Paul's argument in Romans 1:18–32. First, in both passages, the failure to give glory and offer thanksgiving to God amounts to idolatry. In Romans 1, however, a specific example of rebellion from Israel's past becomes illustrative of human sinfulness. Second, Israel's forgetting in Psalm 106 corresponds to the failure to give thanks in Romans 1:21. In Psalm 106, that which is forgotten is God's deliverance of his people from Egypt. In Romans 1, in this general statement of human sinfulness, the climax of salvation history is not explicitly noted. The inclusive emphasis leads, however, to the reference to God's creative

[47] The shift in tenses is noteworthy as Paul points to the universal condition of those who fail to worship God. The aorist is here used to express general truth. See S. Porter 1989: 234–236.

[48] Blessings given freely by the beneficent God are well described in Rom. 3:21–24 where sinful human beings are in turn 'justified freely by his grace through the redemption that came by Christ Jesus' (v. 24). For a further discussion of the Pauline understanding of the beneficent God, see Danker 1988: 84–94.

[49] Moo (1996: 107) points to 2 Sam. 17:15 and Jer. 2:5; 51:17, but cautions that the word is not used in Paul elsewhere in reference to idolatry. 1 Chr. 21:8 should also be included in this list as it is used in reference to sinning against God. In the New Testament, also worth noting is Acts 14:15 where a related form is clearly used to refer to idols (cf. Eph. 4:17).

act in verse 25 where all are accused of worshipping and serving 'created things rather than the Creator'.[50]

Moreover, as in Psalm 106, one can suggest that references to sexual immorality in Romans 1:24, 26–27 are expressions of ingratitude (cf. Ps. 106:28, 39). This leads us back to 1 Corinthians 1:6–10 where one finds the same conglomeration of events: idolatry, sexual immorality and ingratitude/murmuring. In Romans 1, however, Paul does not make explicit references to the specifics of Israel's wilderness experience when he directs his accusations against all humanity.

When the general condition of human sinfulness is defined in terms of idolatry and ingratitude,[51] our discussion on ingratitude can be infinitely expanded to include all the individual sins mentioned in the Pauline corpus. At the root of all these is the refusal to trust God and give him the glory and honour that he alone deserves. In his discussion of Romans 1:21–23, Martin Luther (1959: 26) is correct, then, to suggest that ingratitude is the root of all evil.[52]

'Lovers of themselves'

In Romans 1, ingratitude is defined as the failure to acknowledge God and worship him as the creator of all. The refusal to worship God is to remove him from the centre of one's heart and mind. This is well illustrated by the vice list in 2 Timothy 3:

> But mark this: There will be terrible times in the last days. People will be lovers of themselves, lovers of money, boastful, proud, abusive, disobedient to their parents, ungrateful, unholy . . . lovers of pleasure rather than lovers of God. (vv. 1–2, 4)

---

[50] Hays (1989: 211 n.26) notes the allusion to Gen. 1:26: 'The effect is complex and ironic: God created human beings for "dominion" over these creatures, but fallen human idolaters now bow before the likenesses of animals.'

[51] The all-embracing nature of Paul's statement in verse 21 is illustrated by the threefold reference to God giving them over to sinful desires (v. 24), shameful lusts (v. 26), and a depraved mind (v. 28). Within the third category, Paul also provides a list of vices (29–31). It is with this understanding that Irenaeus, alluding to Rom. 1:25, accuses the 'heretics' of deviating from the truth and 'thus proving themselves ungrateful to Him that created them' (*Adversus haereses*. 1.22 [*ANF* 1:347]).

[52] To highlight this point, Luther (1959: 25) also suggests that 'Lucifer before the Fall was ungrateful to his Creator.'

In this passage, ingratitude appears as one of the vices in this long list that characterizes the end times. Some have attempted to search for the source of this vice catalogue[53] while others have tried to discern the pattern that structures the list.[54] To appreciate the significance of the inclusion of 'ingratitude' in this list, that which frames the list has to be highlighted.

The list begins with the description, 'lovers of themselves' (v. 2), and ends with 'lovers of pleasure rather than lovers of God' (v. 4). The phrase, 'lovers of themselves', provides the essential definition of what it meant to live a life without God. The 'lovers of themselves' are not simply those who possess the will to act in their own way. In its immediate context, the opponents of the gospel are described as those who are in 'the trap of the devil' (2 Tim. 2:26).[55] For Paul, to turn away from God is at the same time to turn to the devil (cf. 1 Thess. 1:9). To be 'lovers of themselves' is therefore to allow oneself to conduct one's living under the control of the evil one. It is precisely in this context that one finds ingratitude mentioned. The failure to offer thanks to the one Lord of all is to follow the one who opposes him.

The implicit call for the believers is to be 'lovers of God'. This recalls the central commandment in the covenantal relationship: 'Hear, O Israel: The LORD our God, the LORD is one. Love the LORD your God with all your heart and with all your soul and with all your strength' (Deut. 6:4–5).[56] Understood in covenantal terms, to love God is to be faithful to him and him alone. Martin Luther (1959: 27) is again correct in noting that only when God's gracious acts are remembered can the love of God be nurtured in a life of worship:

> Gratitude, however, keeps the love for God and thus holds the heart directed toward him. Because it is thereby also illumined, it worships, once it is illumined, only the true God, and to this worship there soon attaches itself the whole chorus of virtues.

---

[53] See, in particular, the discussion in Easton 1932: 10–11; and McEleney 1974: 212–213. See also Furnish (1968: 84–89), who emphasizes the role of the hand of Paul in the structuring of these lists.

[54] See the discussion in Knight 1992: 430–432; and Mounce 2000: 543.

[55] The next phrase, 'who has taken them captive to do his will', is unclear because of the use of a different pronoun. Some have taken the phrase to refer to Satan's will, while others argue that it points to the future when the opponents may follow the will of God. See Knight 1992: 426–427.

[56] Mounce (2000: 547) further notes the use of Deut. 6:4–5 in 1 Tim. 2:5.

With this note this study finds its appropriate conclusion. The Pauline call to thanksgiving centres on the submission of one's will in the presence of the Lord of all. We are called to remember the cross and the resurrection. We are called to submit to Christ's Lordship in our present living. We are called to be faithful till his return. In short, to offer thanks to God is to live a life of worship.

> Almighty God, Father of all mercies,
> we thine unworthy servants,
> do give thee most humble and hearty thanks
> for all thy goodness and loving-kindness to us, and to all men.

> We bless thee for our creation, preservation,
> and all the blessings of this life;
> but above all for thine inestimable love
> in the redemption of the world by our Lord Jesus Christ;
> for the means of grace, and for the hope of glory.

> And, we beseech thee, give us that due sense of all thy mercies,
> that our hearts may be unfeignedly thankful;
> And that we show forth thy praise,
> not only with our lips, but in our lives,
> by giving up our selves to thy service,
> and by walking before thee
> in holiness and righteousness all our days;
> through Jesus Christ our Lord,
> to whom, with thee and the Holy Spirit,
> be all honor and glory, world without end.

> Amen.
> (Standard Book of Common Prayer)[57]

---

[57] This prayer is taken from the edition of Guilbert 1971: 251.

Appendix

Pauline thanksgiving and the Greco-Roman benefaction system

In this study, we have discussed how Paul draws on the Old Testament covenantal traditions in his persistent call to offer thanks to God whose faithfulness cannot be doubted. In any act of interpretation, the world of the audience also plays an important role. Since the Pauline emphasis on thanksgiving was received by communities situated in the Greco-Roman world, the wider structure that governed reciprocal relationships should also be noted.

The Greco-Roman patron-client network

In the most general terms, Greco-Roman society was structured in a way where hierarchical relationships that cut across layers of society provided the instrument through which social identities and roles were constructed. This set of relationships also provided the glue that maintained the stability of the society. Benefits were transferred with the expectation of an appropriate return from those who rely on these 'gifts'.

In examining the structure of reciprocal relationships within the context of the first century Mediterranean world, one should not assume the existence of an abstract and rigid system where certain interactions could be regulated throughout the entire Roman empire. It is common to distinguish between the classical Greek benefactor-beneficiary system and the Roman patron-client system. While in broad historical terms this distinction may be useful, one cannot maintain a strict distinction when one comes to the situation in the Hellenistic cities during the early imperial period.[1] More importantly,

---

[1] It is justifiable to assume that the majority of the Pauline epistles originated from a Hellenistic setting and are addressed to Greek-speaking audiences living in Hellenistic cities. Even the epistle to the Romans can be situated in this context. See, for example, Hendrix (1991: 40–43) who speaks of the 'mutual domestication of the

165

the distinction between 'Greek' and 'Roman' forms of networking is also questionable as the unique elements can be explained by the inherent differences in political structure and historical circumstances. These differences, therefore, may not point to the existence of two independent traditions of social interaction.[2] While one does not wish to reduce the two into a uniform system,[3] for our discussion, we can limit ourselves to the common elements between the two, especially in view of the way 'gratitude' functions at the centre of both traditions.[4]

At the heart of the patron-client network is the understanding of reciprocity as the foundation of social and political relationships. The provision of benefits creates the need for recipients to respond with appropriate acts. Through such acts, the relative status of both the superior party and the inferior party is affirmed and consolidated. This network is understood to form the basis of society.[5] Beyond social interaction, patron-client reciprocity governs various types of relationship. Rulers were understood as benefactors,[6] and reciprocity is considered as the basis of the political machine.[7] Moreover, this principle of reciprocity provides the framework within which historians were able to make sense out of chains of isolated events.[8] As one

---

Greek benefactor-beneficiary phenomenon and Roman patron-client relationship'. Blok (1969: 365–378) also suggests that the two 'systems' are but two forms of the same wider social phenomenon in the Greco-Roman world.

[2] See, in particular, the discussion in Millett 1989: 15–48.

[3] A careful delineation of the differences between the two in terms of form and substance can be found in the recent work of Joubert 2000: 59–68.

[4] In the remainder of this section, we shall use the phrase 'patron-client' in reference to the common emphases of both systems.

[5] Seneca, for example, writes: 'The giving of a benefit is a social act, it wins the goodwill of someone, it lays someone under obligation' (*De Beneficiis* 5.11.5; cf. 1.4.1–6). In this appendix, all quotations from Seneca *De Beneficiis* are taken from the LCL edition (1934).

[6] Bringmann (1993: 7–24) shows that Hellenistic rulers were often considered to be benefactors. In tracing this understanding back to the Classical period, he further claims that 'benefactions are the origin of monarchy' (7).

[7] See, for example, Philo, *Praem* 97 (Colson and Whitaker, LCL): 'For the conduct of their rulers shows three high qualities which contribute to make a government secure from subversion, namely dignity, strictness, benevolence, which produce the feelings mentioned above. For respect is created by dignity, fear by strictness, affection by benevolence, and these when blended harmoniously in the soul render subjects obedient to their rulers.' This, according to Mott (1971: 92), forms the basis for the ruler cult in the Greek East.

[8] Gould (1989: 65), for example, points to the importance of this framework in the writings of Herodotus: 'The obligations of gratitude and revenge are the fundamental human motives for Herodotus just as . . . they are the primary stimulus to the generation of narrative itself.'

APPENDIX

moves from the Hellenistic period through the early imperial period, one finds the similar pervasive presence of this network that continues to provide structure for social relationships in provinces as well as in individual cities.[9]

In the Greco-Roman world, the divine-human relationship is also portrayed within this patron-client framework. This is clearly illustrated in the writings of the Stoic philosopher Seneca where the gods are understood as the benefactors above all benefactors, from whom blessings and material benefits flow. In a statement introduced by a rhetorical question, one reads:

> If a man denies that he has received from the gods the gift of life that he begs from them every day, to whom will he be indebted for his preservation, to whom for the breath that he draws? Whoever, therefore, teaches men to be grateful, pleads the cause both of men and of the gods, to whom, although there is no thing that they have need of since they have been placed beyond all desire, we can nevertheless offer our gratitude. (*De Beneficiis* 2.30.1)[10]

This framework is picked up by, among others, Josephus who expresses the relationship between the God of Israel and his people in terms of the patron-client relationship. God is described as the benefactor who freely blesses his people with gifts and blessings. Likewise, human beings are expected to respond appropriately within this contractual relationship. Covenantal language seems to have been replaced by patron-client language as Josephus expresses the history of the relationship between Israel and her God.[11]

---

[9] In his study of the conception of the relationship between Rome and her neighbours within the framework of the patron-client network, Badian (1958: 1) begins with this statement: 'The relation of patron and client is one of the most characteristic features of Roman life lasting, in some form, from the origins to the downfall of the city and beyond.' See also the detailed discussion in Saller 1982.

[10] The understanding of deities as benefactors can be found throughout the development of the Greco-Roman patronage system. Danker and Jewett (1990: 487) have pointed to Xenophon's *Memorabilia Socratis* (4.3) in which the gifts deities bestowed are listed. Furthermore, to serve as benefactors of humanity is considered as the primary task of deities. The establishment of the cult is therefore to ensure the continuation of this flow of material benefits.

[11] See, in particular, Josephus' treatment of the law in *Antiquitates judaicae* 4.199–308 and the recent discussion in Spilsbury 1998: 172–191.

Gratitude in the patron-client relationship

For our discussion, we need to focus on one side of the reciprocal relationship. When gifts or benefits are received,[12] an 'appropriate' response is expected. Because of the differences in status as well as economic means, what is expected of the recipients is not the mere return of favours received. This expectation is frequently described as the obligation of gratitude. In the words of Seneca, '[t]he person who intends to be grateful, immediately, while he is receiving, should turn his thought to repaying' (*De Beneficiis* 2.25.3). While the recipients are not in the position to repay the benefactor with material gifts, they are expected to offer honour to the their benefactor:

> The greater the favour, the more earnestly must we express ourselves, resorting to such compliment as . . . 'you do not know what it is that you have bestowed upon me, but you have a right to know how much more it is than you think' . . . 'I shall never be able to repay to you my gratitude, but, at any rate, I shall not cease from declaring everywhere that I am unable to repay it.' (*De Beneficiis* 2.24.4)

In the maintenance of the reciprocal relationship, the public honouring of the patron supports his or her standing in society and it also defines the power relationship between the patron and those within the same social class. In the context of the Greco-Roman world, this aspect of the patron-client relationship also reflects the importance of honour and shame as socio-political categories.[13]

In the relationship between deities and human beings, gratitude is also the expected response for the benefits received. The fact that divine beings do not need anything is well recognized, and gratitude in the form of honour is considered as the needed response. Josephus himself provides a clear statement regarding this relationship:

---

[12] In the Greco-Roman patron-client network, gifts can take a variety of forms. It ranges from material benefits to opportunities that the benefactors may offer.

[13] Malina and Neyrey (1991: 26) provide a helpful statement on the function of honour in ancient society: 'Honor . . . serves as a register of social rating which entitles a person to interact in specific ways with equals, superiors, and subordinates, according to the prescribed cultural cues of the society.' For the significance of this context in the interpretation of New Testament texts, see DeSilva 2000a: 23–93.

Not by deeds is it possible for men to return thanks to God for the benefits they have received, for the Deity stands in need of nothing and is above any such recompense. But with that [gift of speech], O Lord, through which we have been made by Thee superior to other creatures, we cannot but praise Thy greatness and give thanks for Thy kindnesses to our house and the Hebrew people. (*Antiquitates judaicae* 8.111 [Thackeray and Marcus, LCL])[14]

Sacrifice should also be considered in light of this reciprocal relationship. Parker's (1998: 105) statement concerning Greek religious practices applies also in Roman cult: 'Almost the whole of Greek cultic practice is in fact founded – not merely by implication, but through numerous explicit statements – on the belief or hope that reciprocity of this kind is a reality.'[15] Thanksgiving becomes a way to repay the deities with the anticipation of further acts of grace.[16]

As gratitude is expected in the patron-client relationship, ingratitude is widely regarded as a shameful vice:

. . . ingratitude is something to be avoided in itself because there is nothing that so effectually disrupts and destroys the harmony of the human race as this vice. For how else do we live in security if it is not that we help each other by an exchange of good offices? It is only through the interchange of benefits that life becomes in some measure equipped and fortified against sudden disasters. (*De Beneficiis* 4.18.1–2)[17]

Ingratitude does not simply reflect on the personal moral life of an individual, it is understood to affect the fundamental existence of society. Various reasons have been provided to explain one's failure to express gratitude, among them the failure to understand one's

[14] Cf. *De Beneficiis* 2.30.2. See also the discussion in Spilsbury 1998: 183.

[15] See also the treatment in Bremer 1998: 127–137.

[16] Mott (1971: 78) points to the explicit statement in Philo: 'For either he is giving thanks for benefits already received or is asking for security in his tenure of present blessings or for acquisition of others to come, or for deliverance from evils, either present or expected' (*De Specialibus Legibus* 1.283 [Colson and Whitaker, LCL]).

[17] In *De Beneficiis* 1.10.4, ingratitude is regarded as the worse of all vices: 'Homicides, tyrants, thieves, adulterers, robbers, sacrilegious men, and traitors there always will be; but worse than all these is the crime of ingratitude, unless it be that all these spring from ingratitude, without which hardly any sin has grown to great size' (cf. 3.1.1).

place in relation to both one's patron and one's peer (*De Beneficiis* 2.26–29). In a system that defines a person through his or her relation with the external world, the issue of gratitude and ingratitude becomes one that transcends personal morality. It is in this way that one finds the subject of gratitude an important one in the Greco-Roman world.

Pauline thanksgiving and the patronage model

The Pauline emphasis on thanksgiving naturally reminds one of the importance of gratitude in the patron-client system. The exact relationship between the two, however, is difficult to determine. On the side of the receptors of the Pauline message, one can probably assume the likelihood of the incorporation of Paul's language into the pervasive patronage system in the early imperial period.[18] Some have further pointed to the parallelism between Paul's thought and Stoicism in particular,[19] especially with Seneca who had written extensively on the patronage network.[20] More relevant for our discussion is the fact that God is indeed portrayed as the benefactor in the Pauline epistles,[21] although the use of the benefactor language is not limited to the Greco-Roman patronage system. These similarities and possible conceptual connections do make it probable that the Pauline language of thanksgiving had been understood within the context of the patronage system.

To suggest that Paul's language is intelligible in the Greco-Roman context of patronage should not, however, be construed to mean that the Pauline call to thanksgiving should primarily be understood within this thought-world. Forms of benefaction and reciprocal relationship are not limited to the Greco-Roman world. The bestowal of gifts and the expectation of some form of response can be found in any culture.[22] In the Old Testament itself, one already finds an independent

---

[18] This is the one of the main arguments used to establish the contact between New Testament authors and the wider Greco-Roman world (e.g., Moxnes 1991: 241–268; DeSilva 1996: 91–116). As we shall see, the limitation of this line of argument should be noted. More importantly, the distinction between what is embedded in the text and how the text is received has to be made.

[19] The most recent example comes from the extensive treatment of Engberg-Pedersen (2000) who suggests that 'there is a single, basic thought structure that is formulated in both Stoic ethics and in Paul' (31).

[20] See the earlier statement in Lightfoot 1956: 270–328 and the discussion in Sevenster 1961. Passages that are frequently mentioned in this regard are Rom. 1 – 2, Acts 7, and the entire epistle to the Philippians.

[21] See Danker 1988: 84–94 and Danker and Jewett 1990: 486–498.

[22] See Gouldner 1960: 171.

form of a blessing-thanksgiving system.[23] Noting Paul's familiarity with the Old Testament, this obvious source cannot be ignored.

As we have discussed in this study, the Pauline call to thanksgiving is linked to a number of themes. These include a call to remember, anti-idol polemic, and an eschatological orientation that is tied to the promises of God. These are covenantal themes that find no parallel in the Greco-Roman context. Furthermore, the basic temporal framework within which the past, the present and the future are evoked in the call to thanksgiving points directly back to Old Testament covenantal traditions. Behind this temporal framework is the affirmation that the God of Israel is one who is active in the history of his people. Even when deities are understood as benefactors in the Greco-Roman patronage system, this affirmation of a personal, sovereign and active God who cares for his own people is missing.

Related to these themes is the striking lack of ethical focus in the Greco-Roman patronage system. The individual life and personal behaviour of the client is not a concern of the benefactor as long as the client is able to fulfil his duty in providing an adequate return for the benefits received. Moreover, the concern of the God of Israel in his attempt to establish a lasting relationship with his people also moves beyond the realm of the patronage system. This relationship is guarded by specific boundaries with the intended result of the creation of a community that is defined by its relationship with its creator and deliverer. This ethical focus in terms of God-centredness in the Pauline call to thanksgiving, together with the emphasis on the identity of the people of God, is again best understood within a covenantal context.[24]

More importantly, the principle of 'reciprocity' that forms the foundation of the Greco-Roman patronage system is inadequate when one comes to the heart of the Old Testament and Pauline messages. The *ḥeseḏ* of the Old Testament and the grace of the Pauline gospel point to the break down of this assumption of reciprocity. Both *ḥeseḏ* and graciousness are attributes of God that emanate from

---

[23] For a discussion of both the Old Testament and the Hellenistic Jewish benefit exchange systems, see Joubert 2000: 93–99.

[24] We are not attempting to deny the importance of ethics in Stoicism that is tied indirectly to the patronage system. The difference between the basis of Pauline ethics and that of Stoicism needs to be highlighted. Instead of a set of abstract rules, Pauline ethics is based on the person of Christ. Sevenster (1961: 106) is correct in noting that 'in Paul there is no place for an autonomous set of ethical principles, and that he does not take the individual human being as his point of departure but always sees him involved in some way or other in the entire salvation-occurrence'.

his very being. The appropriate human response is above all worship. To label the life of worship as merely a 'return' is insufficient at best.[25] Finally, the construction of social reality in terms of the rigid class distinction in the Greco-Roman patronage system is also contrary to the basis of Paul's understanding of ecclesiological structure and the way the church is supposed to interact with the wider culture. Bruce Winter (1994), for example, has shown how Paul encourages the church to transcend the elitist ethos of the benefaction system by having believers function as benefactors to those in need even though their own social identity may not encourage such behaviour.[26] In Paul's emphasis on thanksgiving that is directed solely to God as the one Lord of all, one can also point to the failure of Greco-Roman conceptions of interpersonal relationships in articulating the vision that is introduced by the proclamation of the gospel message.

Since the Pauline epistles are saturated with Old Testament quotations, allusions and imageries, the Scripture of Israel is to take priority in any search for an appropriate framework of interpretation. In addition, the numerous references to the 'covenants' and the emphasis on covenantal institutions provide the reader with sufficient clues to locate Paul's call to thanksgiving within a particular theological context.[27]

[25] This also touches on the point of human merit or the lack thereof. As Danker (1988: 91) has noted, within the patronage system, it is the return of the client that would secure the continuous flow of benefits. In Paul, however, the emphasis is precisely on the inability of human beings to secure benefits from God since God alone is the source of goodness. A comparison with imperial benefaction may be helpful at this point as the initiative of the client is often the reason why the emperor is willing to grant specific favours to individuals according to a particularistic criterion. For a further discussion, see Saller 1982: 33.

[26] In his more recent work on 1 Corinthians, B. Winter (2001: 184–205) has further pointed to the 'detrimental effect' of the patronage system on the Christian community and how Paul is attempting to move beyond the cultural and social norms of the wider world. In this context, one finds an intense effort on the part of Paul as he anticipates ways his gospel could have impacted the thought-structure of its receptors.

[27] In support of this point, one can compare the Pauline epistles with the work of Josephus. In Josephus, explicit reference to Old Testament covenants is missing. Instead, one finds the prominence of the patron-client model in describing Israel's relationship with her God. Some (e.g., Attridge 1976) have concluded that Josephus had replaced the covenantal paradigm with one supplied by the Greco-Roman world. Others (e.g., Spilsbury 1998: 172–191) have suggested that Josephus is simply expressing covenantal ideas through the language of patron-client system. Without attempting to settle the debate, it is sufficient to note that in Josephus we do have a sample of Jewish writings clothed with Greco-Roman cultural symbols. This shows that if the patron-client system were the primary model for Paul in the formulation and expression of his thoughts, it would look very different from what we now find in his writings. When one moves beyond Paul to the early church fathers, the language of Josephus reappears. For a further discussion, see Danker 1988: 84–94.

In conclusion, while we are prepared to acknowledge the formal similarities between Paul's call to thanksgiving and the emphasis on gratitude in the Greco-Roman patronage system, notable differences must not be ignored. In light of the significance of Scripture in diaspora communities, one should assume that the readers might also have been able to read the New Testament in light of God's wider plan of salvation.

Bibliography

Allen, L. C. (1983), *Psalms 101 – 150*, WBC, Waco, TX: Word.

Amato, J. A., II (1982), *Guilt and Gratitude: A Study of the Origins of Contemporary Conscience*, Contributions in Philosophy 20, Westport, CT: Greenwood.

Anderson, G. W. (1963), 'Israel's Creed: Sung, not Signed', *SJT* 16: 277–285.

Anderson, H. (1964), *Jesus and Christian Origins*, New York: Oxford University Press.

Apostolic Fathers (1912), (trans. K. Lake), LCL, Cambridge, MA: Harvard University Press.

Arzt, P. (1994), 'The "Epistolary Introductory Thanksgiving" in the Papyri and in Paul', *NovT* 36: 29–46.

Attridge, H. W. (1976), *The Interpretation of Biblical History in the Antiquitates Judaicae of Flavius Josephus*, HDR 7, Missoula, MT: Scholars Press.

Audet, J. P. (1959), 'Literary Forms and Contents of a Normal Εὐχαριστία in the First Century', in *Studia Evangelica*, 643–662, Berlin: Akademie-Verlag.

Auerbach, E. (1953), *Mimesis: The Representation of Reality in Western Literature* (trans. W. R. Trask), Princeton, NJ: Princeton University Press.

Aune, D. E. (1998), *Revelation 6 – 16*, WBC 52B, Nashville, TN: Thomas Nelson.

Aus, R. D. (1973), 'The Liturgical Background of the Necessity and Propriety of Giving Thanks According to 2 Thess 1:3', *JBL* 46: 432–438.

Badian, E. (1958), *Foreign Clientelae (264–70 B.C.)*, Oxford: Clarendon.

Balch, D. L. (1981), *Let Wives be Submissive: The Domestic Code in 1 Peter*, SBLMS 26, Chico, CA: Scholars Press.

——(1988), 'Household Codes', in D. E. Aune (ed.), *Greco-Roman Literature and the New Testament*, Atlanta, GA: Scholars Press.

Baltzer, K. (1971), *The Covenant Formulary in Old Testament, Jewish, and Early Christian Writings* (trans. D. E. Green), Oxford: Basil Blackwell.

Bandstra, A. J. (1971), 'Interpretation in 1 Corinthians 10:1–11', *CTJ* 6: 5–21.

Banks, R. (1978), 'Romans 7.25a: An Eschatological Thanksgiving?', *Australian Biblical Review* 26: 34–42.

Barcley, W. B. (1999), *'Christ in You': A Study in Paul's Theology and Ethics*, Lanham, MD: University Press of America.

Barker, E. (ed.) (1958), *The Politics of Aristotle*, New York: Oxford University Press.

Barnett, P. (1997), *The Second Epistle to the Corinthians*, Grand Rapids, MI: Eerdmans.

Barr, J. (1977), 'Some Semantic Notes on the Covenant', in R. Hanhart, H. Donner and R. Smend (eds), *Beiträge zur alttestamentlichen Theologie*, 23–28, Göttingen: Vandenhoeck and Ruprecht.

Barth, K. (1957), *Church Dogmatics II.1: The Doctrine of God* (trans. T. H. L. Parker, W. B. Johnston, H. Knight and J. L. M. Haire), Edinburgh: T. & T. Clark.

Barth, M. (1974), *Ephesians*, 2 vols, AB 34, 34A, New York: Doubleday.

Barth, M. and H. Blanke (1994), *Colossians: A New Translation with Introduction and Commentary*, AB 34B, New York: Doubleday.

——(2000), *The Letter to Philemon*, ECC, Grand Rapids, MI: Eerdmans.

Bauckham, R. (ed.) (1998), *The Gospels for All Christians: Rethinking the Gospel Audiences*, Grand Rapids, MI: Eerdmans.

——(1999), *God Crucified: Monotheism and Christology in the New Testament*, Grand Rapids, MI: Eerdmans.

Bauckham, R. and T. Hart (1999), *Hope against Hope: Christian Eschatology at the Turn of the Millennium*, Grand Rapids, MI: Eerdmans.

——(2000), 'The Shape of Time', in D. Fergusson and M. Sarot (eds), *The Future as God's Gift: Explorations in Christian Eschatology*, 41–72, Edinburgh: T. & T. Clark.

Beck, N. A. (1970), 'The Last Supper as an Efficacious Symbolic Act', *JBL* 89: 192–198.

Beckwith, R. T. (1987), 'The Unity and Diversity of God's Covenant', *TynBul* 38: 93–118.

Berger, F. R. (1975), 'Gratitude', *Ethics* 85: 298–309.

Berger, K. (1974), 'Apostelbrief und apostolische Rede: zum Formular frühchristlicher Brief', *ZNW* 65: 190–231.

Best, E. (1972), *The First and Second Epistles to the Thessalonians*, HNTC, New York: Harper.

——(1987), 'Fashions in Exegesis: Ephesians 1:3', in B. P. Thompson (ed.), *Scripture: Meaning and Method*, 79–91, Hull: Hull University Press.

——(1998), *A Critical and Exegetical Commentary on Ephesians*, ICC, Edinburgh: T. & T. Clark.

Beyer, H. W. (1964), '*Εὐλογέω, κτλ*', *TDNT* 2: 754–765.

Bickermann, E. J. (1962), 'Benediction et priere', *RB* 69: 524–532.

Blair, E. P. (1961), 'An Appeal to Remembrance: The Memory Motif in Deuteronomy', *Int* 15: 41–47.

Blank, S. H. (1961), 'Some Observations Concerning Biblical Prayer', *Hebrew Union College Annual* 32: 75–90.

Blok, A. (1969), 'Variations in Patronage', *Sociologische Gids* 16: 365–378.

Bolt, P. G. (2000), 'Paul and the Evangelization of the Stoics', in P. Bolt and M. Thompson (eds), *The Gospel to the Nations*, 309–336, Downers Grove, IL: InterVarsity Press and Leicester: Apollos.

Boobyer, G. H. (1929), *'Thanksgiving' and the 'Glory of God' in Paul*, Borna-Leipzig: Universitätsverlag von Robert Noske.

Bornkamm, G. (1964), 'Lobpreis, Bekenntnis und Opfer', in W. Eltester and F. H. Kettler (eds), *Apophoreta: Festschrift Ernst Haenchen*, 46–63, Berlin: Alfred Töpelmann.

Bossman, D. M. (1995), 'Paul's Mediterranean Gospel: Faith, Hope, Love', *BTB* 25: 71–78.

Bradshaw, P. F. (1982), *Daily Prayer in the Early Church: A Study of the Origin and Early Development of the Divine Office*. New York: Oxford University Press.

Brilioth, Y. (1939), *Eucharistic Faith and Practice: Evangelical and Catholic* (trans. A. G. Herbert), New York: MacMillan.

Bremer, J.-M. (1998), 'The Reciprocity of Giving and Thanksgiving in Greek Worship', in C. Gill, N. Postlethwaite and R. Seaford (eds), *Reciprocity in Ancient Greece*, 127–137, New York: Oxford University Press.

Bringmann, K. (1993), 'The King as Benefactor: Some Remarks on Ideal Kingship in the Age of Hellenism', in E. S. Gruen, A. Bulloch, A. A. Long and A. Stewart (eds), *Images and Ideologies: Self-Definition in the Hellenistic World*, 7–24, Berkeley, CA: University of California Press.

Brown, A. R. (1995), *The Cross and Human Transformation: Paul's Apocalyptic Word in 1 Corinthians*, Minneapolis: Fortress.

Bruce, F. F. (1961), *The Epistle to the Ephesians*, London: Pickering & Inglis.

Brueggemann, W. (1972), *In Man We Trust: The Neglected Side of Biblical Faith*, Atlanta, GA: John Knox.

——(1985), 'Psalm 100', *Int* 39: 65–69.

——(1988), *Israel's Praise: Doxology against Idolatry and Ideology*. Philadelphia: Fortress.

Budd, P. J. (1984), *Numbers*, WBC, Waco, TX: Word.

Bultmann, R. (1955), *Theology of the New Testament* (trans. K. Grobel), New York: Charles Scribner's Sons.

Burkhart, J. E. (1994), 'Reshaping Table Blessings', *Int* 48: 50–60.

Burtness, J. H. (1958), 'Eschatology and Ethics in the Pauline Epistles', Th.D. Diss., Princeton Theological Seminary.

Calvert, N. L. (1993), 'Abraham and Idolatry: Paul's Comparison of Obedience to the Law with Idolatry in Galatians 4.1–10', in C. A. Evans and J. A. Sanders (eds), *Paul and the Scriptures of Israel*, 222–237, Sheffield: Sheffield Academic Press.

Cambe, M. (1963), 'La χάρις chez saint Luc', *RB* 70: 193–207.

Campbell, W. S. (1993), 'Covenant and New Covenant', in G. F. Hawthorne and R. P. Martin (eds), *Dictionary of Paul and His Letters*, 179–183, Downers Grove, IL: InterVarsity Press.

Carasik, M. A. (1996), 'Theologies of the Mind in Biblical Israel', Ph.D. Diss., Brandeis University.

Carman, J. B. (1989), 'Reflections on the Discussion: Diverse Logics and Common Themes in Thanksgiving', in J. B. Carman and F. J. Streng (eds), *Spoken and Unspoken Thanks: Some Comparative Soundings*, 155–167, Cambridge, MA: Center for the Study of World Religions.

Carman, J. B. and F. J. Streng (eds) (1989), *Spoken and Unspoken Thanks: Some Comparative Soundings*, Cambridge, MA: Center for the Study of World Religions.

Carson, D. A. (1991), *The Gospel According to John*, Grand Rapids, MI: Eerdmans.

——(1992), *A Call to Spiritual Reformation: Priorities from Paul and His Prayers*, Grand Rapids, MI: Baker.

——(1993), '"Worship the Lord Your God": The Perennial Challenge', in D. A. Carson (ed.), *Worship: Adoration and Action*, 13–18, Grand Rapids, MI: Baker.

——(2000), 'Paul's Mission and Prayer', in P. Bolt and M.

Thompson (eds), *The Gospel to the Nations*, 175–184, Downers Grove, IL: InterVarsity Press.

Carter, W. (1994), *Households and Discipleship: A Study of Matthew 19 – 20*, JSNTSup 103, Sheffield: Sheffield Academic Press.

Chapple, A. (1992), 'The Lord is Near (Philippians 4:5b)', in D. Peterson and J. Pryor (eds), *In the Fullness of Time: Biblical Studies in Honour of Archbishop Donald Robinson*, 149–165, Homebush West, Australia: Lancer.

Charlesworth, J. H. (ed.) (1985), *The Old Testament Pseudepigrapha*, 2 vols, Garden City, NY: Doubleday.

Chesnutt, R. D. (1995), *From Death to Life: Conversion in Joseph and Aseneth*, JSPSup 16, Sheffield: Sheffield Academic Press.

Childs, B. S. (1962), *Memory and Tradition in Israel*, London: SCM.

Clancy, R. A. D. (1993), 'The Old Testament Roots of Remembrance in the Lord's Supper', *Concordia Journal* 19: 35–50.

Clark, G. R. (1993), *The Word Hesed in the Hebrew Bible*, JSOTSup 157, Sheffield: Sheffield Academic Press.

Coats, G. W. (1968), *Rebellion in the Wilderness: The Murmuring Motif in the Wilderness Traditions of the Old Testament*, Nashville, TN: Abingdon.

Colish, M. L. (1992), 'Stoicism and the New Testament: An Essay in Historiography', *ANRW* II.26.1: 334–379.

Collier, G. D. (1994), 'The Structure and Argument of 1 Corinthians 10 – 13', *JSNT* 55: 55–76.

Collins, J. J. (1997), *Jewish Wisdom in the Hellenistic Age*, OTL, Louisville, KY: Westminster/John Knox.

Collins, R. F. (1998), 'The Function of Paraenesis in 1 Thess 4,1–12; 5,12–22', *ETL* 74: 398–414.

Conzelmann, H. (1975), *1 Corinthians* (trans. J. W. Leitch), Hermeneia, Philadelphia: Fortress.

Craigie, P. C. (1983), *Psalms 1 – 50*, WBC, Waco, TX: Word.

Crook, Z. A. (1997), 'Paul's Riposte and Praise of the Thessalonians', *BTB* 27: 153–163.

Crouch, J. E. (1972), *The Origin and Intention of the Colossian Haustafel*, Göttingen: Vandenhoeck and Ruprecht.

Cruz, H. (1990), *Christological Motives and Motivated Actions in Pauline Paraenesis*, Frankfurt am Main/New York: Peter Lang.

Cullen, P. J. (1995), 'Euphoria, Praise and Thanksgiving: Rejoicing in the Spirit in Luke-Acts', *JPT* 6: 13–24.

Danker, F. W. (1988), 'Bridging St. Paul and the Apostolic Fathers: A Study in Reciprocity', *CurTM* 15: 84–94.

Danker, F. W. and R. Jewett (1990), 'Jesus as the Apocalyptic Benefactor in Second Thessalonians', in R. F. Collins (ed.), *The Thessalonian Correspondence*, 486–498, Leuven: Leuven University Press.

Davies, W. D. (1948), *Paul and Rabbinic Judaism*, London: SPCK.

Davies, W. D. and D. C. Allison (1991), *The Gospel According to Saint Matthew*, vol. 2, ICC, Edinburgh: T. &. T. Clark.

Dawes, G. W. (1996), 'The Danger of Idolatry: First Corinthians 8:7–13', *CBQ* 58: 82–98.

Dawes, S. B. (1995), '"Bless the Lord": An Invitation to Affirm the Living God', *ExpTim* 106: 293–296.

De Vaux, R. (1961), *Ancient Israel: Its Life and Institutions* (trans. J. McHugh), London: Darton, Longman & Todd.

De Vries, S. J. (1968), 'The Origin of the Murmuring Tradition', *JBL* 87: 51–58.

Deeley, M. K. (1989), 'The Rhetoric of Memory: A Study of the Persuasive Function of the Memory Commands in Deuteronomy 5 – 26', Ph.D. Diss., Northwestern University.

Deidun, T. J. (1981), *New Covenant Morality in Paul*, AnBib 89, Rome: Biblical Institute Press.

Derrett, J. D. M. (1995), 'Gratitude and the Ten Lepers', *DRev* 113: 79–95.

DeSilva, D. A. (1996), 'Exchanging Favor for Wrath: Apostasy in Hebrews and Patron-Client Relationships', *JBL* 115: 91–116.

——(2000a), *Honor, Patronage, Kinship and Purity: Unlocking New Testament Culture*, Downers Grove, IL: InterVarsity Press.

——(2000b), *Perseverance in Gratitude: A Socio-Rhetorical Commentary on the Epistle 'to the Hebrews'*, Grand Rapids, MI: Eerdmans.

Dibelius, M. (1953), *An die Kolosser, Epheser an Philemon*, HNT 12, Tübingen: Mohr.

Dippenaar, M. C. (1994), 'Prayer and Epistolarity: The Function of Prayer in the Pauline Letter Structure', *Taiwan Journal of Theology* 16: 147–188.

Dumbrell, W. J. (1997), *Covenant and Creation: A Theology of the Old Testament Covenants*, Carlisle: Paternoster.

Dunn, J. D. G. (1988), *Romans*, vol. 38ab, Dallas, TX: Word.

——(1996), *The Epistles to the Colossians and to Philemon*, NIGTC, Grand Rapids, MI: Eerdmans.

——(1998), *The Theology of Paul the Apostle*. Grand Rapids, MI: Eerdmans.

Duquoc, C. and C. Florestan (1990), *Asking and Thanking*, Philadelphia: Trinity Press International.

Easton, B. S. (1932), 'New Testament Ethical Lists', *JBL* 51: 1–12.

Elliott, M. A. (2000), *The Survivors of Israel: A Reconsideration of the Theology of Pre-Christian Judaism*, Grand Rapids, MI: Eerdmans.

Engberg-Pedersen, T. (2000), *Paul and the Stoics*, Louisville, KY: Westminster/John Knox.

Enslin, M. S. (1957), *The Ethics of Paul*, Nashville, TN: Abingdon.

Faley, R. J. (1997), *Bonding with God: A Reflective Study of Biblical Covenant*, New York: Paulist.

Farrow, D. (1999), *Ascension and Ecclesia: On the Significance of the Doctrine of the Ascension for Ecclesiology and Christian Cosmology*, Grand Rapids, MI: Eerdmans.

——(2000), 'Eucharist, Eschatology and Ethics', in D. Fergusson and M. Sarot (eds), *The Future as God's Gift: Explorations in Christian Eschatology*, 199–215, Edinburgh: T. & T. Clark.

Faur, J. (1978), 'The Biblical Idea of Idolatry', *JQR* 69: 1–15.

Fee, G. D. (1980), '$Εἰδωλόθυτα$ Once Again: 1 Corinthians 8 – 10', *Bib* 61: 172–191.

——(1987), *The First Epistle to the Corinthians*, NICNT, Grand Rapids, MI: Eerdmans.

——(1994), *God's Empowering Presence: The Holy Spirit in the Letters of Paul*, Peabody, MA: Hendrickson.

——(1995), *Paul's Letter to the Philippians*, NICNT, Grand Rapids, MI: Eerdmans.

Fensham, F. C. (1981), 'Neh. 9 and Pss. 105, 106, 135 and 136: Post-exilic Historical Traditions in Poetic Form', *JNSL* 9: 35–51.

Ferguson, E. (1980), 'Spiritual Sacrifice in Early Christianity and its Environment', *ANRW* 2.23.2: 1151–1189.

Fitzmyer, J. A. (1993), *Romans*, AB 33, New York: Doubleday.

Flusser, D. (1990), 'The Ten Commandments and the New Testament', in B.-Z. Segal (ed.), *The Ten Commandments in History and Tradition*, 219–246, Jerusalem: Magnes Press.

Fowl, S. E. (1990), *The Story of Christ in the Ethics of Paul: An Analysis of the Function of the Hymnic Material in the Pauline Corpus*, JSNTSup 36, Sheffield: JSOT Press.

Franzmann, J. W. (1972), 'The Early Development of the Greek Concept of Charis', Ph.D. Diss., University of Wisconsin.

Freund, R. A. (1998), 'The Decalogue in Early Judaism and

Christianity', in C. A. Evans and J. A. Sanders (eds), *The Function of Scripture in Early Jewish and Christian Tradition*, 124–141, Sheffield: Sheffield Academic Press.

Frost, S. B. (1958), 'Asseveration by Thanksgiving', *VT* 8: 380–390.

Furnish, V. P. (1968), *Theology and Ethics in Paul*, Nashville, TN: Abingdon.

——(1984), *II Corinthians*, AB 32A, New York: Doubleday.

Garlington, D. B. (1990), '*ΙΕΡΟΣΥΛΕΙΝ* and the Idolatry of Israel (Romans 2.22)', *NTS* 36: 142–151.

Gebauer, R. (1989), *Das Gebet bei Paulus: Forschungsgeschichtliche und exegetische Studien*, Giessen: Brunnen Verlag.

Georgi, D. (1992), *Remembering the Poor: The History of Paul's Collection for Jerusalem*, Nashville, TN: Abingdon.

Gerrish, B. A. (1993), *Grace and Gratitude: The Eucharistic Theology of John Calvin*, Minneapolis: Fortress.

Gese, H. (1981), *Essays on Biblical Theology* (trans. K. Crim), Minneapolis: Augsburg.

Getty, M. A. (1987), 'Paul on the Covenants and the Future of Israel', *BTB* 17: 92–99.

——(1990), 'The Imitation of Paul in the Letters to the Thessalonians', in R. Collins (ed.), *The Thessalonian Correspondence*, 277–283, Leuven: Leuven University Press.

Gnilka, J. (1980), *Der Kolosserbrief*, HTKNT 10/1, Freiburg: Herder.

Goppelt, L. (1967), 'Paul and Heilsgeschichte: Conclusions from Romans 4 and 1 Corinthians 10:1–13', *Int* 21: 315–326.

Gosnell, P. W. (1993), 'Ephesians 5:18–20 and Mealtime Propriety', *TynBul* 44: 363–371.

Gould, J. (1989), *Herodotus*, New York: St Martin's Press.

Gouldner, A. W. (1960), 'The Norm of Reciprocity: A Preliminary Statement', *American Sociological Review* 25: 161–178.

Grant, R. M. (1940), 'The Decalogue in Early Christianity', *HTR* 40: 1–17.

——(1986), *Gods and the One God*, Philadelphia: Westminster.

Grayston, K. (1990), *Dying, We Live: A New Enquiry into the Death of Christ in the New Testament*, New York: Oxford University Press.

Greenberg, M. (1983), *Biblical Prose Prayer*, Berkeley, CA: University of California Press.

Groh, J. E. (1970), 'The Qumran Meal and the Last Supper', *Concordia Theology Monthly* 41: 279–295.

Gromacki, R. (1991), 'Ephesians 1:3–14: The Blessings of Salvation', in G. T. Meadors (ed.), *New Testament Essays in Honor of Homer A. Kent, Jr*, Winona Lake, IN: BMH Books.

Groß, H. (1960), 'Zur Wurzel *zhr*', *BZ* 4: 227–237.

Guilbert, C. M. (ed.) (1971), *Services for Trial Use*, New York: Church Hymnal Corporation.

Guillet, J. (1969), 'Le langage spontané de la bénédiction dans l'Ancien Testament', *RSR* 57: 163–204.

Gustafson, J. (1981), *Ethics from a Theocentric Perspective*, vol. 1, Chicago: University of Chicago Press.

Guthrie, H. H., Jr (1981), *Theology as Thanksgiving: From Israel's Psalms to the Church's Eucharist*, New York: Seabury.

Hafemann, S. J. (1986), *Suffering and the Spirit: An Exegetical Study of II Cor. 2:14 – 3:3 within the Context of the Corinthian Correspondence*, WUNT II.19, Tübingen: Mohr Siebeck.

Hagner, D. A. (1993), *Matthew 1 – 13*, WBC, Dallas, TX: Word.

Halbertal, M. (1998), 'Coexisting with the Enemy: Jews and Pagans in the Mishnah', in G. N. Stanton and G. S. Stroumsa (eds), *Tolerance and Intolerance in Early Judaism and Christianity*, 159–172, Cambridge: Cambridge University Press.

Hammer, R. (1991), 'Two Liturgical Psalms: Salvation and Thanksgiving', *Judaism* 40: 484–497.

Hanson, A. T. (1968), *Studies in the Pastoral Epistles*, London: SPCK.

——(1987), *The Paradox of the Cross in the Thought of St. Paul*, JSNTSup 17, Sheffield: Sheffield Academic Press.

Hanson, P. D. (1982), *The Diversity of Scripture: A Theological Interpretation*, Philadelphia: Fortress.

Harder, G. (1936), *Paulus und das Gebet*, NTF 10, Gütersloh: C. Bertelsmann.

Harrelson, W. J. (1990), 'Death and Victory in 1 Corinthians 15:51–57: The Transformation of a Prophetic Theme', in C. H. Cosgrove, J. T. Carroll and E. E. Johnson (eds), *Faith and History: Essays in Honor of Paul W. Meyer*, 149–159, Atlanta, GA: Scholars Press.

Harris, M. J. (1983), *Raised Immortal: Resurrection and Immortality in the New Testament*, Grand Rapids, MI: Eerdmans.

Hartman, L. (1987), 'Code and Context: A Few Reflections on the Parenesis of Col 3:6 – 4:1', in G. F. Hawthorne (ed.), *Tradition and Interpretation in the New Testament*, 237–247, Grand Rapids, MI: Eerdmans.

——(1988), 'Some Unorthodox Thoughts on the "Household-Code Form"', in E. Frerichs, J. Neusner, P. Borgen and R. Horsley (eds),

The Social World of Formative Christianity and Judaism, 219–232, Philadelphia: Fortress.

Hattori, Y. (1993), 'Theology of Worship in the Old Testament', in D. A. Carson (ed.), *Worship: Adoration and Action*, 21–50, Grand Rapids, MI: Baker.

Hawthorne, G. F. (1983), *Philippians*, WBC, Waco, TX: Word.

Hays, R. B. (1996), *The Moral Vision of the New Testament*, New York: Harper Collins.

——(1989), *Echoes of Scripture in the Letters of Paul*, New Haven: Yale University Press.

Hendrix, H. (1991), 'Benefactor/Patron Networks in the Urban Environment: Evidence from Thessalonica', *Semeia* 56: 39–58.

Holladay, W. L. (1995), *Long Ago God Spoke: How Christians May Hear the Old Testament Today*, Minneapolis: Fortress.

Holleman, J. (1996), 'Jesus' Resurrection as the Beginning of the Eschatological Resurrection (1 Cor 15,20)', in R. Bieringer (ed.), *The Corinthian Correspondence*, 653–660, Leuven: Leuven University Press.

Hooker, M. D. (1985), 'Interchange in Christ and Ethics', *JSNT* 25: 3–17.

Hort, F. J. A., and J. O. F. Murray (1902), 'Εὐχαριστία – Εὐχαριστεῖν', *JTS* 3: 594–598.

Hugenberger, G. P. (1995), 'The Servant of the Lord in the "Servant Songs" of Isaiah: A Second Moses Figure', in R. S. Hess, P. E. Satterthwaite and G. J. Wenham (eds), *The Lord's Anointed*, 105–140, Carlisle: Paternoster.

Hyde, C. (1988), 'The Remembrance of the Exodus in the Psalms', *Worship* 62: 404–414.

Hyde, L. (1983), *The Gift: Imagination and the Erotic Life of Property*, New York: Random.

Jefford, C. N. (1989), *The Sayings of Jesus in the Teaching of the Twelve Apostles*, Leiden: E. J. Brill.

Jeremias, J. (1966), *The Eucharistic Words of Jesus*, Philadelphia: Fortress.

Jewett, R. (1969), 'The Form and Function of the Homiletic Benediction', *ATR* 51: 18–34.

——(1970), 'The Epistolary Thanksgiving and the Integrity of Philippians', *NovT* 12: 40–53.

Jones, D. (1955), 'Ἀνάμνησις in the LXX and the Interpretation of 1 Cor 11:25', *JTS* 6: 183–191.

Josephus (1934), *Jewish Antiquities Books V–VIII* (trans. H. St J.

Thackeray and R. Marcus), LCL, Cambridge, MA: Harvard University Press.

Joubert, S. (2000), *Paul as Benefactor: Reciprocity, Strategy and Theological Reflection in Paul's Collection*, WUNT II.124, Tübingen: Mohr Siebeck.

Kaiser, W. C. (1978), *Toward an Old Testament Theology*, Grand Rapids, MI: Zondervan.

Kilmartin, E. (1965), *The Eucharist in the Primitive Church*, Englewood Cliffs, NJ: Prentice-Hall.

Kilpatrick, G. D. (1983), *The Eucharist in Bible and Liturgy*, Cambridge: Cambridge University Press.

Knight, G. W., III (1992), *The Pastoral Epistles*, NIGTC, Grand Rapids, MI: Eerdmans.

Koenig, J. (1992), *Rediscovering New Testament Prayer*, New York: HarperCollins.

Koester, H. (1979), '1 Thessalonians – Experiment in Christian Writing', in E. F. Church and T. George (eds), *Continuity and Discontinuity in Church History: Essays Presented to George Huntston Williams on the Occasion of his 65th Birthday*, 33–44, Leiden: Brill.

Kruschwitz, R. B. and R. C. Roberts (eds) (1987), *The Virtues: Contemporary Essays on Moral Character*, Belmont, CA: Wadsworth.

Kuhn, K. G. (1957), 'The Lord's Supper and the Communal Meal at Qumran', in K. Stendahl (ed.), *The Scrolls and the New Testament*, 65–93, New York: Harper & Row.

Lähnemann, J. (1971), *Der Kolosserbrief: Komposition, Situation und Argumentation*, SNT 3, Gütersloh: Gütersloher Verlagshaus/Gerd Mohn.

Lambrecht, J. (1990), 'Thanksgivings in 1 Thessalonians 1 – 3', in R. F. Collins (ed.), *The Thessalonian Correspondence*, 183–205, Leuven: Leuven University Press.

——(1992), *The Wretched 'I' and Its Liberation: Paul in Romans 7 and 8*, Louvain Theological and Pastoral Monographs 14, Leuven: Peeters.

——(1994), 'The Eschatological Outlook in 2 Corinthians 4:7–15', in T. E. Schmidt and M. Silva (eds), *To Tell the Mystery: Essays on New Testament Eschatology in Honor of Robert H. Gundry*, 122–139, Sheffield: Sheffield Academic Press.

LaPorte, J. (1983), *Eucharistia in Philo*, Studies in the Bible and Early Christianity 3, New York: Edwin Mellen.

Laub, F. (1986), 'Sozialgeschichtlicher Hintergrund und ekklesiologische Relevanz der neutestamentlich-frühchristlichen Haus- und Gemeinde-Tafelparänese – ein Beitrag zur Soziologie des Frühchristentums', *MTZ* 37: 249–271.

Ledogar, R. J. (1967), 'Verbs of Praise in the LXX Translation of the Hebrew Canon', *Bib* 48: 29–56.

——(1968), *Acknowledgement: Praise Verbs in Early Greek Anaphora*, Roma: Casa Editrice Herder.

Lee, S. (1993), 'Power not Novelty: The Connotations of נבא in the Hebrew Bible', in A. G. Auld (ed.), *Understanding Poets and Prophets: Essays in Honour of George Wishart Anderson*, 199–212, Sheffield: JSOT Press.

Léon-Dufour, X. (1987), *Sharing the Eucharistic Bread: The Witness of the New Testament* (trans. M. J. O'Connell), New York/Mahwah: Paulist.

Levenson, J. D. (1988), *Creation and the Persistence of Evil*, New York: Harper & Row.

——(1989), 'Liberation Theology and the Exodus', *Midstream* 35: 30–36.

Lightfoot, J. B. (1956), *Saint Paul's Epistle to the Philippians*, Grand Rapids, MI: Zondervan.

Lincoln, A. T. (1990), *Ephesians*, WBC 42, Dallas, TX: Word.

——(1999), 'The Household Code and Wisdom Mode of Colossians', *JSNT* 74: 93–112.

Lindsay, D. R. (1997), '*Todah* and Eucharist: The Celebration of the Lord's Supper as a "Thanks Offering" in the Early Church', *ResQ* 2: 83–100.

Lohse, E. (1971), *Colossians and Philemon* (trans. W. R. Poehlmann and R. J. Karris), Hermeneia, Philadelphia: Fortress.

——(1991), *Theological Ethics of the New Testament* (trans. M. E. Boring), Minneapolis: Fortress.

Longenecker, B. W. (1996), 'Defining the Faithful Character of the Covenant Community: Galatians 2.15–21 and Beyond', in J. D. G. Dunn (ed.), *Paul and the Mosaic Law*, 75–97, Tübingen: Mohr Siebeck.

——(1997), 'Contours of Covenant Theology in the Post-Conversion Paul', in R. N. Longenecker (ed.), *The Road from Damascus: The Impact of Paul's Conversion on His Life, Thought and Ministry*, Grand Rapids, MI: Eerdmans.

Longenecker, R. N. (1985), 'The Nature of Paul's Early Eschatology', *NTS* 31: 85–95.

Lövestam, E. (1963), *Spiritual Wakefulness in the New Testament*, Lund: Gleerup.

Luther, M. (1959), *Lectures on Romans* (trans. W. Pauck), Philadelphia: Westminster.

——(1962), 'Preface to Romans', in J. Dillenberger (ed.), *Martin Luther: Selections from His Writings*, Garden City, NY: Doubleday.

Lyons, D. (1968), 'The Odd Debt of Gratitude', *Analysis* 29: 92–97.

Lyons, G. (1985), *Pauline Autobiography: Toward a New Understanding*, SBLDS 73, Atlanta, GA: Scholars Press.

MacKenzie, R. A. F. (1963), *Faith and History in the Old Testament*, Minneapolis: University of Minnesota Press.

Malherbe, A. J. (1983), *Social Aspects of Early Christianity*, Philadelphia: Fortress.

——(2000), *The Letters to the Thessalonians*, AB 32B, New York: Doubleday.

Malina, B. J. and J. H. Neyrey (1991), 'Honor and Shame in Luke-Acts: Pivotal Values of the Mediterranean World', in J. H. Neyrey (ed.), *The Social World of Luke-Acts: Models for Interpretation*, 25–65, Peabody, MA: Hendrickson.

Martin, M. W. (1996), *Love's Virtues*, Lawrence, KS: University Press of Kansas.

Martin, R. P. (1959), *The Epistle of Paul to the Philippians*, TNTC, Grand Rapids, MI: Eerdmans and Leicester: Inter-Varsity Press.

——(1981), *Reconciliation: A Study in Paul's Theology*, Atlanta: John Knox.

Maschke, T. (1992), 'Prayer in the Apostolic Fathers', *SecCent* 9: 103–118.

McCarter, P. K. Jr (1980), *1 Samuel*, AB, Garden City, NY: Doubleday.

McCarthy, D. J. (1972), *Old Testament Covenant: A Survey of Current Opinions*, Richmond, VA: John Knox.

McComiskey, T. E. (1985), *The Covenants of Promise: A Theology of the Old Testament Covenants*, Grand Rapids, MI: Baker.

McConnell, T. (1993), *Gratitude*, Philadelphia: Temple University Press.

McEleney, N. J. (1974), 'The Vice Lists of the Pastoral Epistles', *CBQ* 36: 203–219.

McFarlane, D. J. (1966), 'The Motif of Thanksgiving in the New Testament', M.Th. thesis, St Andrews University.

McKenzie, S. L. (2000), *Covenant*, St Louis, MO: Chalice.

McWilliams, N. and S. Lependorf (1990), 'Narcissistic Pathology of Everyday Life', *Contemporary Psychoanalysis* 26: 434–449.

Meeks, W. A. (1982), "'And Rose Up to Play": Midrash and Paraenesis in 1 Corinthians 10:1–22', *JSNT* 16: 64–78.

——(1993), *The Origins of Christian Morality: The First Two Centuries*, New Haven, CT: Yale University Press.

Melammed, E. Z. (1990), "'Observe" and "Remember" Spoken in One Utterance', in B.-Z. Segal (ed.), *The Ten Commandments in History and Tradition*, 191–217, Jerusalem: Magnes Press.

Mendenhall, G. E. (1955), *Law and Covenant in Israel and the Ancient Near East*, Pittsburgh: Biblical Colloquium.

Merrill, E. H. (1975), *Qumran and Predestination: A Theological Study of the Thanksgiving Hymns*, vol. 8, Studies on the Texts of the Desert of Judah (ed. by J. van der Ploeg), Leiden: E. J. Brill.

——(2000), 'Remembering: A Central Theme in Biblical Worship', *JETS* 43: 27–36.

Mettinger, T. N. D. (1979), 'The Veto on Images and the Aniconic God in Ancient Israel', in H. Biezais (ed.), *Religious Symbols and their Functions*, 15–29, Stockholm: Almqvist & Wiksell.

Metzger, B. M. (1994), *A Textual Commentary on the Greek New Testament*, Stuttgart: United Bible Societies.

Miller, P. D. Jr (1985), "'Enthroned on the Praises of Israel": The Praise of God in Old Testament Theology', *Int* 39: 5–19.

——(1988), 'In Praise and Thanksgiving', *Theology Today* 45/2: 180–188.

——(1994), *They Cried to the Lord: The Form and Theology of Biblical Prayer*, Minneapolis: Fortress.

Millett, P. (1989), 'Patronage and its Avoidance in Classical Athens', in A. Wallace-Hadrill (ed.), *Patronage in Ancient Society*, 15–48, London: Routledge.

Milton, J. (1983), *The Ethics of Gratitude*, Harrington Lecture 31, Vermillion, SD: University of South Dakota.

Mitchell, C. W. (1987), *The Meaning of BRK 'To Bless' in the Old Testament*, SBLDS 95, Atlanta, GA: Scholars Press.

Mitchell, M. M. (1992), 'New Testament Envoys in the Context of Greco-Roman Diplomatic and Epistolary Conventions: The Example of Timothy and Titus', *JBL* 111: 641–662.

——(1993), *Paul and the Rhetoric of Reconciliation*, Louisville, KY: Westminster/John Knox.

Mócsy, E. (1941), 'De gratiarum actione in epistolis paulinis', *Verbum Domini* 21: 193–201.

Montgomery, J. A. (1939), 'Hebrew Hesed and Greek Charis', *HTR* 32:. 97–98.

Moo, D. (1996), *The Epistle to the Romans*, NICNT, Grand Rapids, MI: Eerdmans.

Mott, S. C. (1971), 'The Greek Benefactor and Deliverance from Moral Distress', Ph.D. Diss., Harvard University.

Motyer, S. (1989), 'The Relationship between Paul's Gospel of "All One in Christ Jesus" (Galatians 3:28) and the "Household Codes"', *VE* 19: 33–48.

Moule, C. F. D. (1973), '"The New Life" in Colossians 3:1–17', *RevExp* 70: 481–493.

——(1987), 'Jesus, Judaism, and Paul', in G. Hawthorne and O. Betz (eds), *Tradition and Interpretation in the New Testament: Essays in Honor of E. Earle Ellis*, Grand Rapids, MI: Eerdmans.

Mounce, W. D. (2000), *Pastoral Epistles*, WBC 46, Nashville: Nelson.

Mowinckel, S. (1962), *The Psalms in Israel's Worship* (trans. D. R. Ap-Thomas), vol. 2, New York: Abingdon.

Moxnes, H. (1991), 'Patron-Client Relations and the New Community in Luke-Acts', in J. H. Neyrey (ed.), *The Social World of Luke-Acts*, 241–268, Peabody, MA: Hendrickson.

Mullins, T. Y. (1984), 'The Thanksgivings of Philemon and Colossians', *NTS* 30: 288–293.

Murphy, F. J. (1988), 'Retelling the Bible: Idolatry in Pseudo-Philo', *JBL* 107: 275–287.

Nash, R. S. (1989), 'Heuristic Haustafeln: Domestic Codes as Entrance to the Social World of Early Christianity. The Case of Colossians', in E. S. Frerichs, J. Neusner and A. J. Levine (eds), *Religious Writings and Religious Systems*, II, 25–50, Atlanta, GA: Scholars Press.

Neusner, J. (1987), *Pesiqta deRab Kahana*, vol. 1, BJS 122, Atlanta, GA: Scholars Press.

Newman, C. C. (1998), 'Ephesians 1:3 – A Primer to Paul's Grammar of God', *RevExp* 95: 89–101.

Nicholson, E. W. (1986), *God and His People: Covenant and Theology in the Old Testament*, Oxford: Clarendon.

Nitzan, B. (1994), *Qumran Prayer and Religious Poetry*, STDJ 12, Leiden: Brill.

O'Brien, P. T. (1975), 'Thanksgiving and the Gospel in Paul', *NTS* 21: 144–155.

——(1977), *Introductory Thanksgivings in the Letters of Paul*, Leiden: E. J. Brill.

——(1979), 'Ephesians 1: An Unusual Introduction to a New Testament Letter', *NTS* 25: 504–516.

——(1980), 'Thanksgiving Within the Structure of Pauline Theology', in D. A. Hagner and M. J. Harris (eds), *Pauline Studies: Essays Presented to Professor F. F. Bruce on His 70th Birthday*, 50–66, Grand Rapids, MI: Eerdmans.

——(1982), *Colossians, Philemon*, WBC, Waco, TX: Word.

——(1991a), 'Divine Provision for our Needs: Assurances from Philippians 4', *RTR* 50: 21–29.

——(1991b), *The Epistle to the Philippians*, NIGTC, Grand Rapids, MI: Eerdmans.

——(1993), 'Benediction, Blessing, Doxology, Thanksgiving', in G. Hawthorne et al. (eds), *Dictionary of Paul and His Letters*, 68–71, Downers Grove, IL: InterVarsity Press.

——(1999), *The Letter to the Ephesians*, PNTC, Grand Rapids, MI: Eerdmans and Leicester: Apollos.

Oepke, A.(1964), Ἐγείρω, κτλ', *TDNT* 2: 333–339.

——(1967), 'Παρουσία, πάρειμι', *TDNT* 5: 858–871.

Oropeza, B. J. (1998), 'Laying to Rest the Midrash: Paul's Message on Meat Sacrificed to Idols in Light of the Deuteronomic Tradition', *Bib* 79: 57–68.

——(1999), 'Apostasy in the Wilderness: Paul's Message to the Corinthians in a State of Eschatological Liminality', *JSNT* 75: 69–86.

Ortlund, R. C. Jr (1996), *Whoredom: God's Unfaithful Wife in Biblical Theology*, NSBT, Grand Rapids, MI: Eerdmans and Leicester: Apollos.

Pao, D.W. (2000), *Acts and the Isaianic New Exodus*, WUNT II.130, Tübingen: Mohr Siebeck.

Parker, R. (1998), 'Pleasing Thighs: Reciprocity in Greek Religion', in N. Postlethwaite, C. Gill and R. Seaford (eds), *Reciprocity in Ancient Greece*, 105–125, New York: Oxford University Press.

Patrick, D. (1995), 'The First Commandment in the Structure of the Pentateuch', *VT* 45: 107–118.

Perkins, P. (1989), '1 Thessalonians and Hellenistic Religious Practices', in M. P. Horgan and P. J. Kobelski (eds), *To Touch the Text: Biblical and Related Studies in Honor of Joseph A. Fitzmyer, S.J.*, 325–334, New York: Crossroad.

Perriman, A. C. (1989), 'Paul and the Parousia: 1 Corinthians 15.50–57 and 2 Corinthians 5.1–5', *NTS* 35: 512–521.

Peterman, G. W. (1991), '"Thankless Thanks": The Epistolary Social Convention in Philippians 4:10–20', *TynBul* 42: 261–270.

Peterson, D. (1993), 'Worship in the New Testament', in D. A. Carson (ed.), *Worship: Adoration and Action*, 51–91, Grand Rapids, MI: Baker.

Petuchowski, J. J. (1957), '"Do This in Remembrance of Me" (1 Cor. 11:24)', *JBL* 76: 293–298.

Philo (1937) (trans. F. H. Colson. and G. H. Whitaker), vols. 1–10, LCL, Cambridge, MA: Harvard University Press.

Piper, O. A. (1954), 'Praise of God and Thanksgiving', *Int* 8: 3–20.

Pleket, H. W. (1981), 'Religious History as the History of Mentality: The "Believer" as Servant of the Deity in the Greek World', in H. S. Versnel (ed.), *Faith, Hope and Worship: Aspects of Religious Mentality in the Ancient World*, 152–192, Leiden: Brill.

Plummer, A. (1915), *A Critical and Exegetical Commentary on the Second Epistle of Paul to the Corinthians*, ICC, Edinburgh: T. & T. Clark.

Porter, C. L. (1994), 'Romans 1.18–32: Its Role in the Developing Argument', *NTS* 40: 210–228.

Porter, S. E. (1999), *The Paul of Acts: Essays in Literary Criticism, Rhetoric, and Theology*, WUNT 115, Tübingen: Mohr Siebeck.

——(1989), *Verbal Aspect in the Greek of the New Testament, with Reference to Tense and Mood*, vol. 1, SBG, New York/Frankfurt am Main.

Porton, G. G. (1988), *Goyim: Gentiles and Israelites in Mishnah-Tosefta*, BJS 155, Atlanta, GA: Scholars Press.

Price, C. P. (1962), 'Remembering and Forgetting in the Old Testament and its Bearing on the Early Christian Eucharist', Th.D. Diss., Union Theological Seminary, New York.

Pryor, J. W. (1991), 'The Great Thanksgiving and the Fourth Gospel', *BZ* 35: 157–179.

Quincey, J. H. (1966), 'Greek Expressions of Thanks', *JHS* 86: 133–158.

Räisänen, H. (1983), *Paul and the Law*, Philadelphia: Fortress.

Reed, J. T. (1996), 'Are Paul's Thanksgivings "Epistolary"?', *JSNT* 61: 87–99.

Reicke, B. (1959), 'Some Reflections on Worship in the New Testament', in A. J. B. Higgins (ed.), *New Testament Essays: Studies in Memory of Thomas Walter Manson*, 194–209, Manchester: Manchester University Press.

Reinhart, A. K. (1989), 'Thanking the Benefactor', in J. B. Carman and F. J. Streng (eds), *Spoken and Unspoken Thanks: Some*

Comparative Soundings, 115–133, Cambridge, MA: Center for the Study of World Religions.

Rendtorff, R. (1998), *The Covenant Formula: An Exegetical and Theological Investigation* (trans. M. Kohl), Edinburgh: T. & T. Clark.

Rengstorf, K. H. (1953), 'Die neutestamentlichen Mahnungen an die Frau, sich dem Manne unterzuordnen', in W. Foerster (ed.), *Verbum Dei Manet in Aeternum*, 131–145, Wittenberg: Luther-Verlag.

Ridouard, A. and J. Guillet (1967), 'Thanksgiving', in X. Léon-Dufour (ed.), *Dictionary of Biblical Theology*, 525–527, New York: Desclee.

Robbins, C. J. (1986), 'The Composition of Eph. 1:3–14', *JBL* 105: 677–687.

Roberts, A. and J. Donaldson (eds) (1994), *Ante-Nicene Fathers*, Peabody, MA: Hendrickson.

Roberts, J. H. (1986), 'The Eschatological Transitions to the Pauline Letter Body', *Neot* 20: 29–35.

Robinson, J. M. (1964), 'Die Hodajot-Formel in Gebet und Hymnus des Frühchristentums', in W. Eltester and F. H. Kettler (eds), *Apophoreta: Festschrift Ernst Haenchen*, 194–235, Berlin: Alfred Töpelmann.

——(1969), 'The Historicality of Biblical Language', in B. W. Anderson (ed.), *The Old Testament and Christian Faith: A Theological Discussion*, 124–158, New York: Herder and Herder.

Rogahn, K. (1975), 'The Function of Future-Eschatological Statements in the Pauline Epistles', Ph.D. Diss., Princeton Theological Seminary.

Rosner, B. S. (1992), '"Stronger than He?" The Strength of 1 Corinthians 10:22b', *TynBul* 43: 171–178.

——(1999), *How to Get Really Rich: A Sharp Look at the Religion of Greed*, Leicester: Inter-Varsity Press.

Roth, W. M. W. (1975), 'For Life, He Appeals to Death (Wis 13:18)', *CBQ* 37: 21–47.

Ruiz, J.-P. (1995), 'Revelation 4:8–11; 5:9–14: Hymns of the Heavenly Liturgy', *SBLSP* 31: 216–220.

Sakenfeld, K. D. (1985), *Faithfulness in Action*, OBT 16, Philadelphia: Fortress.

Saller, R. P. (1982), *Personal Patronage under the Early Empire*, Cambridge: Cambridge University Press.

Sandelin, K.-G. (1991), 'The Danger of Idolatry According to Philo of Alexandria', *Temenos* 27: 109–150.

——(1996), 'The Jesus-Tradition and Idolatry', *NTS* 42: 412–420.

Sanders, E. P. (1976), 'The Covenant as a Soteriological Category and the Nature of Salvation in Palestinian and Hellenistic Judaism', in R. Hamerton-Kelly and R. Scroggs (eds), *Jews, Greeks and Christians: Religious Cultures in Late Antiquity. Essays in Honor of William David Davies*, 11–44. Leiden: Brill.

——(1977), *Paul and Palestinian Judaism: A Comparison of Patterns of Religion*, Philadelphia: Fortress.

——(1983), *Paul, the Law, and the Jewish People*, Philadelphia: Fortress.

Sanders, J. T. (1962), 'The Transition from Opening Epistolary Thanksgiving to Body in the Letters of the Pauline Corpus', *JBL* 81: 348–362.

Schaller, H. (1990), 'Asking and Thanking – A Meaningful Unity', in C. Duquoc and C. Florestan (eds), *Asking and Thanking*, 1–6, Philadelphia: Trinity Press International.

Schermann, T. (1910), '*Εὐχαριστία* und *Εὐχαριστεῖν* in ihrem Bedeutungswandel bis 200n.Chr.', *Philologus* 69: 375–410.

Schieffelin, E. L. (1980), 'Reciprocity and the Construction of Reality', *Man* 15: 502–517.

Schiffman, L. H. (1994), *Reclaiming the Dead Sea Scrolls: The History of Judaism, the Background of Christianity, the Lost Library of Qumran*, Philadelphia: Jewish Publication Society.

Schottroff, W. (1964), *Gedenken im Alten Orient und im Alten Testament*, Neukirchen-Vluyn: Neukirchener Verlag.

Schröder, D. (1959), 'Die Haustafeln des Neuen Testaments: Ihre Herkunft und ihr theologischer Sinn', D.Th. Diss., University of Hamburg.

Schubert, P. (1939), *Form and Function of the Pauline Thanksgivings*, Berlin: Alfred Töpelmann.

Seaford, R. (1998), 'Introduction', in N. Postlethwaite, C. Gill and R. Seaford (eds), *Reciprocity in Ancient Greece*, 1–11, New York: Oxford University Press.

Seifrid, M. A. (1985), 'The Subject of Rom. 7:14–25', *NovT* 34: 313–333.

——(1992), 'The Subject of Rom 7:14–25', *NovT* 34: 313–333.

——(2000), *Christ, Our Righteousness: Paul's Theology of Justification*, NSBT 9, Downers Grove, IL: InterVarsity Press and Leicester: Apollos.

Seneca (1935), *Moral Essays* (trans. J. W. Basore), vol. 3, Cambridge, MA: Harvard University Press.

Sevenster, J. N. (1961), *Paul and Seneca*, NovTSup 4, Leiden: Brill.

Shead, A. G. (2000), 'The New Covenant and Pauline Hermeneutics', in P. Bolt and M. Thompson (eds), *The Gospel to the Nations*, 33–61, Downers Grove, IL: InterVarsity Press.

Shedd, R. P. (1987), 'Worship in the New Testament Church', in D. A. Carson (ed.), *The Church in the Bible and the World*, 120–153, Exeter: Paternoster.

Shipp, R. M. (1993), '"Remember His Covenant Forever": A Study of the Chronicler's Use of the Psalms', *ResQ* 35: 29–39.

Silva, M. (1988), *Philippians*, Chicago: Moody Press.

Smiga, G. (1991), 'Romans 12:1–2 and 15:30–32 and the Occasion of the Letter to the Romans', *CBQ* 53: 257–273.

Smit, J. F. M. (1997a), '"Do Not Be Idolaters": Paul's Rhetoric in First Corinthians 10:1–22', *NovT* 39: 40–53.

——(1997b), 'The Function of First Corinthians 10,23–30: A Rhetorical Anticipation', *Bib* 78: 377–388.

Smith, E. W. Jr (1971), 'The Form and Religious Background of Romans VII 24–25a', *NovT* 13: 127–135.

Soares-Prabhu, G. M. (1990), 'Speaking to "Abba": Prayer as Petition and Thanksgiving in the Teaching of Jesus', *Concilium* 3: 31–43.

Spilsbury, P. (1998), 'God and Israel in Josephus: A Patron-Client Relationship', in S. Mason (ed.), *Understanding Josephus: Seven Perspectives*, 172–191, Sheffield: Sheffield Academic Press.

Spykerboer, H. C. (1976), *The Structure and Composition of Deutero-Isaiah: With Special Reference to the Polemics against Idolatry*, Franeker, Netherlands: T. Wever.

Stählin, G. (1965), 'Ἴσος, ἰσότης, ἰσότιμος', *TDNT* 3: 343–355.

Standhartinger, A. (2000), 'The Origin and Intention of the Household Code in the Letter to the Colossians', *JSNT* 79: 117–130.

Stevenson, T. R. (1992), 'The Ideal Benefactor and the Father Analogy in Greek and Roman Thought', *CQ* 42: 421–436.

Stoessel, H. E. (1963), 'Notes on Romans 12:1–2', *Int* 17: 161–175.

Streng, F. J. (1989), 'Thanksgiving as a Worldwide Response to Life', in J. B. Carman and F. J. Streng (eds), *Spoken and Unspoken Thanks: Some Comparative Soundings*, 1–9, Cambridge, MA: Center for the Study of World Religions.

Stuart, D. (1987), *Hosea-Jonah*, WBC, Waco, TX: Word.

Stuhlmacher, P. (1968), *Die paulinische Evangelium, vol. 1: Vorgeschichte*, FRLANT 95, Göttingen: Vandenhoeck & Ruprecht.

Talbert, C. (1987), 'Paul on the Covenant', *RevExp* 84: 299–313.

——(1989), *Reading Corinthians: A Literary and Theological Commentary on 1 and 2 Corinthians*, New York: Crossroad.

Tate, M. E. (1990), *Psalms 51–100*, WBC, Dallas, TX: Word.

Thesaurus Linguae Graecae: CD ROM #D (1992), Irvine, CA: University of California.

Thiselton, A. C. (2000), *The First Epistle to the Corinthians*, NIGTC, Grand Rapid, MI: Eerdmans.

Thrall, M. E. (1982), 'A Second Thanksgiving Period in II Corinthians', *JSNT* 16: 101–124.

Tinker, M. (2001), 'Last Supper/Lord's Supper: More than a Parable in Action?', *Them* 26: 18–28.

Tripp, D. (1990), 'The Prayer of St. Polycarp and the Development of Anaphoral Prayer', *Ephemerides Liturgicae* 104: 97–132.

Tsirpanlis, C. N. (1983), 'The Structure of the Church in the Liturgical Tradition of the First Three Centuries', *Patristic and Byzantine Review* 2: 44–62.

Tunyogi, A. C. (1962), 'The Rebellions of Israel', *JBL* 81: 385–390.

Vacek, E. C. (2000), 'Gifts, God, Generosity, and Gratitude', in J. Keating (ed.), *Spirituality and Moral Theology: Essays from a Pastoral Perspective*, 81–125, New York: Paulist.

Van der Watt, J. G. (1986), 'Colossians 1:3–12 Considered as an Exordium', *JTSA* 57: 32–42.

Van Wees, H. (1998), 'The Law of Gratitude: Reciprocity in Anthropological Theory', in N. Postlethwaite, C. Gill and R. Seaford (eds), *Reciprocity in Ancient Greece*, 13–49, New York: Oxford University Press.

Versnel, H. S. (1981), 'Religious Mentality in Ancient Prayer', in H. S. Versnel (ed.), *Faith, Hope and Worship: Aspects of Religious Mentality in the Ancient World*, 1–64, Leiden: Brill.

Volf, M. (1993), 'Worship as Adoration and Action', in D. A. Carson (ed.), *Worship: Adoration and Action*, 203–211, Grand Rapids, MI: Baker.

Von der Osten-Sacken, P. (1977), 'Gottes Treue bis zur Parusie: Formgeschichtliche Beobachtungen zu 1 Kor 1:7b–9', *ZNW* 68: 176–199.

Von Rad, G. (1966), *The Problem of the Hexateuch and Other Essays* (trans. E. W. Trueman Dicken), New York: McGraw-Hill.

Von Rad, G. (1968), *The Message of the Prophets* (trans. D. M. G. Stalker), London: SCM.

Wainwright, G. (1981), *Eucharist and Eschatology*, New York: Oxford University Press.

——(1986), 'Praying for Kings: The Place of Human Rulers in the Divine Plan of Salvation', *ExAud* 2: 117–127.

Waltke, B. K. (1992), 'The Fear of the Lord: The Foundation for a Relationship with God', in J. I. Packer and L. Wilkinson (eds), *Alive to God: Studies in Spirituality presented to James Houston*, 17–33, Downers Grove, IL: InterVarsity Press.

Walton, J. H. (1994), *Covenant: God's Purpose, God's Plan*, Grand Rapids, MI: Zondervan.

Wanamaker, C. A. (1990), *Commentary on 1 and 2 Thessalonians*, NIGTC, Grand Rapids, MI: Eerdmans.

Ware, J. (1992), 'The Thessalonians as a Missionary Congregation: 1 Thessalonians 1,5–8', *ZNW* 83: 126–131.

Watson, N. M. (1983), '"To Make Us Rely Not on Ourselves but on God who Raises the Dead" 2 Cor. 1,9b as the Heart of Paul's Theology', in U. Luz and H. Weder (eds), *Die Mitte des Neuen Testaments: Einheit und Vielfalt neutestamentlicher Theologie*, 384–398, Göttingen: Vandenhoeck & Ruprecht.

Weatherly, J, A. (1991), 'The Authenticity of 1 Thessalonians 2.13–16: Additional Evidence', *JSNT* 42: 79–98.

Weinfeld, M. (1990), 'The Uniqueness of the Decalogue and its Place in Jewish Tradition', in B.-Z. Segal (ed.), *The Ten Commandments in History and Tradition*, 1–44, Jerusalem: Magnes Press.

Weippert, H. (1979), 'Das Wort vom Neuen Bund in Jeremia xxxi 31–34', *VT* 29: 336–351.

Weitzman, S. (1994), 'Lessons from the Dying: The Role of Deuteronomy 32 in its Narrative Setting', *HTR* 87: 377–393.

Wenham, D. (1988), 'The Paulinism of Acts Again: Two Historical Clues in 1 Thessalonians', *Them* 13: 53–55.

——(1995), 'How Jesus Understood the Last Supper: A Parable in Action', *Them* 20: 11–16.

Westermann, C. (1965), *The Praise of God in the Psalms* (trans. K. R. Crim), Richmond, VA: John Knox.

——(1981), *Praise and Lament in the Psalms* (trans. K. R. Crim and R. N. Soulen), Atlanta, GA: John Knox.

White, J. L. (1972), *The Form and Structure of the Official Petition: A Study in Greek Epistolography*, Missoula, MT: Society of Biblical Literature.

——(1987), 'New Testament Epistolary Literature in the Framework of Ancient Epistolography', *ANRW* II.25.2: 1730–1756.

Whiteley, D. E. H. (1974), *The Theology of St. Paul*, Oxford: Basil Blackwell.

Whybray, R. N. (1978), *Thanksgiving for a Liberated Prophet: An Interpretation of Isaiah Chapter 53*, JSOTSup 4, Sheffield: JSOT.

Wilckens, U. (1974), *Die Missionsreden der Apostelgeschichte: Form- und traditionsgeschichtliche Untersuchungen*, WMANT 5, Neukirchen-Vluyn: Neukirchener.

Wiles, G. P. (1974), *Paul's Intercessory Prayers: The Significance of the Intercessory Prayer Passage in the Letters of St. Paul*, Cambridge: Cambridge University Press.

Wilkes, J. R. (1981), 'Remembering', *Theology* 84: 87–95.

Williamson, H. G. M. (1985), *Ezra, Nehemiah*, WBC, Waco, TX: Word.

Wilson, A. (1986), *The Nations in Deutero-Isaiah*, Lewiston, NY: Mellen.

Wilson, W. T. (1997), *The Hope of Glory: Education and Exhortation in the Epistle to the Colossians*, NovTSup, Leiden: E. J. Brill.

Winter, B. W. (1994), *Seek the Welfare of the City*, Grand Rapids, MI: Eerdmans.

——(1997), *Philo and Paul among the Sophists*, SNTSMS 96, Cambridge: Cambridge University Press.

——(2001), *After Paul Left Corinth: The Influence of Secular Ethics and Social Change,* Grand Rapids, MI: Eerdmans.

Winter, S. (1987), 'Paul's Letter to Philemon', *NTS* 33: 1–15.

Witherington, B., III (1994), *Paul's Narrative Thought World*, Louisville, KY: Westminster/John Knox.

Wright, N. T. (1996), *Jesus and the Victory of God*, London: SPCK.

Zeidman, R. (1997), 'A Time to Mourn: Methods of Reading Intertextuality in the Laws of Idolatry', in J. Neusner (ed.), *Approaches to Ancient Judaism*, 1.125–144. Atlanta, GA: Scholars Press.

Index of modern authors

Wilson, W. T.   89
Winter, B. W.   172
Winter, S.   118

Witherington, B., III   15
Wright, N. T.   72
Zeidman, R.   93

Index of biblical references and ancient sources

Index of subjects

Abraham 41–42, 44, 49, 45, 53, 56,
61, 63, 70, 94
approach
form-critical 19
history-of-religion 16
source-critical 16–17, 19
atonement 47–48, 72–74, 88,
100–101, 133
authority 75, 98, 108–116, 158, 172
benediction 17, 29, 31–32, 75
benefaction system 165–173
blessing 29–32, 157
comfort 74–75, 89, 120
community 43, 55, 67, 116–118,
171
confession 17, 64–66, 84, 86, 89, 99,
105, 107, 111, 144
covenantal traditions 21, 39–58,
59–64, 86–88, 91–94, 119–126,
145–153, 171–172
creation 19, 33–35, 37, 57, 67, 73,
120
cross 36, 73–74, 77, 88, 103, 106,
114, 128, 131, 136, 143, 157, 164
cultural distance 19–21
David 36, 41–43, 46, 51, 55
debt 19, 22, 103
deliverance 51–52, 65–67, 70, 79, 84,
87–88, 98–99, 120–122, 128–133,
145–149, 161
doxology 32–34, 68
duty 112, 116–117, 171
election 50–52, 76, 78, 81, 99,
130–131
eschatology 20, 45–47, 52–53,
57–58, 119–144

ethics 16, 17, 20, 21, 28, 44–45,
51–52, 56–57, 86–118, 139–144,
171–172
etiquette 20, 28
exodus 42, 46, 57, 61, 63–69, 73–74,
91–98, 145–159
faith 37, 71, 80
faithfulness 43, 45–47, 53, 57,
59–64, 76, 86–88, 91, 107, 117,
119–122, 126–127, 130, 140, 143,
152–153
fear 54–55
forgetfulness 53–54, 61, 149–153,
161
Gentiles 21, 46, 50, 66, 82–83,
93–94, 97, 127, 160
gift 20, 25, 28, 37–38, 59, 70, 82–84,
91, 103, 116–117, 119, 165, 168
God
as benefactor 161, 167–169, 171
as creator 24, 32, 33–36, 54, 73,
91, 97, 107, 116, 159–162, 171
as king 41, 52, 56
as Lord 47, 52, 54, 56, 62, 68, 70,
86, 91–98, 120, 138, 145,
149–153, 172
-centredness 29, 33–38, 97, 107,
137, 144, 163–164, 171
glory of 16, 29, 31–34, 79, 83, 94,
97–98, 105, 155, 161
jealousy of 44, 61, 93, 154
relationship with 25, 31–32, 37,
39–42, 55, 61, 80–81, 91,
116–118, 120, 158, 171
gospel 51, 74–81, 88, 116, 130,
171